To
Gwen Kilvert for her unfailing support
and dedication to excellence

Contents

BEST
Girlfriends Getaways
WORLDWIDE

BEST
Girlfriends Getaways
WORLDWIDE

By Marybeth Bond

NATIONAL GEOGRAPHIC

WASHINGTON, DC

Live Life to Its Fullest

Women travel differently from men. We seize opportunities to meet other women, take the time to slowly meander through a flower garden, devote time in a spa, take a cooking lesson in a local woman's kitchen, or shop without the pressure of someone waiting for us outside the store. If you buy this book for yourself or a loved one, you understand the powerful experience of traveling with women. It's the easiest way to reconnect with our deepest female soul mates—our girlfriends. Whether we're single or married, career women or stay-at-home moms, traveling with girlfriends is great fun. We laugh, we're silly, and we're blissfully free of our responsibilities to anyone but ourselves. We return home rejuvenated, recharged, and recommitted to our families and work. Best of all, we encourage each other and get out of our own shells.

Girlfriend getaways, however, aren't just limited to gal pals. Mothers, daughters, and sisters are also traveling together. A girlfriend getaway can celebrate milestones and changes, from graduation and retirement to beating cancer. Sometimes we just want to escape the daily grind.

What do women want when they go away with each other? Flip through the chapters to find out. How about a cooking class in Tuscany? Or a hike and fondue in Zermatt? Or culture, art, fine dining, and a personal shopper in Paris? Or a guided tour of a London museum? Or a ginger oil massage in Thailand?

This book is organized by the places we want to visit and the things we want to do. I've arranged the trips by themes, such as exotic escapes, wonderful walks, culinary classes, volunteer trips, education travel, or cosmopolitan cities. You can use this book as a resource to learn about a style of travel or a specific location. Do you want to devote a trip to volunteer work, spas, gardens, or staying in a castle? This book will help you decide and offer you advice on which countries are the best to visit for your interest.

Let's face it, the world is a big place, and it can be hard to narrow down all of your choices. Luckily, I've done that for you. I recommend exotic "once-in-a-lifetime" adventures from the Galápagos to Turkey, and old-world palaces where we'd love to lay our heads, in Ireland or India. In other chapters I select some of the best trails worldwide from Zermatt to Machu Picchu; culinary classes in Tuscany, Provence, or Thailand; and volunteer trips where we can lend a hand and make a difference in Guatemala, Cambodia, or Kenya.

Like most experienced travelers, I have become very picky. I have traveled on a limited budget and in extreme luxury. Because I've had mediocre meals, hotels, guides, tours, and some rotten travel experiences, I want to save you time and, in some places, money so you won't have similar negative memories. I wrote this book for you: a sophisticated, open-minded, adventurous woman who hungers for the world's most incredible locales and trips. You will want to grab a girlfriend or two and just make it happen. In compiling this book, I have tossed out the average places, accommodations, and experiences. I have selected what is truly worthy, in my opinion, of your money and limited travel time.

Each destination is scrupulously examined through a female lens. What will women travelers appreciate in Sydney, Buenos Aires, Cape Town, or on a barge trip in Holland? Destination descriptions include female-friendly activities and places, such as best farmers' markets, best outdoor cafés for people watching, best venues for afternoon tea, best cooking classes, best private shopping guides (in Paris), best music or art festivals.

"Have you visited all these places?" is the most frequent question I am asked by readers. Yes, I have visited, hiked, biked, eaten, slept, and shopped in almost all (98 percent) of the destinations I recommend in my books. I'm a gypsy at heart and a zealous traveler, who has dedicated her life to exploring—and who can tolerate lots of long flights in the course of a year. Over the past four decades, I have lived in Europe for six years, the South Pacific for one year, and traveled, at my leisure, for two years around the world (alone).

You'll see in the introduction to Chapter One that I have been to India seven times in the past 25 years, most recently last summer. I explain how India has changed and why it is still a "must" destination for every curious traveler. Nepal, where I have worn out hiking boots on nine treks in different regions, is included in Chapter Three, wonderful walks of the world. But in Chapter Two I admit that no one can be a true expert on Paris. Although I lived on rue Jacob, in the 6th arrondissement, for four years, and I visit Paris often, I recognize that I can't possibly come up with the most up-to-date information myself. For this book, I asked expats living in Paris to share their secrets with us. Although I've been to Sydney, Cape Town, and London, I'm not up on the latest hot places to dine, hear a free concert in a park, or buy curios in a neighborhood market. That's when I call upon my loyal network of girlfriends. For example, my friend Suzy was transferred to Sydney 25 years ago. She broke the glass ceiling, working her way to the top of an investment banking firm. She's a sophisticated woman who entertains often, so I asked her for "women-friendly" suggestions for best places to go to the beach, shop, stroll safely, get cultured, watch the sunset, cruise, and dine in Sydney. She invited a group of "with it" women friends to the boardroom of her office, and over wine and cheese, and much negotiation, they hammered out a list of "Best Places" for Sydney. Two weeks later, she sent me a five-page email with ideas. I owe a debt of gratitude to my countless sophisticated, well-traveled friends like Suzy whose advice I trust and who have "been there and done that" recently.

Best Girlfriends Getaways Worldwide is not a cookie-cutter guide-book. Like my first book, *50 Best Girlfriends Getaways in North America*, it contains dozens of sidebars with advice by women, for women, from how to pack to what to look out for and how not to offend the locals. Many of the short intimate stories and interviews in this book describe the inner journey of exploring the world with a close female friend or relative. They are meant to coax you out of your everyday routine and possible apprehension and just book a darn flight! I have learned that many times it's that easy: Get your plane tickets and the rest will fall into place (after a carefully reading of my suggestions, of course).

Like me, you may start at the back of the book and skim through it, reading snippets here and there. Take a moment to peruse the inter-views at the beginning of each chapter. They will give you a glimpse of the gutsy women who are out there living life to its fullest. Let these ideas begin to take shape and start to solidify into actual travel plans.

Thanks to all of the courageous women for sharing their stories, and thereby sharing their strength. We are role models for each other. I hope this book gives every woman the example, advice, and encour-agement to step out the door and explore the world. So don't wait, call a girlfriend, daughter, sister, or mother, and go now!

See you on the road.

—*Marybeth Bond*

CHAPTER ONE

Exotic Escapes

Chris and Peg have been close friends for more than 30 years. Both are bird ladies. They've spent many extended days, binoculars in hand and birding field guides in their packs, slogging through wetlands and meadows in search of the world's rare birds. Over the years, they've shared this love of bird-watching on trips to Alaska, Kenya, and Tanzania. And for Peg's retirement, they decided to raise the stakes, narrowing it down to two of the most renowned and remote wildlife destinations in the world: South America's Amazon and Galápagos Islands.

"We were fascinated by Ecuador's biodiversity," says Chris. "There's the rain forest, indigenous people and cultures, the colonial city of Quito, and of course, the curious endemic species of the Galápagos Islands." It became apparent to them that a hot, humid, roughing-it adventure in South America might not fit every woman's idea of a vacation, but they were pretty sure Sherry and Ann, occasional travel tagalongs and neighbors in their small northern California town, wouldn't miss out on this once-in-a-lifetime journey. And they were right. This was a foursome whose passions drove them to seek out the corners of the world: Chris was the bird lady; Ann, the monkey enthusiast; Peg, the aquatic gal; and Sherry, the photographer. And without saying as much, they knew that each of them would share in the other's excitement for these things, as women tend to do, making sure they all came home satiated. They nicknamed themselves the "Galápagos Gals."

From the capital city of Quito, they flew to a teeny town on the Napo River in the Amazon. There they boarded a small motorized boat for a journey down the river to the Napo Wildlife Center, an eco-lodge tucked deep into the jungle. Within minutes of settling into the boat, the indigenous Anangu guides, who spoke very little English, handed them ponchos. And, as if on cue, the rain started falling. It didn't let up for the entire three-hour trip. Hey, they *were* looking for an exotic adventure.

When they arrived at the lodge, they were delighted, if not relieved, to find comfy thatch-roofed bungalows perched on a hillside in the thick tropical rain forest. This would be their base camp for five days of hiking, birding, and river trips. "We'd wake up at 5 a.m. to a roaring sound, similar to planes taking off," says Sherry. "It was the choir of howler monkeys greeting the day and foraging for food in the canopy." At dawn and dusk, the ladies would navigate narrow tributaries in dugout canoes, watching for birds and animals. Between river trips, Chris would sit with her binoculars and a gin-and-tonic on the observation deck at the lodge and spy more unusual birds. "We saw 135 species of birds in five days," she boasts. "To put this in perspective, my Life List of birds, which represents ten years of observation, is 985."

The monkey lover in the group, Ann, had it even better. One day, as the gals floated in the dugout, they could hear the leaves rustling in the dense jungle canopy. Their guide pointed to a troop of spider monkeys moving through the forest more than a hundred feet above them. As the boat rounded a corner in the creek, they spotted more canopy commotion: a band of capuchin monkeys quietly stalking behind the spider monkeys. And then the guide pointed to pint-size squirrel monkeys and red howler monkeys. Within the next few days, they had spotted the pygmy marmoset, the world's smallest monkey; the golden-mantled tamarin, which the Napo Wildlife Center uses as its logo; and although they didn't actually see the red howlers in residence across the lagoon from the lodge, every morning and evening they heard the creature's magnificent cries reverberate over the water.

The next stop for the Galápagos Gals was, fittingly, the archipelago they named themselves for. Peg, the self-proclaimed water girl, slipped into her wet suit every day to dive from the yacht they slept on into water busy with penguins, sea turtles, sea lions, and marine iguanas. "I even saw a ten-foot whitetip shark!" she says. The ladies were warned to be careful around the playful sea lions—and for good reason. A plump, wet-suit-clad woman in a nearby group was bitten on the derrière by a sea lion that mistook her for a potential mate. "We watched while her travel companions pulled down the bottom part of her wet suit to reveal a long, bloody gash on her commodious butt," Ann laughs.

Sherry, the group's photographer, had a field day with the amazing photo ops—and the almost ethereal light—in the Galápagos. Feeling just like a *National Geographic* photographer on assignment, she captured blue-footed boobies, the famous finches of Charles Darwin, lumbering giant tortoises, sunsets, sunrises, cactus-covered islands, sandy beaches, and—most important—her closest friends.

"We have developed a special bond because we've had so many adventures together," Chris says. There is something about traveling with each other that has allowed them to be so intensely focused on their own passions and hobbies. Yet these women take so much joy in one another's joys. They encouraged one another's hunger to see the world, and they collectively share the thrill of catching sight of an orange-cheeked parrot or capturing a sunset perfectly on film. "I think we'll be friends forever."

ॐ India ॐ

From the moment you step off the plane, India will start working its magic on you. The air swirls with smoky sandalwood and spices, and streets teem with people, cars, and cows. Experiencing India with girl-friends, you allow yourselves to become completely enchanted by its customs, history, spirituality, and grandeur. A visit is tantamount to a pilgrimage. It's a journey of reflection. And nowhere do I think you can take this personal journey better than in the country's largest state, Rajasthan, in the northwest corner. It's one of India's most exotic and colorful regions—and one of my favorite places—on Earth. Prior to

British rule (which began in the early 1800s), Rajasthan was a collection of princely states, each with its own maharaja (king) and warrior clans. But first, you can't avoid a visit to India's other premier highlights: the city of Delhi, which pulses with life and has fabulous museums and shopping, and the iconic Taj Mahal monument, in Agra. Then you can continue on to the colorful capital of the Rajasthan region, Jaipur, dominated by pink-sandstone palaces and equally vibrant locals decked out in jewelry from head to toe, hot-pink and crimson saris,

GETTING THE FEEL OF INDIA

∽

To prepare for our trip to India, my mom and I went to the library. We borrowed movies and watched *Gandhi*, *Monsoon Wedding*, and all ten segments of *The Jewel in the Crown*. The films of Deepa Mehta are incredible. *Water* was gorgeous and really tugged at my heartstrings. I also recommend a couple of books that illuminated some of the country's contradictions and gave us a lot of useful background information:

We read *In Spite of the Gods: The Strange Rise of Modern India* by Edward Luce. Using scholarship and history, he explains India's rise in global power and future prospects. *Holy Cow: An Indian Adventure* is by Sarah Macdonald, an Australian radio correspondent who lived for two years in India traveling around the country, sampling India's "spiritual smorgasbord." *The City of Joy*, by Dominique Lapierre, mixes history and fiction and offers glimpses from the lives of a French priest, a rickshaw driver, and an American doctor in the slums of Calcutta. *Heat and Dust*, by Ruth Prawer Jhabvala, is a Booker Prize–winning short novel set in the 1920s in India. The story, which revolves around an Anglo-Indian romance, discusses class and colonialism.

—JC Sheppard, 20, Student, Cornell University,
Ithaca, New York

and Easter-egg colored turbans. If you're on a fairly tight schedule, you can fly from city to city within the region, but if you have a week or more to spare, hire a car and driver (a safe and very feasible option) for the most exotic girlfriend road trip of your lives. Almost every town is dominated by a huge fort with imposing walls and turrets that once protected incredibly luxurious palaces; there are world-class heritage hotels sprinkled throughout, which means you can always finish off a day of sightseeing with spa treatments and superior fine dining. Fall and winter are fantastic in India—days are pleasantly warm and nights are cool. It's also a great time to catch Rajasthan's fairs and festivals. (December is the height of India's wedding season, so it can be a busy month. If you go at this time, make reservations a few months ahead of time.) The advantages of off-season travel in the summer—which, I might add, spells incredibly hot days not for the faint of heart—are deep discounts, lush green landscapes, and very few Western tourists.

MUST-SEE MUSEUMS OF DELHI

Delhi is a city of 13 million people. It's mind-boggling in its diversity: It's home to Hindus, Sikhs, and Muslims. You'll hear at least ten different languages spoken on the streets. Harkening back to another age, Old Delhi boasts intricate streets packed with temples and bazaars. Hop into a bicycle rickshaw for a ride through the old city, soaking in sights like the Red Fort and Jama Masjid (India's largest mosque). Another way to get to know Delhi's cultural makeup is to visit its museums, which mirror its diversity. To trace the progression of Indian art through the past century, visit the National Gallery of Modern Art (*www.ngmaindia.gov.in*). Or explore millennia-old sculptures, Buddhist art, and Indian jewelry and miniature paintings at the National Museum (*www.nationalmuseumindia.gov.in*). One of my favorites is the little-known National Handlooms and Handicrafts Museum, which has a massive collection of sculptures, toys, wood carvings, and fabrics from all over India, as well as an outdoor area where artisans conduct demonstrations (no website; located on Pragati Maidan, just off Bhairon Road, New Delhi).

WONDER OF THE WORLD

Many people go to India solely to see Agra's renowned tribute to lost love—the Taj Mahal. The Taj is the most popular attraction in all of India, and a quick flight from Delhi, drawing two million visitors each year. The king Shah Jahan started building this stunning monument in the 17th century, after his beloved wife died during childbirth. With snow-white marble, intricate inlaid patterns of precious stones, and shapely domes, it's no surprise this is a UNESCO World Heritage site. You'll witness some of the most stunning sunsets and sunrises of your lives. Gather around in the garden with your cameras to watch the sky ignite behind the Taj's iconic minarets and domes. The ultimate splurge is a room with a view of the Taj Mahal's great onion dome and four slender minarets (from your window as well as your bathtub) at the luxurious Oberoi Amarvilas (from $600 for doubles; 800-562-3764, *oberoiamarvilas.com*).

THE GIRLS' GUIDE TO JAIPUR
Known as the pink city because of its ubiquitous pink-sandstone buildings, kaleidoscopic Jaipur is a photographer's dream. Rajasthani women wearing saffron-, turquoise-, and vermilion-colored saris and scarves and men in white tunics and pink-and-orange turbans glide among camels, sacred cows, and rickshaws in the streets and alleys of its old town. This neighborhood is still encircled by the original thick, crenellated walls with seven imposing gates. And the most spectacular architectural site within those walls is the Hawa Mahal, aka the Palace of the Winds, whose façade of 953 delicate sandstone windows resembles a gigantic honeycomb. The palace was built by a poet-king for the ladies of his court, who used the windows to gaze out at the action on the street. (If you're wondering whether 953 windows mean 953 courtesans, all I can say is, I certainly hope not!) After your exploration of the old town, be sure to let yourselves simply meander—and stimulate the local economy. By this, I mean shop: You can expect to stock up on lightweight clothes, decorated purses, rings for fingers and toes, bangles, handmade paper, vibrant textiles, and whimsical puppets carefully crafted by local artisans.

BEST ADVENTURE
Every tour of Rajasthan should include a visit to Amber Fort, a palace seven miles from Jaipur. You can easily hire a taxi to deliver you. But the most exotic mode of transport is an elephant. Unless you're completely pooped from all the sightseeing (or afraid of heights), you must do the elephant ride—it's a once-in-a-lifetime experience and perspective. The fortress of ivory-colored marble and red sandstone is situated on a steep hillside overlooking a lake that reflects its massive walls and gateways. Inside, explore the many intricately decorated buildings, including the Palaces of Women, the separate quarters for all of the maharaja's wives.

Don't travel too cheaply in India. Stay in middle to upscale hotels to be safe and comfortable. All five-star hotels are safe and offer superb service. In the large cities you can wear Western clothing—pants, skirts, dresses. Outside the urban areas you will rarely see Indian women showing their shoulders, legs, or cleavage. To avoid unwanted attention or appearing insensitive to local customs, dress conservatively. I wear a *salwar kameez* (a traditional outfit of pants and a flowing, loose top), which feels cool, goes anywhere, and looks great on women of any size!

—Marybeth

INDIA'S RETAIL HIGHLIGHTS

The tiny shops of Janpath Market, in central Delhi, are stuffed with bright cotton garments, lovely textiles, leatherwork, curios, and fine jewelry. Everything is inexpensive: It's possible to bring back gifts for everyone back at home, which you can prepare for by packing an empty duffle bag (to bring home filled). And negotiating is expected. On the other hand, when you shop at the State Emporiums and Cottage Industries (government-operated stores with set prices), you don't bargain. Two that I've been to recently that I especially like are the State Emporia on Baba Kharak Singh Marg and the Central Cottage Industries Emporium on Janpath. You could spend days at Chandni Chowk, the buzzing center of Delhi's bazaars that sells everything from spices to silver, but it's congested and crime-ridden, so I recommend limiting your time to a rickshaw ride through the market's tiny lanes.

If you're a serious shopper, you could organize an entire trip to Rajasthan around the hobby. For 30 years, the Anokhi stores have pioneered hand-block printing for textiles (a labor-intensive technique used on bold-colored cotton). With 16 locations in India (including Jaipur, Udaipur, and Delhi), Anokhi sells top-quality clothing, home textiles, and accessories in Eastern and Western styles (*www.anokhi.com*). Fabindia sells classic Indian goods including hand-woven and hand-block-printed textiles and hand-sewn embroidery. Stores are located across India; in Agra, Delhi, and in Rajasthan, where you'll find them in Jaipur (*www.fabindia.com*). I've returned home from both of these stores loaded with exquisite clothing with appliqué, embroidery, patchwork, and beadwork.

continued on page 22

HEALTH TIPS FOR INDIA AND OTHER
EXOTIC DESTINATIONS

∾

See your health care provider at least four to six weeks before you travel to India. If your doctor is not familiar with travel medicine, you may need to visit a specialized travel clinic. Although there are no compulsory vaccinations for travel to India, the Centers for Disease Control strongly recommends you be up-to-date on routine vaccines, such as influenza, chickenpox (or varicella), polio, measles/mumps/rubella (MMR), and diphtheria/pertussis/tetanus (DPT).

Rarely do childhood diseases, such as measles, occur in the United States; however, they are still common in many parts of the world. A traveler who is not vaccinated can be at risk for infection. Many state and local health departments throughout the U.S. provide travel immunizations. To find the closest private or public travel clinic to you, go to the CDC website: *wwwn.cdc.gov/travel/content TravelClinics.aspx.*

Safe Eating and Drinking

Since diseases from food and water are the leading cause of illness in travelers, follow these tips:

* Avoid raw vegetables, stick to cooked foods, and peel all fruit before eating it.
* Carry antibacterial alcohol-based hand gel (with at least 60 percent alcohol) and use it often to wash your hands, especially before eating. Although you may find soap and water, there may not be towels.
* Do not drink tap water at all costs! Drink only bottled or boiled water, or carbonated (bubbly) drinks in cans or bottles. Make sure the waiter opens the bottled

water in front of you. Avoid ice cubes in drinks.
- Indian beer is very good and so are Indian gin and vodka, which you can drink without ice.
- Avoid eating food prepared by street vendors.
- Make sure food is fully cooked.

Stomach upsets from contaminated food and water often cause diarrhea. Make sure to bring over-the-counter diarrhea medicine with you so that you can treat mild cases yourself.

Pesky Mosquitoes — Malarial Protection

Malaria remains a risk in all areas throughout India, including urban areas, such as Delhi and Mumbai. Non-malarial areas are in the mountains above 6,561 feet. To prevent mosquito bites:

- Try to remain indoors in a screened or air-conditioned area during the peak biting periods, which are dusk and dawn. Sleep under mosquito nets if there is no air-conditioning or screens.
- When you go outdoors at dawn and dusk, wear long-sleeved shirts and long pants and use insect repellent that contains DEET.

Prevent Accidents

The number one source of injury among world travelers is motor-vehicle accidents. Poorly trained drivers, substandard roads, unmaintained vehicles, and dangerous driving habits such as passing on blind curves or speeding are common in many developing countries. Wear seatbelts and travel during daylight hours. Firmly insist that the driver slow down, drive more carefully, and pull over to talk on a cell phone.

—Marybeth

YOUR CHARIOT AWAITS

Hire a driver—alternatively, a chauffeur, tour guide, and savior—for this packed itinerary in the region from Welcome Rajasthan, a tour company based in Jaipur. You can either customize your own stops or sign on for an established tour (from $30 per day; *www.welcome rajasthan.com*).

INDIA'S VERSION OF SAFARI

For the spine-tingling thrill of a lifetime, get yourselves over to Ranthambore National Park, about 80 miles from Jaipur, for a glimpse at endangered Bengal tigers in the wild. Since the park is closed to tourists from July to September, the best time to see these beasts is during the winter months. After this exhilarating adventure, pamper yourselves in wild luxury at the high-end tents of the lavish Oberoi Vanyavilas located in the jungle on the edge of the Ranthambore Tiger Reserve. There's no roughing it here: You'll enjoy divine linens, a king-size, four-poster bed, and a bath ($700 per night for doubles; 800-562-3764, *www.oberoivanyavilas.com*). It might be your biggest splurge, but it's worth it.

EVENTS TO FLY IN FOR

There are volumes to read about the Pushkar Camel Fair in November; however, with more than 10,000 observers descending upon it, it can be a real zoo. Instead, I recommend going to the four-day Nagaur Fair, which is the second largest camel fair held in Rajasthan each January or February. Doesn't sound like your idea of a good time? While livestock and camel traders with long elegant mustaches and colorful turbans conduct business, you'll lose yourselves in horse and camel races, markets, and tug-of-war matches. Think county fair with a twist. As the sun sets over the desert sands, folk musicians play traditional instruments and sing. Ibex Expeditions offers a 15-day Rajasthan Royal Cities cultural tour that includes the Nagaur Camel Fair. The dates are set according to the lunar calendar (trips start from $4,900; *www.ibexpeditions.com*).

The International Folk Festival is held every year; Jodhpur and Jaipur alternate as the host city. You and the girls can marvel at the foreign sounds of Rajasthani folk ensembles, Hindi hip-hop, Indian ragas, flamenco, and a version of jazz. There are puppet shows, photo exhibits, a literary reading, an afternoon elephant polo match, and stalls selling local crafts. All of you should get involved (and your hands dirty) and sign up for workshops in jewelry-making, block printing, painting, poetry, or cooking (*www.jodhpurfolkfestival.org* and *www.jaipurfestival.org*).

BEST TOUR OPERATORS

My advice to first-timers to India is to book your trip through a reputable tour operator—one that includes Rajasthan in its itinerary. They will take care of all the details, including ones you'd never think of, such as hiring a personal shopper to help you navigate the local shops and markets. In 2007, I used the services of India specialists Ibex Expeditions and Greaves Tours—and I was impressed. You can book a private trip with Chicago-and-London-based Greaves or sign on for their 11-day "Marvels of Rajasthan" tour (from $6,587 [in January]; 800-318-7801, *www.greavesindia.com*). Ibex Expeditions, in New Delhi, specializes in cultural itineraries, heritage properties, ecotourism, safaris, and luxury travel. You can book a custom trip or select their 15-day "Window to Rajasthan's Heritage" tour, which includes some palace stays, visits to women's nonprofit projects, and interaction with the local Bishnoi Tribes (from $5,340; *www.ibexpeditions.com*).

The crème de la crème of hospitality, the Oberoi Hotels and Resorts and Taj Hotel Groups offer off-season specials from mid-April to the end of September. The eight-night packages with Oberoi hotels in Delhi or Mumbai let you design your own India tour, choosing from the other Oberoi properties in Jaipur, Udaipur, Agra, Shimla in the Himalaya, and Ranthambore (from $3,300, including transfers from airports or railway stations; 800-562-3764, *www.oberoihotels.com*). Moderately priced hotels in Rajasthan include the Umaid Bhawan in Jaipur, (from $40-90; *www.umaidbhawan.com*); Mandawa Haveli in Jaipur (from $80-120; *www.castlemandawa.com*); and in Udaipur, the Jagat Niwas Palace; (from $35-130; *www.jagatniwaspalace.com*) and Mewar Haveli, (from $25; *www.mewarhaveli.com*).

ONE CLICK AND YOU'RE OFF

For more information about Rajasthan, try *www.rajasthantourism.gov.in*. An introduction to all of India can be found at *www.incredibleindia.org*.

≈ Turkey ≈

Turkey, a country with one foot in Europe and one in Asia, has something for everyone: a spicy tempest of history filled with Oriental splendor, mystery, intrigue, and whirling dervishes; more Roman archaeological sites than all of Italy; more Greek ruins than Greece; 5,000 miles of coastline along four seas offering a treasure chest of coves, bays, beaches, and idyllic cruising; and historic cities—from Istanbul to Ephesus.

Mosques and minarets, bazaars and palaces—not to mention fantastic new restaurants and a buzzing nightlife—make Istanbul a crowd-pleaser. In the old city, or Sultanahmet, you can take a trip back in time. To find the sleek modernity of the city's fine restaurants and nightspots, cross the Golden Horn, a freshwater estuary shaped like a horn that divides old and new Istanbul. From Istanbul, I recommend sampling the country's highlights by flying to Cappadocia (in central Turkey), hopping south to Antalya to sail the Turquoise Coast, then heading west to visit the 3,000-year-old ruins at Ephesus. You can hop from place to place via short flights or tap into Turkey's extensive network of air-conditioned buses. Throughout the country, you'll be met with legendary Turkish warmth and hospitality, and you'll enjoy it all the more in the company of your best pals. The country's top tourist destinations—especially the Turkish coast—fill with visitors during the summer. If you and the girls can hold off until the fall or spring, you'll have a better chance of seeing the country at an easier pace, with fewer crowds, and out of the summer heat.

SIGHTSEE, SHOP, SOAK IN ISTANBUL

Byzantine art and architecture's tour de force has always been Istanbul's Hagia Sophia, a massive structure with a dome of 40 arched windows built by Byzantine Emperor Justinian almost 1,500 years ago. When the Turks took over Constantinople (now Istanbul) in 1453, this basilica was converted to a mosque, and today it's a museum. You'll gape at the elaborate mosaics and gigantic marble pillars. And at sunset, you'll hear the call to prayer echoing over the city from its minarets. Second to Hagia Sophia in beauty, the Sultan Ahmed Mosque (known as the Blue Mosque, for the sapphire-colored tiles on the inside), shows off its eye-catching array of domes and minarets.

Taxis are a great way to get around Istanbul, but they are not for the timid, the fainthearted, or those who insist on wearing a seat belt. Before you get into a taxi, ask the driver if he uses the meter. If he refuses to use the meter, find another cab. The price he quotes is invariably higher than the metered fare.

The term "hard sell" may as well have been invented in Istanbul's Kapali Carsi, one of the largest covered bazaars in the world. Here vendors encourage you—strongly—to come into their shops. There's no harm accepting their invitation for tea, from, say, the Turkish equivalent of a carpet salesman, because you might learn about the history of the craft.

Turkey is also well known for *hammams*, or baths, which often have gorgeous architectural details. At the historic Cemberlitas Hamami in Istanbul, guests sit and sweat in a hot chamber and can treat themselves to an exfoliating scrub and a 30-minute massage ($56 including bath, scrub, and massage; *www.cemberlitashamami .com.tr*). If it's in the budget, the Four Seasons Istanbul is the city's finest offering—especially for gals with packed days looking to spoil themselves (from $390 for two for the bed-and-breakfast package; *www.fourseasons.com/istanbul*).

ANOTHER PLANET

Underground cities, cave churches, and rock figures that look like Dr. Seuss characters—find them all in the central region of Cappadocia. The photogenic geology here takes on bewildering forms ranging from the fairy chimney rock formations to the strik- ing red-rock gorge of the Ihlara Valley. This supernatural landscape also serves as a window to a rich, complex history: You'll marvel over the underground cities of Derinkuyu and Kaymakli, which may be close to 4,000 years old, and churches adorned with centuries- old Byzantine frescoes.

SAILING THE TURQUOISE COAST

Surrounded by water on three sides, Turkey practically begs you to take to its waters. With almost 5,000 miles of coastline along four seas, its coast is a treasure chest of coves, inlets, bays, and beaches. The sunny skies and warm waters of the Turquoise Coast on the Mediterranean beat all your other options. You and the girls need to rent a *gulet* (the Turkish take on a sailboat) or book a cruise with a local company to access hiking trails to coastal ruins, ports, and historic monuments. In the midday sunshine, you can snorkel, swim, or lounge on deck spying dolphins and sea turtles. If you decide to charter a boat—usually for 6 to 12 passengers—the onboard cook will likely whip up some amazing fresh seafood dishes while you and your friends have a glass of wine on the deck. It can be a great way to celebrate a birthday or retirement or simply get some quiet time with the girls.

MUST-SEE RUINS

The lay historians and archaeologists among you won't want to miss a visit to Ephesus, on the Aegean Sea in the west. Here you will explore the ruins of a city that was founded close to 3,000 years ago, and follow in the footsteps of its famous visitors: Alexander the Great came in 334 B.C.; early Christians St. John and St. Paul centuries later. To some, Ephesus might be too crowded and feel somewhat hokey (and hot, so bring a hat and a water bottle). If this is the case, you can find solitude farther inland in the ancient town of Aphrodisias, dedicated to the Greek goddess Aphrodite. It's home to a beautifully preserved Roman theater, an odeum, and the columns of the temple to the goddess of love and beauty, Aphrodite. You may find that it could just be you and the girls strolling through history.

EVENTS TO FLY IN FOR

Istanbul has fantastic international festivals to suit arts lovers of all stripes: a film festival (March), theater (May), music (June), and jazz (July). Learn about them all at *www.istfest.org*.

BEST TOUR OPERATORS

U.S.-based Overseas Adventure Travel runs an 18-day trip that combines a gulet along the Turquoise Coast with visits to historic Ephesus, Istanbul, Cappadocia, and more (from $2,995 including flight from New York; 800-493-6824, *www.oattravel.com*). The cultural travel experts at Wilderness Travel, based in San Francisco's Bay Area, have arranged an 11-day trip that combines a cruise along the gorgeous Turquoise Coast. The trip includes visits to Ephesus, Istanbul, and Cappadocia (from $3,895; *www.wilderness travel.com*).

ONE CLICK AND YOU'RE OFF

Visit Turkish Tourism at *www.tourismturkey.org*.

Expect a lot of attention from Turkish men, especially touts in the bazaars. Many shopkeepers will insistently call out to you and use high-pressure sales tactics. They may even follow you down the street after you show interest in their goods. To avoid problems, don't look them in the eye or respond unless you intend to enter their shop.

ᵔᵕ Vietnam ᵔᵕ

From war-torn country to irresistible exotic travel oasis—an admirable comeback for the people of Vietnam. Stretched out more than a thousand miles from north to south along the eastern edge of Southeast Asia, the country today entices travelers with magnificent sandy beaches along the South China Sea, emerald-colored rice paddies, and bustling cities with divine artistry and delectable cuisine. Add to that 54 ethnic groups and a French influence, and you've got a rich vacation awaiting you. It's this variation of culture (and dare you forget its past) that has drawn so many girlfriends of mine to its borders. But the real hard sell is its tropical climate and insanely tasty gastronomy (think of it as the lightest and brightest tasting Chinese food possible). I suggest to everyone to start in the north, in the capital of Hanoi (where your plane will land), where the culture-vultures among you will be bowled over by both the traditional art and architecture and the modern additions. The way to go from here is southward, along the coast through the small city of Hoi An (with a stop at Nha Trang's photogenic beaches) until you reach Ho Chi Minh City, which you may know as Saigon. You can either fly between the major cities, or board a train that runs between Hanoi and Ho Chi Minh City, stopping at the most scenic cities along the coast. An option for a small group is to hire a driver to navigate the wild roads of Vietnam—you and the gals can gaze at the scenery while the driver worries about the water buffalo in the middle of the road. And from north to south (and everywhere in between), you will positively salivate over the food: Imagine bowls of steaming noodles, fresh fish and vegetables, lemongrass and lime. The weather is most reliably cool and dry here in the spring and fall, but no matter when you go, Vietnam's lush rain forests will be…rainy. Your best friend will be a lightweight, packable rain jacket.

BIG CITY THRILLS

Hanoi, in the middle of the Red River Delta, is one of Asia's most alluring capital cities. The ideal way to see it, as far as I'm concerned, is to pack yourselves into a bicycle rickshaw. There are 600-plus pagodas and temples here, many of them hundreds of years old, and stunning buildings that reflect France's presence in Vietnam, including the spectacular Opera House. Ladies, you must get tickets to a performance here, even if just to peek inside at the ornate staircases and gilded mirrors. The Old Quarter is a particular treat, with 36 streets named for artisans' guilds—silversmiths and bamboo craftsmen, for instance. More so in Hanoi that anywhere else in the nation, a healthy art scene is synthesizing both an obligation to a rich history and to modernity. And day trips to some of the villages outside of Hanoi will afford you a look back at its untouched ancient art forms. Bat Trang is known for its traditional pottery; while Van Phuc is a silk village, where you might see silkworms spinning their magic fibers. Whereas Hanoi offers you a host of galleries representing Vietnam's young talent. Start your gallery-hopping with the city's best: Hanoi Studio exhibits works by up-and-coming Vietnamese artists (*www.arthanoistudio.com*).

HALONG BAY BEACH BREAK
Northwest of Hanoi, Halong Bay presents a landscape foreign to many. Limestone karst islands, jungle-covered mounds of gray-stone rock sculptured by weather to form fantastic towers, are scattered across its turquoise-colored water. Caves and grottos make for a kayaker's playground. Duck inside them and you'll feel like you're in the core of the Earth. And beaches here are long swaths of silky yellow sand. Find the secluded ones (and maybe a monkey or two) on an overnight boat trip (from $101 per person per night; *www.handspan .com*) or arrange with a local merchant to rent kayaks.

SHOP, SHOP, SHOP
Formerly Vietnam's most important port, Hoi An boasts 844 historic landmarks—among them 400-year-old merchant houses. Combine them with white-sand beaches and picturesque streets perfect for strolling. But what you'll be talking about long after you leave will be what you bought. Hoi An's tailors are world famous: You can walk into any of them with a photo of the budget-blowing suit or gown you saw in *Vogue* and they'll whip it up for you. It's possible to revamp an entire wardrobe for less than a thousand dollars! Yaly Couture is especially good—the prices are slightly higher, but for the craftsmanship it's well worth it (located on Nguyen Thai Hoc, *www .yalycouture.com*).

SPA BREAK
At the Evason Ana Mandara & Spa in Nha Trang, you and the girls can step out of sightseer mode with a session of tai chi on the beach or with an Eastern-style facial and massage. For a decadent spa retreat, visit the Evason Hideaway, accessible only by boat. There

The scars of war aren't too far beneath the surface in Vietnam. I went underground into the Cu Chi tunnel networks in which millions of Vietnamese once lived and fought American GIs. The tunnel system was an underground city with kitchens, living areas, storage rooms, weapon factories, tiled hospitals, and command centers. You'll crawl through narrow passageways to see bunkers with bunk beds, a hospital, and kitchens with cooking stoves. Located 45 miles northwest of Saigon, the tunnel system stretched from the edge of Saigon to the Cambodian border, about 150 miles, at the height of the Vietnam War. Up to 10,000 people lived for years underground—getting married, having babies, going to school. They only came out at night to furtively take care of their crops. My visit was a moving and somewhat uncomfortable experience, but I don't regret it for a minute.

My advice: Hire a taxi in Saigon and go visit these subterranean warrens. It's an adventure you'll never forget. It's well worth the effort.

—Marybeth

you get spoiled by the same wonderful spa treatments but in peaceful seclusion. Imagine soaking in a Vietnamese herbal bath with the jungle on one side and a white sandy shore on the other (services at Evason Ana Mandara begin at $252, Evason Hideaway starts at $667; *www.sixsenses.com*).

HOW TO HO CHI MINH

You'll find Ho Chi Minh City to be quite a change of pace after you've been out in the Vietnamese countryside or unwinding at a tranquil spa. Go from zero to 80 mph upon arrival in this bustling metropolis in the south and dive right in with a trip to the Ben Thanh Market, burgeoning with flowers, produce, jewelry, clothing, and porcelain. You and the girls will get a kick out of eating alongside the locals from steaming stalls after a hard day of shopping. Another marquee activity to do here is a visit to the Cu Chi tunnels (see above), an extensive network of underground passageways outside the city, used during the war with the French and, later, the Americans. After hours, the group should get gussied up for a familiar Western tradition: cocktails on the roof of a retro-chic hotel. The posh Rex Hotel has a place on the world's "Top Ten" lists (*www.rexhotelvietnam.com*).

IT'S ALL ABOUT THE FOOD

On this trip, you can look forward to soothing bowls of stringy and filling pho noodles with fresh vegetables, meats, and sprigs of mint, the freshest spring rolls you've ever tasted, and the occasional buttery Parisian baguette and croissant. And all for cheap, cheap, cheap. Never be afraid to stumble into small local restaurants: It could be the best meal in Vietnam. (That said, one you must wander into is Brothers Café Hoi An.) Where there's excellent food, not far are notable cooking schools. Also in Hoi An, the Red Bridge Restaurant and Cooking School (*www .visithoian.com/redbridge.html*) or the Morning Glory Cooking School (*www.hoianhospitality.com/morning.html*) are among my favorites. And Ho Chi Minh City's Vietnam Cookery Center escorts you to a market to select your ingredients (*www.expat-services.com*).

BEST TOUR OPERATORS

Myths and Mountains, based in Nevada, guides both a classic tour and an adventure version of Vietnam and Southeast Asia. My pick: their 15-day "Classic Vietnam" trip by way of Saigon, Vietnam's coast, and Hanoi with an emphasis on food and the arts (from $4,795 for 3-5 people, $4,295 for 6-9; 800-670-6984, *www.mythsandmountains.com*). The Californians at Classic Journeys have put together a wonderful walking trip focusing on Ho Chi Minh City, rice fields, and a visit to Cambodia's Angkor Wat (from $3,895; 800-200-3887, *www.classicjourneys.com*).

ONE CLICK AND YOU'RE OFF

Start planning with a visit to Vietnam Tourism online at *www.viet namtourism.com*. If you'll be taking the train, schedules and fares can be found on *www.vr.com.vn/english*.

❧ Ecuador ❧

They say variety is the spice of life, and in Ecuador, you'll find the spice cabinet well stocked, particularly if you're an outdoorsy gal. The northernmost country in South America, Ecuador is located right on the Equator (as you might have guessed). It's probably best known for its treasured Galápagos Islands, located about 600 miles offshore and reachable via a three-hour flight from the capital city of Quito. This trip is epic—with a capital "E." For girlfriends there's no bigger trip to take. And you can expect a wildlife experience like no other in the world—you'll watch giant tortoises crawl at the pace of, well, a tortoise, in search of a leafy lunch. From boats, curious visitors spy on blue-footed boobies in the midst of a comical mating dance. You can snorkel among penguins, and literally everywhere you go, you'll be accompanied by a troop of playful young sea lions eager to make friends. You'll start your equatorial adventure by flying into Quito, nestled among Andean volcanoes. Do not skip the museums and churches of this historic center. If you have an extra day, hire a taxi for the two-hour drive to the town of Otavalo, where you'll find a lively market filled with affordable handmade textiles, wood carvings, leather goods, and alpaca blankets. (My policy of packing an empty bag to get all your purchases home with you applies.) The Galápagos deserve about a week of your time—your camera's memory card will have long been used up by then and it's the length of most cruises in the region. But if you can, I'd stay in Ecuador just a bit longer. Chances are, you won't make it down this way very many times in your life, and the Amazon jungle is a "life list" item. Extend your trip and indulge yourselves with a stay at a jungle eco-lodge, where you'll spend days traipsing after many of the 400-plus

EASY ECUADOR

✑

Ecuador is such an easy destination because they use U.S. currency and electrical outlets. When the country was on the verge of bankruptcy in the early 2000s, the government decided to adopt the U.S. dollar. North American tourists love the electrical plug adaptability because you can easily recharge your digital camera batteries or use a hair dryer anywhere there is an electrical connection—even in the Amazon jungle.

Quito is located at an elevation of 9,300 feet, so headaches are a common occurrence on the first day. Allow two days in Quito to acclimatize. If you have had altitude problems in the past, see a travel doctor for medication, which you should take before arriving at altitude.

—Marybeth

bird species in the Amazon. Having been to what will seem like the edge of the universe, you'll all return with a renewed connection to the natural world. And the warm weather will leave you feeling revived—and tan. Since this an equatorial region, any time of year is a good time to visit. But from January to June, water temps are slightly warmer in the Galápagos—perfect for snorkeling with the seals sans the wet suit.

ISLAND HOPPING

When your flight touches down at Baltra airport in the Galápagos, you've arrived at the world's most fascinating wildlife destination—Charles Darwin sure seemed to think so. The Galápagos are a chain of islands, and the best way to see them and their magnificent animals is by boat. If you charter your own yacht, you and your seafaring sisters can have your own expert naturalist guide to show

GALÁPAGOS ESSENTIALS

ॐ

High-quality binoculars are a must on wildlife and nature cruises, such as those in the Amazon and Galápagos. Each person should have her own pair. Affix a label on the binoculars, as well as on the case, so if they're misplaced, they can easily be returned to you.

Brightly colored clothing should be avoided when viewing wildlife. Red makes you very conspicuous to wildlife. Pack khaki, brown, or olive safari clothing because you'll want to get as close as possible to photograph the amazing wildlife that can't be found anywhere else in the world. You can approach the giant tortoises, marine iguanas, penguins, and colonies of sea lions and their young pups because they have a remarkable lack of fear and are unaffected by people. Keep your eyes open for the red Sally lightfoot crab, one of 118 species of crab found in the Galápagos Islands, who "skip" across the water.

—Marybeth

you the islands' best spots, a chef to whip up freshly caught seafood, and a deck from which to watch the sunset after days of snorkeling, hiking, and sea kayaking. If you're bird enthusiasts, you've got it made here. During your cruise you'll see waved albatrosses, pink flamingos, Galápagos ducks, blue-footed boobies, and the occasional penguin. Most cruises follow the same route, and all include a stop in Puerto Ayora so that you can study up on local flora and fauna at the Charles Darwin Research Station. Here, a breeding center raises giant tortoises to be released into the wild. The most famous resident is Lonesome George, a tortoise who's the last of his subspecies. Another highlight is Bartolomé Island. If you've seen the movie *Master and Commander*, picture its gorgeous, stark island scenery. Well, this is where it was filmed. I recommend the short hike to the top of the island at sunrise for an amazing panoramic vista of the Galápagos's moon-like landscape. If you and the gals are up for some underwater sightseeing, don masks and fins and snorkel along the Galápagos's equatorial reefs. You'll be accompanied by playful sea lions everywhere you go, and you'll spot sea stars, reef fish, hammerhead sharks, whale sharks, and rays. For the divers among you, Scuba Iguana, based in Puerto Ayora, offers single and multiday scuba diving trips (from $90 for single day; *www.scubaiguana.com*).

TOP ISLAND LODGES

For those of you who are prone to serious seasickness, I'd recommend sleeping in a hotel on land and taking day trips among the islands. But even if you don't get queasy, you might want to treat yourselves to a pre- or post-cruise night of luxury at the Royal Palm Hotel's tropical forest resort. Here you can indulge in foot massages and whirlpools and visit an art gallery featuring Ecuadorian artists (from $345; *www.royalpalmgalapagos.com*). Another great option is the adventure-focused Finch Bay Eco Hotel, which arranges day tours of the islands by yacht, kayak, mountain bike, or foot (three-night packages start at $976; *www.finchbayhotel.com*).

AMAZON ADVENTURE

After your dose of the Galápagos, you and the girls might still have a thirst for more adventure. And there isn't a better place to get it than the Ecuadorian Amazon, a short flight to the east of Quito. As you fly in, you'll get a breathtaking aerial view of one of the world's lushest landscapes. The Amazon is home to birds seen nowhere else in the world. The eco-lodges in this area are dedicated to sustainable

I'd never leave home without calorie-free, powdered Crystal Light lemonade, my hard Nalgene water bottle, and vodka. When we were cruising in the Galápagos, we had cocktails on the deck each evening. The drinks aboard were expensive, so we mixed the powder, vodka, and ice made from bottled water.

—Chris Bard, 50s, Retired Teacher, Birder, Skier, Kayaker,
Adventure Traveler, Alameda, California

---

operations, preserving the nature around them. And the indigenous people working at them open your eyes to their jungle world. One lodge I really loved, the Kapawi Ecolodge and Reserve, began in partnership with the regional Achuar people. And during your stay in one of the guest cabins (all built using Achuar architectural principles), you can visit local villages to learn more about their ways (three nights start at $670 for double occupancy; *www.kapawi.com*). Overlooking the Napo River, the Yachana Lodge will appeal to the sybarites among you—especially the chocoholics who can learn about and sample the Yachana Jungle chocolate (three nights from $405; *www.yachana.com*).

BEST TOUR OPERATORS
Wilderness Travel, operating since 1978, leads an active trip that maximizes your time with Galápagos wildlife—you'll get plenty of snorkeling excursions and expert naturalist-led hikes each day when you charter one of their 84-foot sailing yachts, the *Sea Cloud* or the *Rachel*. Depending on the trip you choose, you can take an extension to one of several eco-lodges in the Amazon, too (from $3,695 per person for groups of seven or eight; 800-368-2794, *www.wildernesstravel.com*). Myths and Mountains's unique multiday trips include visits with Ecuadorian shamans, aka healers, and to the country's best spas. Combine these special journeys with one of their Galápagos cruises. With several boats at their service, they'll find just the right one for you and the ladies (from $3,895 per person, $3,450 per person, and $2,995, respectively; 800-670-6984, *www.mythsandmountains.com*).

ONE CLICK AND YOU'RE OFF
Go to Ecuador's Ministry of Tourism online at *www.purecuador.com*.

Morocco

Perhaps Humphrey Bogart and his "Here's looking at you, kid" line did more for Morocco's image in the West than any tourism board could have. But there's also this image of a North African nation with snake charmers, bazaars, camels, dusty alleys in ancient villages, and the dunes of the Sahara desert. If you can't shake the intrigue, then Morocco is a must. Girlfriends with an intrepid streak can look forward to an adventure woven with dichotomies: desert and sea, French and Spanish influences, African and Middle Eastern ways, and old-world Berber and Muslim customs colliding with modernity. While the country may seem worlds away, the flight to Morocco actually isn't much longer than a trip to Europe. Now to set those romantic notions (and Bogart fans) straight, Casablanca is not worthy of a visit: It's not particularly scenic. Instead, when you land on Moroccan soil, make a beeline to colorful Marrakesh in the foothills of the Atlas Mountains to kick off your journey with some superlative shopping, people-watching, and exotic gardens. From there, I recommend traveling in a loop, crossing from Marrakesh west to the beach town of Essaouira (an 18th-century fortified town now with an energetic beach resort scene), then heading south to the dramatic Atlas Mountains and the Sahara beyond them, and finally returning through Fez, with its fascinating spiderweb of medieval streets. It's possible to travel the country by train (those who prefer to take in the landscape at this pace will get a kick out of hopping aboard, pressing play on their iPods, and zoning out to the Crosby, Stills and Nash song "Marrakesh Express"). But if you're not up for this kind of adventure (and it will challenge you), I advise most women to sign up with a U.S-based travel company. If you have a large enough group, you may consider your own private trip. The best time for your visit is from November to March, when the weather is cool. But be careful, because it *really* cools down at night in the Atlas Mountains and the Sahara. You'll want to pack warm clothes, but, since this is a Muslim country, you should always respect local customs by covering up: long-sleeved shirts, pants, and skirts wherever you go.

MEET UP IN MARRAKESH

Lively Marrakesh has long been a trading hub—it's a crossroads where cultures meet, mingle, and sell their finest merchandise. As you wander past rose-colored buildings and browse the souks (markets) for brightly colored skeins of wool, essential oils, and golden slippers, you and the girls will find yourselves entranced by it all. You can spend hours here combing through crafts, haggling with merchants, and taking in the smells of the turmeric, cumin, and paprika on display. For a drastic change of scene, pay a visit to the Majorelle Garden—a plume of French elegance in the heart of Marrakesh. Three hundred species of palm, bamboo, and aquatic plants are contained within its brilliant blue walls. French designer extraordinaire Yves Saint Laurent is one of Marjorelle's owners, and his personal Islamic art collection is housed in a small museum on the grounds (www.jardinmajorelle.com). A must for girlfriends is flagging down a *calèche*, a horse-drawn carriage, and trotting through the city. If you time it to sundown, you can witness how the golden rays cast a splendid glow onto its red-ochre walls. And if you thought the city was electric during the day, at night it gets a second wind and presents some unparalleled experiences. After dark, Djemma el Fna, Marrakesh's renowned square, transforms into a stage for snake charmers, storytellers, fire-eaters, and acrobats. Plan for at least one ladies' night on the square, where you can either take a seat in one of the streetside cafés and watch the action unfold or stroll around for an active dining tour of the delicious food stalls.

FIT FOR A QUEEN

Those of you who take luxury seriously can look to a *riad*, or Moroccan palace, for a heavenly retreat after a day spent walking the busy city streets. Girlfriends can look forward to spending some

When I think of dining in Morocco, all I can think of is—*tagine! tagine! tagine!* We ate lamb tagine, chicken tagine, goat tagine, and unidentifiable tagines—all delicious and served in beautiful ceramic pots with long chimneys. We were planning to buy pots to bring home, but by the end of our visit, we were "tagined out" and didn't!

Recently I took a Moroccan cooking course and learned how to make tagine. The pots are all the rage now and I ended up buying them in a glitzy kitchen supply store in Arizona, at a huge markup, of course. My advice: don't hesitate. Buy whatever you like while you're there.

—Pat Watt, 60s, World Traveler, Writer, Toronto, Canada

time together unwinding and really feeling pampered. And the best thing about them is the price: For one night in a riad in Marrakesh, for example, you might only spend $80 for a room with two single beds. To rent out the entire riad would cost just $45 per person for a group of 16 ladies. And there are plenty of palaces to choose from throughout the country (*www.riadsmorocco.com*).

HIT THE BEACH

On the Atlantic coast, about a hundred miles west of Marrakesh, you can recharge in Essaouira, an artsy, laid-back community. Windsurfers and kiteboarders gather here to get a lift from the northeast trade winds that blow through between March and November. It also has an impressive music scene. (Both Jimi Hendrix and Cat Stevens graced its stages.) There's something for every lady: Laze on the sand, have a go at one of the many water sports offered, or get into its side streets.

MOUNTAIN HIGH

It may come as a surprise that Morocco is home to a mountain range of jagged peaks and snowy caps. Once you lay your eyes on the majestic high Atlas Mountains, they'll be etched in your minds forever. Marrakesh is the gateway to these mountains sprinkled with towns made up of kasbahs—a high-walled fortress that once protected it from attacks. Some kasbahs are now historic sites that you can visit. One not to miss is the Kasbah Ait Benhaddou, which appeared in the film *Lawrence of Arabia*. The Kasbah du Toubkal, a restored kasbah turned hotel nestled at the base of North Africa's highest peak: 13,665-foot Mount Toubkal ($220 per night for doubles; *www.kasbahdutoubkal.com*). The hikers among you can ask at the front desk to have a trek arranged into the mountains.

SAHARAN SPECIAL

After you cross through the mountains, you are delivered to the world's largest desert. To immerse yourselves in the Saharan experience (perhaps familiar from Paolo Coehlo's *The Alchemist*), set out with a guide on camelback (many tours of Morocco incorporate this into their itineraries). By day, you'll cross the Sahara on the back of these funny creatures, stopping to hunt for fossils from the Paleozoic era and scramble up 300-foot dunes to gaze out at the vast sea of sand. To top it off, you'll visit Erg Chebbi, the largest expanse of dunes in Morocco, with brilliantly orangey sand. That night you'll camp in comfy tents, watch the sun drop on the Sahara, take in the desert sounds, and stay up way past your bedtimes, gaping at the pitch-black sky teeming with constellations.

GET LOST IN FEZ

Fez, considered Morocco's intellectual touchstone, is the world's largest medieval town in use today. A fun alternative to a walking tour of its labyrinthine streets, stunning mosques, imposing palaces, souks, and ornate fountains is letting a donkey be your transport. You and the girls will likely laugh your way through it. And for whatever you compromised in comfort (and maybe a bit of pride) on your tour, you'll make up for with a stay at the exquisite La Maison Bleue. Retire to an elegant room for a nap (or indulge in an orange blossom water massage or soak your limbs in a traditional hammam), which should prepare you for the feast that awaits you. Served by waiters in traditional garb, you'll receive course after course ranging from couscous to lamb tagines to mint tea. Good thing you'll have pillows all around you because you'll need to lie back and rest in between courses (from about $242 per night for doubles; *www.maisonbleue.com*).

EVENTS TO FLY IN FOR

If anyone is in need of a spirit booster, a must is the Fez Sacred Music Festival. Fez turns itself over each June to a week of international performances (past guests have included Johnny Clegg and Angelique Kido) that includes Sufi musicians, sunrise performances at the Merinides Quarry, and healing Gregorian chants (*www.fesfestival.com*).

BEST TOUR OPERATORS

Adventurous gals should join Mountain Travel Sobek's 14-day trip through Morocco's hot spots; it includes a four-day camel trek and four-wheel-drive spree into the Atlas Mountains and the Sahara (from $4,595; 888-687-6235, *www.mtsobek.com*). On an Overseas Adventure Travel trip you'll take in Morocco's cities and really connect with Berber culture during their 15-day tour with an overnight in the Sahara (from $2,595, including flight from New York; 800-493-6824, *www.oattravel.com*). If your time is limited (and your legs are strong), cycle with Backroads on their six-day biking and walking combo between Marrakesh and Essaouira (from $3,998; 800-462-2848, *www.backroads.com*).

ONE CLICK AND YOU'RE OFF

For more on Morocco, start by visiting *www.visitmorocco.org*.

CHAPTER TWO

Cosmopolitan Cities

∾ **CLAIRE'S STORY** ∾

"Can you meet me in the Amazon in two weeks?" Claire's former college roommate asked her in a middle-of-the night, long-distance phone call from Brazil. "What airport do I fly into?" was her response. Claire and Claudine are cut from the same mold; they're spirited, bold, successful, and adventurous women who meet, once a year, in an exotic place. Although they live on opposite coasts—Claire is in Los Angeles and Claudine is in Miami—the geographic distances haven't hindered their girlfriend getaways for the past 15 years. When they met in college, in upstate Vermont, they discovered they were both fascinated with the language and Latin culture of Central and South America. They naturally gravitated south of the border for reunions because they're both fluent in Spanish. Claudine, who is also fluent in Portuguese, works for an international credit card company and travels for weeks at a time in South America, including numerous visits to Buenos Aires.

Last fall, when Claire changed jobs and discovered she had a window of freedom, she caught the next plane to Buenos Aires to meet Claudine for a week of walking, dancing the tango, feasting, and shopping.

"Buenos Aires is a safe walking city—we hit the pavement with comfortable shoes and strolled in the Recoleta area through neat little parks, the cemetery, and a craft fair," says Claire. "The area reminded me of New York's Madison Avenue; clean and manicured, nice boutiques with an upscale ambience.

"We visited in November when the purple jacaranda was blooming and the city was a lush garden. It was as beautiful as Paris or Florence," states Claire.

No one can leave Buenos Aires without indulging copiously in steak. In Argentina cattle eat well and steak houses cook grass-fed beef from cattle of British origin, mostly Aberdeen Angus, Shorthorn, or Hereford. Even the most modest steak house takes pride in grilling it until the outside crust has a smoky caramelized flavor and the inside is still rosy red and moist. "The meat was so delicious we ate it at least once a day. I don't think I had ever eaten grass-fed steak before. I could actually taste the mellow grass flavor," says Claire. "They put great effort and passion into preparing the perfect steak on the bar-be-que."

For the past decade Claudine has shopped her way through Europe, Asia, and Latin America on business trips. "The shopping was truly amazing and very affordable," Claire says. "Even Claudine, my sophisticated, shopaholic friend, couldn't get enough of the inexpensive, but very high-quality products, especially leather. When we finally tired of shopping, we'd stop in a café for a snack of chicken empanadas (stuffed pastries) and a glass of chilled Malbec wine."

"It's a great place for women, because it's safe, you're treated with respect, there's a lot to do and buy," adds Claire. "I've been to New York, Paris, London, and other cosmopolitan cities. In Buenos Aires you feel you're on a different continent and it's a very sophisticated and cultured city."

"We always have two or three more trips in the works. Sometimes they don't pan out, but we enjoy the planning. For us, travel is about celebrating our freedom," says Claire. "Next year we're thinking about Tokyo and Santiago, Chile."

~ Paris ~

Paris promises something for every woman—sophistication, beauty, culture, cuisine, art, escape, and that indefinable quality called ambience. Generations of artists, from Monet to van Gogh, painted it from high and low; authors and poets from Molière to Hemingway and Henry Miller portrayed their vision of the City of Lights. French films have charmed us and we know the songs of Maurice Chevalier and Edith Piaf by heart—but every woman must discover *her own* Paris. After the first visit to the City of Lights, when everyone tries to see all the tourist attractions, you realize you cannot fully appreciate the ambience of Paris unless you curb your frenetic pace, to become a *flaneur*—an aimless stroller in a town ideal for aimless walking. You must allow time to wander, to sit, to savor sensations, to tune in and be surprised by Parisian daily life.

For four years in my 20s I lived on rue Jacob, in the 6th arrondissement, and I return to Paris as often as I can; regardless of the season or the exchange rate. I've seen it through the eyes of my daughters, my mother, my husband, my goddaughter, and my girlfriends. Let me offer you a glimpse of the Paris I love: It is waking to the eight o'clock bells of the St.-Germain-des-Prés church, meandering along the Seine pausing to browse for old postcards in the quayside outdoor bookstalls, watching the barges as they cruise up and down the river, visiting Monet's water lily paintings in the Musée de l'Orangerie, strolling by my favorite Maillol sculptures in the Tuileries Garden, lunching on a baguette and Brie sandwich in the Place des Vosges, wandering the quaint neighborhoods of the Left Bank, sipping a kir in a sophisticated café, and savoring *steak frites* and chocolate mousse. And of course there are countless other world-class sights and attractions to lure you for a gathering with your friends. Visit the mansions on the Île St.-Louis, spend an afternoon in Luxembourg Garden, hit the major museums, go to a Vivaldi concert at Ste.-Chapelle, take a French cooking class, and shop at outdoor street markets for cheese and fruit, or in stores like the famed Le Bon Marché—all of which, lets face it, are eminently more fun to do with your girlfriends. Paris gets a lot of attention for being one of the most romantic cities in the world—and it is. But it's also a get-up-and-go metropolis. Paris is a walker's city, and navigating your way around the 20 neighborhoods, or

continued on page 44

MYTHS ABOUT PARIS:
TRUE OR NOT?

∽

1. Paris is really, really expensive.
   Of course, as in any city of the world, the sky's the limit when it comes to what you can pay for things. But it is completely possible to find quality, fashionable goods, meals, and other items for bargain and affordable prices. You just have to know where to look!

2. Paris is not safe, especially for women.
   In general, European cities are safer than North American ones, since guns, gangs, personal property/bank robberies, and drugs are not as common. The most common hazard, particularly for tourists, is pickpockets, who prey on easy targets. Simply don't provide these opportunities or make it easy to be a target. The most common hazard for women in Paris is encountering the odd *drageur*, local men who profess their undying love to foreigners. These men are more a source of mild amusement or irritation than a threat.

3. You can't wear jeans in Paris.
   Paris may be considered one of the fashion capitals of the world, but jeans are worn everywhere, by everyone, even Galeries Lafayette sales staff! Parisians wear their jeans with flair: Try pairing yours with great shoes and accessories.

4. It is unsafe to take the Métro, especially at night.
   The Paris Métro system and buses are filled with tourists and Parisians at all hours of the day and night and are considered safe. Métro, city, and national police patrol public areas frequently, ensuring the public's safety.

5. Parisian sidewalks are filthy.
   There is dog *merde* (poop) all over the streets of Paris, but it's not as bad as it was a decade ago.

6. Parisians are unfriendly and rude.
   This myth couldn't be further from the truth, since the majority of Parisians are helpful and friendly. Upon first meeting, Parisians can appear to be less casual and more reserved than Americans; however, this does not translate to unfriendliness. Take the time to understand the cultural differences and behave accordingly.

7. Secondhand smoke will negatively impact your culinary, bar, and café experiences.
   Full antismoking laws were instigated in January 2008 that ban puffing in restaurants, bar-tabacs, clubs, and hotels.

8. There is very little to no air-conditioning in France.
   This is absolutely true. Luckily, only in the peak of summer does the weather warrant the need for air conditioning.

9. Your hotel quarters will be cramped.
   Many hotels occupy buildings erected decades ago, if not more than a century ago. In those hotels, guest-rooms and elevators are generally much smaller than you would expect. Walls may be paper-thin, and the floors and ceiling may not match and may be crooked.

10. Public restrooms are awful.
    There are very few free public washrooms in Paris in the style we are accustomed to. Each washroom will be different and many public washrooms, including those in cafés, can range from really good to poor. There still exist some "Turkish-style" squatters in Parisian cafés and restaurants.

—Karen Henrich, 48, Personal Shopper, Nuit Blanche Tours,
Paris, France

arrondissements, is an adventure in itself. The beauty of its clean, efficient Métro system is that if you get tired of walking, you can always hop a train. In the tourist areas of central Paris, people are out at all hours of the day and night, and the streets and Métro are safe.

WHEN TO GO

Paris's weather is similar to London's—which is to say, warm and gorgeous in the summer, but chilly and drizzly the rest of the year. September and October, after the summer heat subsides and shopkeepers and restaurateurs return from their summer holidays, is my favorite time to visit. But I'll go anytime I can find a reasonable plane ticket.

FIRST TIMER ORIENTATION

It certainly won't come as a surprise that I'm suggesting a cruise along the Seine or a tour of the Eiffel Tower, but I simply don't know of a better way to get the lay of the land than with a trip to the top of the city's tallest structure or drifting along the river looking up. Take turns posing for pictures at the base of the tower—your friends back home will be so jealous! At the top, when you circle around the observation deck, you're high enough to get a bird's-eye view, but not so high you can't make out the landmarks below, and on a clear day, the views stretch well past the city limits. If you're contemplating walking to the second level (the highest visitors can go on foot), I have one thing to say: try it! I climbed the 704 steps behind my laughing daughters a decade ago, and we avoided the long lines of tourists at ground level waiting for the expensive elevator ride to levels two or three (tickets to the top via elevator are $17; *www .tour-eiffel.fr*). Go at 9 a.m. for the 9:30 a.m. opening or wait until dinnertime, when the lines will be shorter.

If there are big crowds and your heart isn't set on going up the Eiffel Tower, change plans and hop on one of the Bateaux Mouches sightseeing boats at the foot of the tower, at the Pont de l'Alma. You and your girlfriends will understand why Paris is called the City of Lights particularly if you go at sunset or after dark, when many of the city's most stunning monuments, historic buildings, and ornate bridges are illuminated. The narrated tour will educate you as you lounge on the open-air deck and drift by Notre-Dame, the Louvre, the Orsay Museum, and the belle-époque grand palace. Or begin your cruise from the Pont Neuf near the tip of the Île de la Cité. Take a normal cruise on either the Bateaux Mouches or the Vedettes, located under the bridge. Boats run every day of the year and leave about every 30 minutes. You arrive and queue and take the next boat. The dinner cruises, which need to be booked in advance, are very expensive, crowded and very few diners get a window seat ($15 for the one-hour cruise; *www.bateaux-mouches.fr* or *www.vedettesdupontneuf.com*. Discount coupons are available on the Vedettes website).

BEST PLACE FOR SUNSET

The café on the roof of La Samaritaine department store treats you to a breathtaking 360-degree view of Paris. It's free to enter and look, but you'll want to linger with a glass of wine or an express coffee. Last October, as I was walking across the Seine River on the Pont Neuf at dusk, I noticed a tangerine ball of light close to the horizon; it was the setting sun. I hurried to the department store, took the elevator to the top and arrived just in time to watch the orange disk descend behind the Eiffel Tower. The only sounds in the café were hushed whispers and clicking cameras. La Samaritaine is located along the right bank of the Seine River at the Pont Neuf (1st arrondissement), Métro Pont Neuf.

MUST-SEE MUSEUMS

If you have to narrow down your museum visits to just a few, here are my picks. Begin with the Louvre and the Musée d'Orsay. One word of advice: Beware of the crowd on the ticket line at the d'Orsay—I recommend buying your tickets online in advance (*www.musee-orsay.fr*). There are also a bunch of smaller gems you shouldn't miss. The Musée de l'Orangerie, located at the opposite end of the Tuileries Garden from the Louvre, is a tribute to Monet, showcasing eight of the French master's gigantic water lily paintings in a far more intimate setting than the big museums. Enjoy the masterpieces of Picasso, Renoir, Matisse, Modigliani, and others (*www.musee-orangerie.fr*). You'll find the Rodin Museum and its exquisite garden equally special, with 6,600 works, including the famous "Thinker" and "Kiss" sculptures. Bronze and stone statues are exhibited in an 18th-century mansion filled with many of Rodin's personal belongings, including artwork by van Gogh and Renoir (*www.musee-rodin.fr*). The Cluny Museum, housed in an incredible 15th-century Gothic mansion, is located on the Left Bank next to La Sorbonne (University). It features an amazing selection of art from the Middle Ages, including stained-glass windows, textiles, jewelry, leather shoes, and the famous "Lady and the Unicorn" tapestries. Don't miss the third-century Gallic-Roman baths on the lower level. Like most museums in Paris, it's closed on Tuesdays and holidays (6 place Paul Painlevé,

5th arrondissement, Métro Cluny–La Sorbonne, Saint-Michel, or Odéon, *www.musee-moyenage.fr*).

BEST GARDENS

Paris has some of the most wonderful city parks in the world, and if I had to pick just two, I'd send ladies to the Luxembourg Garden on the Left Bank and Bois du Boulogne. There's nothing like sitting on a bench in a lavishly landscaped park to restore your inner calm amid the chaos of the city. You won't be able to miss Luxembourg Palace, originally built for Marie de Médicis in the 1600s. On sunny days in warmer weather, find a chair by the octagonal boat basin with the fountain and watch artists paint, students kiss, and kids sail their boats. Take time to find the children's attractions: pony rides, a merry-go-round, and a puppet show. You might get lucky and arrive just in time to see "Pinocchio." I never visit Luxembourg Garden without a pensive rest by the romantic Fontaine de Médicis, set in a little grove of dripping greenery. Luxembourg Garden is located on Boulevard St. Michael in the 5th arrondissement, near Métro Luxembourg.

In the Bois du Boulogne, the Bagatelle Rose Garden boasts 1,150 varieties of roses, which make up the French National Collection of Roses. Visit in May or June when the blossoms peak and enjoy the tapestry of color, texture, and form. Download Edith Piaf's classic "La Vie En Rose" on your iPod before cruising the 60 acres of mani-cured grounds of this magnificent garden, located on the route de Sèvres in the 16th arrondissement. Métro Pont de Neuilly (Line 1), then bus 43 or 244; get off at the main gate.

BEST DAY TRIPS

The gargantuan palace of Versailles, King Louis XIV's decadent digs, is a must-see—it's a 45-minute train ride from the center of Paris. It can be exhausting to tour the entire palace, but you don't want to miss the Gothic- and baroque-style Chapelle Royale, where the king attended daily mass amid spectacular stained-glass windows and watchful gargoyle statues. If you start feeling claustrophobic inside Versailles, escape outdoors to stroll the mag-nificent gardens (*www.chateauversailles.fr/en*). I also recommend piling into the train for an excursion to the town of St.-Germain-en-Laye, birthplace of Louis XIV, located 30 minutes west of Paris. The chateau here is where Louis XIV lived pre-Versailles. It's far less opulent—in fact it's now the site of an archaeological museum, but it's worth the trip to look at the chateau and stroll its gardens (*www.ville-st-germain-en-laye.fr*).

BEST CAFES AND TEAHOUSES ON THE LEFT BANK

While you're out strolling the boutiques of the St.-Germain-des-Prés neighborhood, you must stop in for a treat at Ladurée, an historic sweetshop and teahouse that takes macaroon baking to another level (21 rue Bonaparte in the 6th arrondissement, *www.laduree.fr*). The rose-petal macaroon is to die for! Two additional Ladurée tea rooms are located in the 8th and 9th arrondissements. To relax with a hot chocolate or a coffee in a historic coffeehouse, hit Café de Flore, also in St.-Germain-des-Prés. Famous past patrons include Trotsky, Picasso, Hemingway, and Capote. But you're just as likely to have a celebrity sighting these days as you would have been in the 1930s, so you and the ladies should keep your eyes peeled (*www.cafe-de-flore.com/indexa.htm*). If you're a tea lover, find your way to the most famous teahouse of them all: Mariage Frères, the oldest tea importer in France. You may get lost among all the temptations; more than 500 varieties of tea, teacups, teaspoons, tea containers, tea-scented candles, tea-flavored cookies, tea candy, tea books, and, of course, teapots. Relax over tea or lunch amid the potted palms and natural rattan. The extensive menu includes quiches, salads, cakes, scones, and madeleine pastries, many flavored with tea. There are three Mariage Frères teahouses in Paris: in the Marais quarter in the 4th arrondissement, in the 8th arrondissement, and my favorite location in the 6th arrondissement, at 13 rue des Grands-Augustins.

BEST SORBET AND ICE CREAM

Just a two-minute walk from Notre-Dame, in the narrow streets of l'Île St.-Louis, you'll find Bertillion, Parisians' favorite ice cream and sorbet store. If there's a long line at the first Bertillion store you see, walk another block down the same street and you'll find other tiny stores selling this French delicacy. The sorbets are made of the freshest fruits in season; my favorites are passion fruit and black current. The primary store is located at 31 rue Saint-Louis-en-l'Île.

OUT OF THE ORDINARY ANTIQUES AUCTION

Paris is a great hunting ground for antiques, and Drouot, the famous French auction house open since 1852, is easier to visit than Christie's and Sotheby's in London or New York City. No appointment is necessary, just stop by. Valuable and unusual antiques, from Old Masters paintings to grandma's silver tea set, are regularly put up for sale. Even if you don't want to buy anything (and there are affordable knickknacks as well as antiques), it's great fun to view the fast-paced auction or wander through the glitzy rooms to see the antiques that will be up for sale. Open for viewing daily except Sunday. Check the website for auction days (9 rue Drouot, in the 9th arrondissement, Métro Richelieu-Drouot, *www.drouot.fr*).

BEST SPLURGE

If you're planning to drop a hefty sum of euros on a meal, there's no better place than a restaurant owned by Alain Ducasse, recipient of more Michelin stars than any chef in history. At Restaurant Alain Ducasse, in the luxurious Hotel Plaza Athenée, the chef's obsession with choosing the very best ingredients and his unswerving commitment to traditional cooking methods result in a culinary epiphany for diners. Feast on an exquisite fish stew featuring fresh turbot from Brittany or a mouthwatering smoked pigeon served with turnips. Dining at Michelin-starred restaurants is less formal and less expensive at lunchtime (entrees are $100 to $215; *www.alain-ducasse.com*).

TAKE A COOKING CLASS

At L'Atelier des Chefs, you and your pals can take a stab at creating fine French cuisine, and savor it at a communal table with chefs and other students. Classes are as short as 30 minutes (you'll learn to make one dish) and as long as four hours (you'll perfect a three-course meal). Learn how to choose fresh ingredients to cook the likes of tuna perfectly sautéed to medium-rare in olive oil, and ladyfingers topped with foamy sabayon and fresh fruit. The cooking school has four locations in Paris (classes start at $21; *www.atelierdeschefs.com*).

The first thing we do, when I go visit my sister in Paris, is to buy the *Pariscope* magazine at a newsstand—called a *tabac*. We look through it and choose chamber music performances in old churches or at Ste.-Chapelle. We like the performances at Chatelet because it's easier to get tickets at the last minute and the concerts are usually in the afternoon.

—Jane Hope Gordon, 60s, Owner Salon des Artistes,
Sausalito, California

When you get home, you'll have some fabulous new recipes, and you should take the opportunity to stock your kitchen with hard-to-find items. E. Dehillerin, which has sold pots, pans, molds, and every kind of cooking utensil or accessory under the sun since 1820, is a Paris institution. The store is simple and charming, with a hardware store vibe. Even the non-chefs among you will marvel over the mind-boggling variations on, say, a tartlet pan (*www.e-dehillerin.fr*).

EVENTS TO FLY IN FOR

Pick a month and there's an event worth hopping a flight to Paris for. You'll go gaga for the shopping deals you can find in Paris in January. Department stores like Colette, Le Bon Marché, and Printemps offer deep discounts in the middle of the month. In February, the Great Wines Fair brings representatives from more than a hundred châteaux showing off the country's top *grands vins*, and at the end of the month, you'll have the chance to sample 300-plus blends of the finest coffee in the world at the Paris Café Show, a free event at the Carrousel du Louvre. You've got a wide window of opportunity to snap up some reasonably priced fine art at the Bazart art show, held from late May to late August at La Samaritaine, that department store with the rooftop cafe and 360-degree killer view of Paris. Get your appetites ready in mid-October, when each region of France celebrates its gastronomic specialties at the food and wine festival La Semaine du Goût (*www.paris.eventguide.com, www.semaine-du-gout.cityvox.com*).

BEST TOUR

There's no better way to explore Paris than by foot. And with a guide on hand, you can turn your stroll into an eye-opening history lesson. A popular tour led by Paris Walks, a company specializing in English-speaking itineraries, traces Parisian history back to the very beginning. You'll start on l'Île de la Cité, the city's birthplace, walk over to the Notre-Dame Cathedral, wind through the streets of the Marais quarter, and end at the picturesque square Place des Vosges (most tours are $14 for two hours; *www.paris-walks.com*).

PERSONAL SHOPPER IN FASHION HEADQUARTERS

For a dedicated shopaholic, there is never enough time in Paris. How do you find designer showrooms, French fashion stores, fashion-specific street markets, or the off-the-beaten-track boutiques and shops

continued on page 52

MULTIGENERATIONAL PARIS

❦

My energetic eight-year-old great-niece, Elizabeth, has wanted to see the "Mona Lisa" since she was five. Her 40-something mom, Dione, has been waiting for her to develop sufficient maturity and attention span so that we could go together. I am their 60-year-old Aunt Sandy and have enjoyed many trips to France over the past 40 years. I have always taken a credit card and Michelin guide, but never once taken a child.

I knew the temples of haute cuisine my husband and I had visited on previous trips would not be part of our itinerary, yet I wanted to find dining opportunities where children were welcome. I had hoped this would not prove too challenging as I had often read how the French prize decorum and find less-than-perfectly mannered children in a restaurant about as distasteful as a burnt brioche.

We found kids' menus at several places, like The Café in the Musée d'Orsay and the comfortable chain restaurant Léon de Bruxelles. These menus also feature un cadeaux with a little game or puzzle to entertain the petite guest. Most sidewalk cafés offered the ever popular hamburger and frites for young diners, and patisserie stops offered sumptuous sweet and savory takeaway treats when instant gratification was needed.

As a docent in the Fine Arts Museums of San Francisco, I learned early on that the more senses you involve with children, the more memorable the experience. I bought each of us a little moleskin sketchbook that could be tucked into a small purse along with colored pencils and pens. There's a handy pocket in the back to save ticket stubs, receipts, and paper memorabilia. As soon as I began to sketch a sculpture at the Musée Picasso, Elizabeth found a tiny painting in the corner and went to work in earnest.

After seeing "Mona" at the Louvre, we spent four more

hours viewing art, sketching, and lunching in the first-floor café. When our feet were too tired to walk, we sat on gallery benches and quietly made up our own narratives about what was going on in a painting. Then we read the case notes and were sometimes surprisingly on target.

The sketchbook fulfilled several functions. Drawing forces a person, be she young or more mature, to really look at the details in an artwork. The physical act of even a quick gesture sketch reinforces the image in memory. We used the book for notes and for written recollections, as well, which also allowed Aunt Sandy the opportunity to sit and rest her feet more frequently. At the end of each day we used the scissors and glue stick I had packed to paste in our paper treasures to accessorize our day's sketches and field notes.

In years to come it will be fun to revisit our books and compare impressions.

For a nominal fee, most museums offer audio guides that children use quite adeptly. They also provide another sensory stimulant. Elizabeth loved putting on the headsets or using the handheld acoustiguide to select which artwork she wanted to hear about and in a sequence of her own choosing. At one point she exclaimed, "Oh, punch in number 133, I'll bet this is going to be so interesting." It was van Gogh's "Portrait of Artist." When she saw one of the several Degas ballerinas, I heard her gasp, "We have one of these in our museum in Houston!"

It was very cost effective to buy a pass for unlimited entries for the desired number of days. With the four-day pass, we enjoyed many thoughtful hours in six museums. Dione went on line to find the days they opened and planned our museum strategy in advance. At each museum we visited, we purchased a publication about the collections to learn more at our leisure and so that Elizabeth could show her grandparents what she had seen.

continued on page 52

continued from page 51

In addition to encouraging Elizabeth to sketch what she was seeing and to keep journal notes of her impressions during the trip, we had been encouraging her to use some basic French vocabulary: *Bonjour, merci, au revoir.* Heretofore, she had chosen to utter only the occasional "*merci beaucoup.*" On our last evening in Paris, we braved an upscale restaurant with white tablecloths and formally set tables.

That night at dinner she seamlessly included "*s'il vous plaît,*" in her meal order. When she requested, "*mousse au chocolat,*" for dessert, the waiter responded in English, "O.K., the chocolate mousse." Suddenly she whipped open her menu and blurted out, "*Excusez-moi, monsieur,* it says, '*mousse au chocolat.*'" The expressionless waiter made no comment, but returned and presented a flat crystal dish filled with the dark, velvety mousse topped with a double portion of Crème Chantilly. "Merci," she smiled demurely.

Plane ticket to de Gaulle Airport: A bundle. Museum Pass: 90 euros. Dinner at Ristorante Dell'Angelo: $75. Paris with a child: Priceless.

—Sandy Javaras, 60, Museum Guide, San Francisco, California

with inexpensive but good-quality items? Karen Henrich, a Canadian who divides her time between Paris and Vancouver, helps women buy exactly what they want by providing a customized personal shopping service. For women unfamiliar with Paris, she includes an orientation of the *grands magasins* such as Galeries Lafayette, and shows them the areas around these stores where real bargains can be found. For people wanting to find French and other European labels at incredibly low prices, she leads them to stock stores and other discount shopping areas. She can also make appointments to visit designer showrooms.

As part of each customized tour, Karen gives a rundown of French fashion stores and labels. She finds products that can only be purchased in Paris and are not exported to North America. Karen understands that some North Americans are a wee bit larger than the tiny French women, so she has a list of labels/stores that are suitable for larger sizes ($210 per person per day, or 175 euros for more than one person; *www.nuitblanchetours.com*).

WHERE TO STAY

If it's a special occasion and you're willing to make a bit of an investment, Relais Christine won't be trumped for elegance, service, and proximity to beautiful tree- and café-lined streets in the St.-Germain-des-Prés neighborhood. The rooms are decorated in modern and traditional furniture with deep-red accents, combining the best of old and new French aesthetics. And if you really feel like treating yourselves, you can get one with a gardenside terrace. Added bonus: Luxembourg Garden is just a short stroll away (from $520 for doubles; *www.relais-christine.com*).

Also in the St.-Germain-des-Prés neighborhood, but more moderately priced, is Hôtel des Saints-Pères. But you won't feel any less decadent—the hotel is the former residence of King Louis XIV's architect. Wooden-beamed ceilings, frescoes, and 17th-century elegance are ubiquitous (from $235 for doubles; *www.paris-hotel-saints-peres.com*).

Bargain prices in one of Paris's toniest neighborhoods, the historic Marais quarter, is what you'll find at Hôtel Caron de Beaumarchais at 12 Vieille-du-Temple, a few steps off rue Rivoli. It's a ten-minute walk from l'Île St.-Louis and close to the Saint-Paul and Hôtel-de-ville Métro stops. The hotel's 19 rooms were renovated in 2004 and they added soundproofing and air-conditioning (from $177; *www.carondebeaumarchais.com*).

RENT AN APARTMENT

A pied-à-terre (temporary lodging) lets you experience Paris not as tourists coming and going from a hotel, but as residents who get to know the neighborhood. The first thing you do is shop at the local greengrocery, bakery, and open-air market. You'll strike up a conversation with the owners of the mom-and-pop stores and the market vendors who will tell you what to try and what to avoid. If another shopper overhears the conversation they will usually add their personal recommendations. If you have your hair done at a local beauty salon, you'll get the whole scoop on the neighborhood.

Minimum rental time is a week. Several of my girlfriends, who have rented numerous times, give high marks to two organizations; Paris Attitude (*www.Parisattitude.com*), a licensed real estate agency, and At Home In France (*www.athomeinfrance.com*), a company owned by two Americans who will conduct an extensive interview with you before recommending a specific apartment in Paris or villa in the countryside. Consider exchanging your home for a pied-à-terre in Paris or elsewhere (*www.intervac-online.com*). Be sure the person you work with has firsthand knowledge of the properties and ask for references.

ONE CLICK AND YOU'RE OFF
The Paris Convention and Visitors Bureau website can be found at *en.parisinfo.com* or *http://en.parisinfo.com.*

⁓ London ⁓

Big Ben, Buckingham Palace, Westminster Abbey, double-decker red buses, manicured gardens, immaculately tailored suits, proper posture and elegant English accents, old and modern architecture, the Queen, and tea and crumpets. That's what most of us think about when we think of London. And we're not wrong. But there's so much more to the refined capital of the United Kingdom. Arranged around the Thames River and broken into more than a dozen neighborhoods, London is a delight for art lovers, shoppers, history buffs, foodies, and bookworms alike. Yes, the weather can be cold and drizzly, but from April to September, it's a lot warmer and a touch less damp. And if you can brave the elements (and you can with the right winter coat) you'll find airfare and hotel deals in the winter months. That's not an insignificant factor considering the strength of the British pound and the high prices this city is known for. Two points of consolation are that museums are free and the public transportation system is as efficient as they come (buses are fabulous for sightseeing—you can jump on and off as you choose—and the Tube, or subway, is convenient when covering longer distances). The main tourist attractions are close enough together that you can easily walk or take short bus rides between them, and if you base yourselves in a neighborhood like Kensington or Knightsbridge, which are in the heart of the city, you'll have more time to explore and fewer logistical details to worry about.

SHOP TILL YOU DROP
Portobello Road Market, in the Notting Hill neighborhood, bills itself as the world's largest antiques market, and I have to say, given the fact that 1,500 dealers converge to sell here, I wouldn't argue with that. On Fridays and weekends, the outdoor market is themed: Fridays

are for art-deco antiques, Saturdays are for fashion, and Sundays for a traditional flea market with clothes and bric-a-brac (*www.portobelloroad.co.uk*). London is also home to several world-famous department stores, Harrods, Harvey Nichols, and Selfridges among them. If you've been searching for a hard-to-find lipstick color or want to learn how to shade your eyes to look smoky, corral the girls for an afternoon of beauty at Selfridges, which boasts one of the largest cosmetics departments in Europe (*www.selfridges.com*). To impersonate a proper Englishwoman, pop into Turnbull & Asser, London's premier shop for custom shirt-making. Snap up a few colorful scarves, cashmere cardigans, and button-down shirts, and set off into the streets of London. Now all you need to do is perfect your accent and no one will be able to tell you're not a local (*www.turnbullandasser.com*).

TOP MUSEUMS

The National Gallery (*www.nationalgallery.org.uk*), which showcases one of the world's largest collections of Western European paintings, and the Tate Modern, opened in 2000 (*www.tate.org.uk*), housed in a hulking former power station, should be on your list of top London museums. Add to that list the little-known Geffrye Museum. Instead of showcasing British décor in all its finery, this museum shows what life was like for regular folk living from the Victorian era to the present. A series of re-created interiors provide a peek at what the

MAKING THE MOST OF A MUSEUM

◈

If you're a museum buff like me, check out what special exhibits are showing at museums in the European city (or cities) you'll be visiting. What's your passion? History, painting, photography, archeology, modern art, music, film? Click on *www.euromuse.net*, type in your interests, the dates you'll be abroad, and the city you'll be visiting. Within seconds you'll be overwhelmed with museum goodies.

—Marybeth

homes of the middle class looked like—a satisfying experience for both the voyeurs and the history buffs in your group (*www.geffrye-museum.org.uk*). I also recommend the Victoria and Albert Museum, an astonishingly comprehensive art and design museum with more than four million objects spanning 5,000 years of cultural history. I always check the museum websites to learn about the permanent collections and special exhibitions. The free museums in London are the Victoria and Albert Museum (*www.vam.ac.uk*), the British Museum (*www.britishmuseum.org*), the Natural History and Science Museums (*www.nhm.ac.uk*, *www.sciencemuseum.org.uk*)), Sir John Soane's Museum (*www.soane.org*), the Imperial War Museum (*www.iwm.org.uk*), and the National Maritime Museum (*www.nmm.ac.uk*). Check each museum's website for free days or hours when admission is free (after 3:30 p.m. for some museums on some days).

If you love history, as I do, don't miss the Museum of London, which begins with the time when London was nothing but tundra, and the local population would fit on a double-decker bus. It follows London's history through the Roman times, the medieval period of Chaucer and Becket into Tudor and early Stuart London (from 1485 to 1666). The museum regularly adds new material, including finds from archaeological digs. It's not all about ancient history—take time to peruse the galleries with 24,000 dresses, accessories, and fashion objects dating from the Tudor period to the present day. You'll see royal clothing, costumes related to the theater, music hall, opera, ballet, circus, cabaret, and television, and fashions by popular, contemporary London-based designers. If you're a history buff, I promise you won't want to leave when the museum closes. It's open until 9 p.m. on the first Thursday of each month (*www.museumoflondon.org.uk*). And it's free.

BEST WAY TO VISIT THE CHURCHES OF LONDON

London's churches are spectacular; Westminster Abbey and St. Paul's top my list. They are both free if you attend evensong services. Even if you are not religious, evensong services are a wonderful way to experience a church as a place of reflection, fabulous organ and choral music, and worship. The nonsectarian evensong service at Westminster Abbey begins at 5 p.m. (3 p.m. on weekends) and lasts about an hour. The abbey is closed to tourists for most of the day, so you enter through the main church doors. After the service, there is some time to walk around the church. Evensong services at St. Paul's are often held at 5 p.m. (*www.westminster-abbey.org*, *www.stpauls.co.uk*).

THE REGAL PARKS

The royal parks of London—Kensington Gardens, The Green Park, St. James's Park, and Hyde Park—connect to each other, forming one large green zone in the center of the city. Each has its own unique character. If you have the time, stroll through all of them, but if your time is limited, don't miss Hyde Park, famous for Speaker's Corner, Marble Arch, and Wellington Arch. It's hard to believe you're in the middle of London when you meander through Hyde Park, sprawled over 50 acres with more than 4,000 trees, a lake, a meadow, boating on the Serpentine (a large artificial lake), tennis courts, bowling green, and horse rides. For information on the stables, lawn tennis, court tennis, swimming at the Serpentine Lido and Paddling Pool, bicycling, jogging, rollerblading, and skateboarding, click on *www.royalparks.org.uk/parks/hydepark*.

WORTH YOUR TIME

Where do you spend your time and money in London? If you haven't already seen it, I recommend you do spend a little money to visit the Tower of London, which has dominated the city for over 900 years as a fortress, prison, palace, place of execution, and home to the crown jewels—encased in glass and displayed in a vault-like room. If you don't want to make a day of waiting in lines, arrive before the opening hour (9 or 10 a.m., depending upon the season and day), take the first Beefeater Tour, go immediately to view the Crown Jewels, then visit the White Tower ($33; *www.hrp.org.uk/TowerOfLondon*).

A SPOT OF TEA

I can't think of a better way to impersonate a queen than to take afternoon tea at Kensington Palace's Orangery Restaurant. The tea tradition is one you certainly shouldn't miss, but I must say, "Afternoon tea" is a bit of a misnomer. Tea time is really more like snack time with cakes, sandwiches, and tea served. Tea at the Orangery comes with access to Kensington Palace, the 17th-century residence of the British royal family, and gives you a special peek at the Orangery building itself, which was commissioned as a greenhouse by Queen Anne in the early 1700s (drinks from $3, cakes from $5; *www.hrp.org.uk/KensingtonPalace*).

CATCH A SHOW

London offers some of the world's best theater and musicals. Since I believe that going to the theater in London is one of the few reasonably priced things to do, I have skipped many dinners to afford theater tickets for a show in the West End (theater district). If you want to see a popular production (one of the top ten musicals), you'll need to book in advance. If specific shows are part of your vacation plans, buy your tickets online as early as possible. If you want to "wait and see," you can still get discount tickets, for same-day performances, at the TKTS booths in Leicester Square and Canary Wharf. Most tickets are sold at exactly half price plus a service charge of $5 per ticket. Some additional shows may also be available at a 25 percent discount or at full price. Not all West End shows have tickets on sale at TKTS—but there is always a large selection, including some of the top musicals. Here's my advice for the best way to play this game: Keep track of what they offer everyday on their website (click on "What's on Sale Today" on the TKTS website, *www.officiallondontheatre.co.uk/tkts*) for about a week before you leave home. You'll see 35-45 choices for matinées and evening shows, and you'll have time to read the reviews and make a wish list with your girlfriends. The ticket booths open at 10 a.m. and there will be a line by 9:30 a.m., so arrive early. When I went to London with my daughters we didn't plan ahead, but on the spot we decided we wanted to see *The Phantom of the Opera* (our third time), and the tickets weren't available at TKTS. We managed to snatch up individual tickets for the matinée directly from the theater box office when it opened at 10 a.m. for a matinée the same day. Midweek matinées are usually less expensive than weekend evening shows. Other useful sites for theater news, gossip and reviews, seating plans, and phone order discounts: *www.theatremonkey.co.uk*, *www.theatrenet.co.uk*, and *www.lastminute.com*.

One of the most glorious outdoor venues on the planet (truly) is Regent's Park's Open Air Theatre, which produces Shakespeare plays every summer. You can enter the theater grounds, which are nestled in the leafy beauty of Regent's Park, with your picnic dinner up to 90 minutes before curtain time. To score tickets for yourselves, you'll have to get aggressive. My advice is to mark your calendar for early January, which is when tickets go on sale, and go online to get first dibs on the coming season's shows (*www.openairtheatre.org*).

FREE THEATER
Don't miss the free street entertainers in Covent Garden (under the porch of the Actors' Church where Britain's first Punch & Judy show

was performed) and those who perform at the many London festivals. The free events at the Southbank Centre and Barbican are usually of the highest artistic standard. And if you wish to see the theater of life, head for the markets. (*www.londontourist.org/free.html*)

DOUBLE-DECKER AND FREE BUS TOURS

When I calculated the price of a Big Bus Tour for myself and my daughters ($120), I decided to save the money for theater tickets, and searched for another way to see the same sights. It's easy to use public transportation to combine a few scheduled bus routes and hit the major attractions. We bought a Travelcard for Zones 1 and 2 and hopped on and off the bus. Best of all, we sat at the top of the red double-decker bus with gregarious Londoners who gave us a running commentary on what we were seeing. Take bus number 11, which runs through the City past the Bank of England, St. Paul's Cathedral, Fleet Street, The Strand, Trafalgar Square, Whitehall, 10 Downing Street, the Horseguards, Parliament, and Westminster Abbey It goes by Westminster Cathedral, close to Buckingham Palace, through Pimlico to the Chelsea Hospital and Physic Garden, Sloane Square, and King's Road (for a map and more details click on *www.londontourist.org/free.html*). The one-day Travelcard ($20) gives you access to unlimited travel on the underground trains, buses (also night buses), or regular trains within London. Tickets for the Hop On/Hop Off Big Bus Tour are valid for 24 hours, and some routes have audio tours, some have live guides ($40 per person; *www.theoriginaltour.com* or *www.bigbus.co.uk*).

BEST DINING

A trip to London wouldn't be complete without a taste of the original British take-out food: fish-and-chips. The Fish Club has turned this classic typically served wrapped in newspaper into an art form. You choose the type of fish from a menu that changes daily (it might include yellowfin tuna, skate, or cod), and you also choose the style of cooking (sautéed, steamed, panfried, or grilled). Don't be surprised if you see customers at a fish-and-chip shop put vinegar on their chips (aka fries); that's popular among the Brits. If you're worried about your cholesterol, you can make some healthier choices here: sushi, for one ($11; *www.thefishclub.com*).

Over the past decade a gastro revolution has hit London, thanks to multicultural immigrants. It began with an invasion of ethnic food—quality curries and Thai pub cuisine. London is reputed to have more Indian restaurants than Bombay and Delhi combined, and you're in for a treat if you order the most popular Indian dish, chicken *tikka masala*. Many chefs inject turmeric, chili powder, and other spices into typically bland British dishes. London is very cosmopolitan in its food culture, so enjoy the potpourri of eclectic styles and locally grown, organic produce. If you want a light meal in London, many pubs offer salads consisting of rocket (aka arugula), heirloom tomatoes, and tangy vinaigrette.

The discerning eaters among you will delight in the food at the swanky Fat Duck. Try cauliflower risotto with chocolate jelly, radish ravioli, and crab biscuits at this It restaurant ($160 for a three-course meal; *www.fatduck.co.uk*). For a brush with a celebrity chef, make a reservation for you and the ladies at the chef's table in the kitchen of Gordon Ramsey at Claridge's. You'll watch Chef Ramsey (the crotchety star of the TV show *Hell's Kitchen*) perfect monkfish, foie gras, and Cornish lamb, and you'll be tended to by the restaurant's head sommelier ($133 for three courses; *www.gordonramsay.com/ukrestaurants*).

MONEY MATTERS

❧

Traveling overseas recently, I have noticed that many merchants ask me if I would like to have my credit card bill converted from the local currency (euros, pounds, Argentine pesos, etc.) into dollars on the spot. It seems as if they are offering you a nice service, when in fact, it's a moneymaking scheme for them and costly for me. They set the exchange rate five or six cents more per dollar than the official bank rate and they keep the difference as a "service fee." To avoid these extra charges, read the fine print on the sales invoice, which will say that you agree to have your charge converted to dollars. Tell the merchant you do not want this service and refuse to sign.

—Marybeth

BEST CRUISE

For a special occasion, gather the girls and board a Bateaux London lunch-and-jazz cruise along the Thames River. A live jazz band will serenade you with Dixieland and traditional jazz while you munch on a terrine of salmon and green peppers, a roast with fresh vegetables, and a baked pear frangipane with clotted cream while you catch up on old times or celebrate a special occasion, and watch Big Ben and the Tower of London go by (from $50 per person; *www.bateauxlondon.com*).

WHAT'S FREE IN LONDON?

Accommodations, meals, and almost everything else in London are expensive, but the good news is that many of the best things in London are (mostly) free. It is possible to see many of the best attractions in London and not pay for admission to anything, including galleries, museums, and historic buildings. There are many free concerts, open-air films, and entertainment along the river, at the National Theatre, on Coin Street, and near Tower Bridge. Most of the major museums are free: the National Gallery; the Tate galleries; the Science, Natural History, and Imperial War Museums; the British Museum; the Sir John Soane's Museum; and the Museum of London. Museums that do charge usually have a free day or period of a day. Put on your dancing shoes and join a free salsa class on Charing Cross Road on Wednesday evenings; you'll enjoy a half-hour introduction to lambada, merengue, and salsa (*www.londontourist.org/free.html*).

EVENTS TO FLY IN FOR

More than 600 gardeners show off their work at the Chelsea Flower Show each May (*www.rhs.org.uk/chelsea*). It's a sell-out event every year, so buy your tickets early. If you can't score a ticket, the Chelsea Week Garden Tours, put on by the Museum of Garden History each July, should satisfy your green thumb. Each day, participants tour different gardens around London. The bookworms among you should fly in for the London Book Fair, held in spring. You'll find rare books, eclectic authors, and publishers at this literary bonanza. Be sure to pack your best and brightest whites when you hop the pond for a trip to the Wimbledon tennis tournament in late June and early July. To get tickets, you have to enter a lottery (*www.wimbledon.org*).

BEST OVERNIGHT TRIP

Shakespeare is everywhere in London, but to get an up close look at the life of the bard, head about a hundred miles north of the city, by train or bus, to his birthplace, Stratford upon Avon. Here, you and the gals can see where he was born, at the Shakespeare's Birthplace museum, which is decorated in furnishings from Shakespeare's time. And you can also get a glimpse of where he spent his final days, at a home called New Place. My recommendation is to buy a combined ticket for entry to all of the Shakespeare sites here (*www.shakespeare .org.uk*). At lunchtime, stop in at Lambs on Sheep Street for everything from local sausages to Scottish beef carpaccio to salmon fish cakes (*www.lambsrestaurant.co.uk*). If you can, catch a show at the Royal Shakespeare Company, which has a stage in Stratford (*www. rsc.org.uk*). What better place to see a play than in the author's hometown? Turn in for the night at the Twelfth Night Guest House bed-and-breakfast, a brick house set amid a sea of Tudor buildings in downtown Stratford (from $140 for doubles, including breakfast; *www.twelfthnight.co.uk*).

WHERE TO STAY
Melia White House Hotel, a four-star hotel next to Regent's Park, has location on its side. It's within walking distance of Piccadilly Circus and great restaurants and bars (among them is Longfords Bar, which features live jazz). Sites like the Tower of London and Westminster Abbey are a little farther, but still walkable. Rooms are deluxe (you'll be presented with a pillow menu!) and include a full hearty English breakfast (from $570 for doubles; *www.melia-whitehouse.com*).

In the West End, near Piccadilly Circus and Trafalgar Square, the Bloomsbury branch of the Jenkins Hotel is a fantastic value. Rooms are small, but if you're of the mind that it's what's out the door that counts, this is the place for you and friends (from $180 for doubles; *www.jenkinshotel.demon.co.uk*).

Why not organize a trip to London with your ladies book club? If you like this idea, check in at the Arran House Hotel, located in Bloomsbury in a 200-year-old Georgian town house. Rent the suite and stage your discussions here; then trot over to the British Library to take a gander at Jane Austen's writings or the original Magna Carta (from $155 for doubles; *www.arranhotel-london.com*).

ONE CLICK AND YOU'RE OFF
For more information on visiting the U.K., try *www.visitbritain.com*; for more information on London, *www.visitlondon.com* and *www.visitlondon.com/events/theatre*.

Sydney

This lively city on the eastern coast of the island continent of Australia is really a glorified beach town. But it's a beach town with a world-class opera house, restaurants serving innovative cuisine, and sleek hotels. Sydney's cosmopolitan vibe is partly due to the fact that it's a cultural melting pot, with large populations of Chinese, Italian, Greek, Turkish, and Irish immigrants. Add to that the Aboriginal influence and the city's longtime commitment to fine arts, and you've got a fascinating cultural blend. The iconic sites—the Sydney Harbour Bridge and the Sydney Opera House—are downtown, and the many beaches, shopping neighborhoods, and parks stretch in all directions from there. Must-see sights are the colonial buildings of the historic Rocks neighborhood, the opera house, the shops and museums of the Darling Harbour neighborhood, and as many beaches as you have sunscreen for. Your two feet are the best way to navigate the city, but a convenient bus-and-rail transportation system comes in handy when you get weary. Avoid the extreme temperatures of summer and winter, instead planning your trip for March or April (autumn Down Under, or September through November, which is their springtime). Sydney is a lady's town with a youthful energetic vibe and sophistication—we can visit a museum in the morning, shop the boutiques in a tiny bay in the afternoon, then head for a swim at the beach before a fresh fish dinner.

DON'T-MISS BEACHES

Bondi Beach is the most famous of Sydney's 37 stretches of sand. And it's certainly one of the best: It's a mecca for surfers, sunbathers, and as of late, café-goers. Bondi has recently morphed into a hotel and restaurant hot spot, with eateries such as the Icebergs providing a perch for some of the world's best people-watching. If you prefer to stay out of the sun (as you should!), settle into a beachside booth at Icebergs for a refreshing lunch of tuna tartare with Tuscan dwarf peaches and salt-crusted suckling lamb (main courses from $25; *www.idrb.com*). I happen to go out of my way for quieter beaches with dramatic natural scenery, like Balmoral Beach, northeast of Sydney proper. A white-sand crescent in an inlet protected from ocean waves, Balmoral is a mellow swimmers' beach (the shark net here provides some added peace of mind). Pack up your sunblock and beach reading and hop on a bus for a relaxing afternoon beach outing.

NEW HARBORSIDE PARK

When you and your girlfriends are looking for a place to spend a sunny afternoon, head for Chowder Bay—the newest waterfront park in Sydney. In the 1800s, whalers who anchored in the bay collected oysters from the rocks at low tide and made chowder from the seafood, which gave the bay its name. For many years the area was the headquarters of the Australian Navy's submarine fleet and torpedo workshops and was closed to the public. The area was recently released for public use. Ripples restaurant occupies a lovely historic building overlooking the middle harbor. As you dine on the deck you'll watch scuba divers slip into the bay and kayakers glide by. Ripples is on the Taronga Zoo to Balmoral Harbour shore walk, a perfect stop for an alfresco breakfast, lunch, a plate of fresh oysters, or dinner. Here you'll dine a few feet above the sandy beach and pristine waters of Clifton Garden's Beach (main courses from $20, and BYOB keeps the price down, corkage fee $5.50; *www.ripplescafe.com.au*).

GET ACTIVE

I would argue that Sydney Harbour looks more beautiful from a sea kayak than from any other vantage point. Form a kayak flotilla with friends and set off for a gentle, two-hour morning tour, basking in the early light and sipping a cup of joe—provided by your guide when you stop for a coffee break halfway through the paddle. If you have previous kayaking experience, you can rent a boat and explore on your own (from $20 per hour for rentals; *www.sydneyharbourkayaks.com.au*).

BEST NEIGHBORHOODS FOR A STROLL

Visitors can get so distracted by Sydney's beaches that they forget the city is surrounded by wilderness and parks. Just to the north of a neighborhood called Watsons Bay (about seven miles northeast of downtown), in Sydney Harbour National Park, the cobblestoned South Head Heritage Trail follows sandstone cliffs and showcases views of the harbor and the historic Hornby Lighthouse. It's a short stroll—less than a mile—and the views are priceless (*www .nationalparks.nsw.gov.au*). Make some time for exploring Sydney's Chinatown, a colorful neighborhood packed with delicious authentic food and street after street of shopping—just like the other Chinatowns you know and love. You can walk off the calories from the fried pork dumplings you gorged on at lunch while perusing inexpensive Chinese clothing, housewares, and herbs. When you need a break from all the walking, rest up in the Chinese Garden of

Friendship, located at the southern end of Darling Harbour, with a pot of jasmine tea by the lotus pond (*www.chinesegarden.com.au*).

A BIT OF CULTURE

No doubt you've laid eyes on an image of the Sydney Opera House, a waterfront theater topped by semicircular domes that jut dramatically into the sky. The opera house is a fabulous photo op for all of you, and now's your chance to see it in the flesh. But here's the glitch: Tickets to performances can be very hard to come by. Shows routinely sell out. To get tickets to the opera, ballet, jazz, and classical musical performances—all of which take place here—my best advice is to buy your tickets even before you book your flight to Australia (*www.sydneyoperahouse.com*). If you're more interested in the architecture than you are in seeing a show, stop by for a drink at the Opera Bar. Similarly, the Museum of Contemporary Art is a must-see, with works by 20th-century icons like Andy Warhol, Roy Lichtenstein, and Edward Ruscha in its permanent collection, and a rotating cast of contemporary artists from around the world exhibiting their work (*www.mca.com.au*).

BEST DINING

You're surrounded by water here, and I guarantee you'll be jonesing for seafood at some point during your stay. The most famous Sydney seafood restaurant is Doyles. Lucky for you, there are several branches, so reservations are fairly easy to come by. For the freshest fish in the city, visit the Doyles restaurant located at the Sydney Seafood Market. You'll pick out prawns, lobster, and scallops to devour on the spot. Of the three Doyles restaurants in Sydney, my favorite is located in Watsons Bay, where you can walk along the coast, swim in secluded beaches, or wander through the historic town before a long lunch and a cool beer (from $12; *www.doyles.com.au*).

For wraps and sandwiches, I like the casual elegance of Tilbury Hotel's café. Relax at your table, which peeks into a courtyard, with a cup of post-lunch organic peppermint tea (it's good for your digestion). You might also stroll over to the bar, which serves up jugs of sangria and apple mojitos to the tunes of live R&B music (*www.tilburyhotel.com.au*).

Fine dining Sydney-style doesn't get any better than Guillaume at Bennelong. This restaurant also has the benefit of a world-class location: It's in the front two shells of the Sydney Opera House. Dress up in your finest, and then prepare for a feast you'll remember for years—the menu includes dishes like freshly shucked oysters in shallot vinegar, basil-infused tuna, and risotto with braised baby octopus. Enjoy the culinary talents of Guillaume Brahimi, the Michelin-trained French chef who has won awards nationally and internationally (from $169; *www.guillaumeatbennelong.com.au*).

BEST SUNSET VIEWS

The view from the Sydney Harbour Bridge is the best in the entire city, looking out over the harbor and the opera house. But it's not for the faint of heart—or those of you with vertigo. For one of the most incredible sunsets of your life, and thrilling stunts of your life, sign on to climb the bridge (from $225 for a sunset climb; *www.bridgeclimb.com*).

BEST OVERNIGHT TRIP

Thanks in part to the Hunter Valley, located a hundred miles from Sydney, Australian wines have become a hot export. With some 90 vineyards growing the oldest grapes in the country, I'd say Hunter is Sydney's answer to Napa. My advice? Pile in the car in Sydney and drive two hours north for a vino tour, stopping to swill the Chardonnay, Shiraz, and Semillon wines this region is known for. Drop in for a tasting at Brokenwood and Tyrrell's vineyards, which are two of the best. If you time your visit right, you can hit Tyrell's annual Jazz in the Vineyards event in October (*www.bro kenwood.com.au* and *www.tyrrells.com.au*). To round out the day, make a lunch or dinner reservation at The Cellar Restaurant, a favorite with locals, for a charcuterie platter of meats and cheeses paired with local wines (*www.the-cellar-restaurant.com.au*). If you've a big enough group and some spare time, a wonderful treat is renting out the entire Vintry Country House, an exquisite hotel and vineyard with four bedrooms that have private decks and views of the Brokenback Mountains (from $730 per night for the entire house; *www.thevintry.com.au*). Don't blame me if you never want to leave!

WHERE TO STAY

You'll get great bang for your buck at Ibis Hotel Darling Harbour, one of the most affordable—yet comfortable—options in the Darling Harbour neighborhood. A stay here puts you in walking range of museums, shopping, the Sydney Aquarium, and Chinatown (from $155 for doubles; *www.hotelibisdarlingharbour.com.au*).

Bed & Breakfast Sydney Harbour has made its home in a restored mansion decked out with stunning hardwood floors in the historic Rocks neighborhood. It's a hop, skip, and jump away from the Museum of Contemporary Art and the Royal Botanical Gardens. Ask for the Philip Room, which has views of the opera house (from $140 for doubles, including a three-course breakfast; *www.bbsydneyharbour.com.au*).

Staying in an apartment gives you far more flexibility and privacy than a hotel (you have your own kitchen and laundry machines)—and can be a great money-saver when you're traveling in a group. Meriton Serviced Apartments has properties sprinkled across the city. You can rent out a studio, one-bedroom, or two-bedroom apartment. I like the location of the new Kent Street property, smack in the middle of Sydney's best nightlife. But the Bondi Junction location is fantastic too—wedged between Bondi Beach and Sydney Harbour (from $160; *www.meritonapartments.com.au*).

EVENTS TO FLY IN FOR

If you can get off work during the middle three weeks of January, the Sydney Festival will be a crowd-pleaser for your whole gang. More than 500 performers gather for various free music, dance, theater, and film events throughout the city, among them the Sydney Symphony Orchestra and Symphony Opera. On January 26, it all culminates with multiple concerts, tall ship parades, and ferryboat races in Sydney Harbour (*www.sydneyfestival.org.au*). The Sydney Royal Easter Show, the week after Easter, is Australia's version of a state fair and loads of fun, with prizes going out to the best cattle, flowers, woodchoppers, and winemakers (*www.easter show.com.au*).

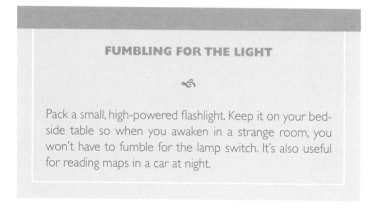

FUMBLING FOR THE LIGHT

Pack a small, high-powered flashlight. Keep it on your bedside table so when you awaken in a strange room, you won't have to fumble for the lamp switch. It's also useful for reading maps in a car at night.

BEST TOUR

The Sydney Opera Afloat Dinner Harbour Cruise lets you and the gals multitask: You'll see the harbor in all its sunset glory, listen to the arias of the Sydney Opera company performed aboard, and eat a scrumptious meal of Tasmanian smoked salmon and asparagus, eggplant and tomato gratin (from $98 per person for a two-and-a-half-hour cruise; *www. www.sydney.com.au/cruises.htm*).

ONE CLICK AND YOU'RE OFF

Learn more at the Tourism Australia website at *www.australia.com*; for Sydney Tourism, visit *www.sydneyaustralia.com*.

⤳ Cape Town ⤳

Perched on a peninsula that juts into the Atlantic Ocean at the very southern tip of the continent of Africa, Cape Town presents visitors with unusual contrasts, found nowhere else in the world. It's an historic outpost and a destination for the rich and famous; cosmopolitan but also an African safari gateway; at once African and European; affluent and still bearing the scars of its county's intense poverty and disease. It's these separations and the exotic, relaxed, and welcoming ambience that make women fall so deeply in love with Cape Town.

The city's youthful energy, enchanting vineyards, dazzling beaches, sheer cliffs, and the ever looming Table Mountain draw photographers and nature lovers—and will hook you immediately. And then you'll be seduced by a delicious mix of Malaysian flavors, barbecue tradition, and ubiquitous fresh seafood. You'll find that the diverse population of Cape Town is open, friendly, and curious about visitors. But it won't be all fun and games for you and your friends; there's much to be learned about South African history. Apartheid isn't that distant a memory, and a visit to Nelson Mandela's prison—an island off the coast of Cape Town—is one of the best history lessons of our time. Cape Town's various neighborhoods emanate from the base of Table Mountain, with the City Bowl (business district) nestled at the very bottom of the mountain. The Waterfront neighborhood reminds me a bit of San Francisco's harbor, with shops, an aquarium, and restaurants clustered together. Weather is usually stellar, except in spring (our fall), when winds pick up and temperatures drop.

MUSEUM BREAK

District Six is the one Cape Town museum worth working into your schedule. Exhibitions tell the stories of the inhabitants of the District Six neighborhood who were banished from their homes during apartheid. Housed in a 170-year-old former church, the museum has served as a centerpiece for community healing, initiating art projects by locals that run the gamut from sculpture to multimedia (www.districtsix.co.za).

BEST SHOPPING

Traditional and contemporary tribal art from across Africa is best found at African Image, in the Table Bay Mall. The collectors in your group will snatch up their masks, jewelry, pots, and sculptures as mementos of your trip or gifts (www.african-image.co.za). In the Cape Quarter (www.capequarter.co.za), quaint coffee shops, boutiques, antique shops, and design studios line the streets. Stop in at Africa Nova for traditional paintings, block prints, and mosaic animals (www.africanova .co.za), or hit Fusion for contemporary glass art and furniture.

MUST-DO DAY TRIPS

During the apartheid years, prisoners were sent to Robben Island—Nelson Mandela among them. This island, seven miles from Cape Town, housed prisoners and freedom fighters for nearly 400 years. Now it's a museum, and one of the best places to learn about South Africa's troubled past. Former prisoners serve as guides on the three-and-a-half-hour tour, which includes ferry transportation from Cape Town (www.robben-island.org.za).

A trip to Cape Point, 36 miles south of Cape Town, is a must for any visitor. While it is not the place where the Atlantic meets the Indian Ocean, nor is it the southernmost point of Africa, it is spectacular and a lot more accessible than the actual tip at Cape Agulhas (138 miles from Cape Town). At Cape Point, giant cliffs tower above the battering ocean. Hold on to your hats so the fierce winds won't whisk them out of sight. The shore is littered with shipwrecks, testimony to violent storms and dangerous rocks. Lace up your hiking boots and enjoy the well-marked paths to the lighthouse, or the shortest trail, a 15-minute ramble, to Smitswinkel viewpoint. Warm your toes in the sand along the Shipwreck trail, which leads you to the remains of shipwrecks buried along the shore. And breathe some of the cleanest air in the world—blown in from Antarctica. If you prefer to retreat from the wind and catch a bit to eat, without the annoying presence of the curious and overly friendly baboons, settle in at Two Oceans Restaurant for lunch and an awesome view from the huge windows over a dizzying drop to the turbulent ocean below. Cape Point is located within Table Mountain National Park, which boasts a variety of animals including baboons and Cape Mountain zebra as well as more than 250 species of birds and indigenous flora that are found nowhere else in the world ($8 entrance fee to the National Park; *www.san parks.org/parks/table_mountain* or *capepointroute.co.za*).

WHERE TO STAY

Cape Heritage Hotel, located in the historic district's Heritage Square, delivers the best of old and new: four-poster beds and fireplaces, plus free DVD rentals and plush mattresses. All of which makes me think: girlfriends' slumber party! The hotel is surrounded by top-notch restaurants and beautiful historic Dutch and Georgian houses (from $185 for doubles; *www.capeheritage.co.za*).

You won't get more for your money than you can at the Hemingway Lodge, in the Western Cape. The hotel is both glamorous and intimate—and some rooms have to-die-for views of Table Mountain. There are only four rooms, so you and your pals could easily take over the entire hotel (from $90 per person per night; *www.hemingwayhouse.co.za*).

For a big gift to yourselves, stay at Cape Grace, voted best hotel in the world by *Condé Nast Traveler* several years ago. In addition to the expected luxuries, the Cape Grace has a fabulous spa that combines understated elegance with treatments that hark back to ancient Africa—when massage and aromatic spices were used to cure a thousand ills. The spa, as well as rooms at the Cape Grace enjoy views of Table Mountain to the south or Victoria and Alfred Waterfront and the Indian Ocean to the north (from $620; *www.capegrace.com*).

BEST DINING

The Nose Restaurant and Wine Bar, in Cape Quarter, might actually have more wine on its menu than food—it has a daily selection of 40 wines available by the glass. If you're not too tipsy when it comes time to order, I'd go with the Camembert and cranberry chicken burger or the summer swimmer dish—the best of what's come in off the fishing boats that day ($10; *www.thenose.co.za*). You'll need to start thinking outside the box before you sit down at Caveau Wine Bar and Deli, in the historic part of town. (You'll notice a trend here: Most restaurants double as wine bars.) The ingredients here are local and therefore a bit unusual, and the preparation is ultracreative, which means you

can expect dishes like ostrich with Parmesan potatoes, springbok pie
(aka antelope pie), and herb-crusted kingklip fish fillets (*www.caveau
.co.za*). For a primer on local wines, join them for their monthly wine-
tasting event. At the Western Cape hot spot Wakame, sushi, dim
sum, and other Asian delights are on the menu: tea-smoked salmon,
crispy duck pancakes, and prawn California rolls wrapped in salmon
and tuna. You'll savor the dishes with stunning views of Table Bay,
and chances are you'll spot dolphins (*www.wakame.co.za*).

BEST CLASSIC SAFARIS

Let's face it, you can't leave Africa without going on safari. Give
yourselves enough time to see Africa's Big Five: lion, leopard, elephant, rhino, and buffalo. And that's not all: There are zebras, wilde-
beests, ostriches, and baboons prowling the corners of South Africa's
national parks. Plan a trip to Kruger National Park and private
game reserves and luxury lodges of Ngala and Phinda or Londolozi.
Thornton Safaris specializes in these areas, and founder Mark
Thornton personally leads all custom safaris (*www.thorntonsafaris
.com*). With 35 years of experience, the highly regarded Conservation
Corporation Africa operates luxury safaris to more than 40 deluxe
African Safari camps (*www.ccafrica.com*).

BEST HIKES

Marvelous 3,563-foot-high Table Mountain is a must for hikers. The
aerial tram will whisk you to the summit in ten minutes and you can
hike for hours along the wooden walkways and well-marked paths that
protect the unique plant life. Bring a warm jacket because it can get
windy and cold very quickly on top of the mountain.

EVENTS TO FLY IN FOR

Plan to bring a bottle of wine, a picnic blanket, and your closest girlfriends to the Summer Sunset Concerts at Kirstenbosch National Botanical Gardens every Sunday from December through March. Set against the eastern slope of Table Mountain, this is one of the best ways to end the day—watching the sun create a red glow behind the mountain while listening to jazz, blues, or R&B (*www.sanbi.org/frames/kirstfram*).

ONE CLICK AND YOU'RE OFF

For more on South Africa, visit *www.southafrica.net*; detailed information about Cape Town can be found at *www.tourismcapetown.co.za*.

❧ Buenos Aires ❧

People often refer to Buenos Aires, the capital city of Argentina, as the Paris of South America, but I don't think that exactly captures its essence. Yes, it's a cosmopolitan city filled with boutiques, fine restaurants, beautiful architecture, and cultural sophistication, but unlike its European counterpart, prices are jaw-droppingly inexpensive, the weather is deliciously temperate, and Latin culture adds a free-and-easy vibe. The city has many different neighborhoods, each with its own distinctive look and feel. It can be tricky to orient yourselves, so let me help you out: The main neighborhoods to focus on are Recoleta (with its upscale shops, restaurants, and hotels), Palermo (with trendy boutiques and tapas eateries), and San Telmo (a historic district with open-air markets and street tango performances). You'll find parks hidden in every pocket of the city, and cafés buzzing with people out for an afternoon glass of local Malbec wine or a snack of chicken empanadas. Cultural landmarks you should put on your must-see list are Casa Rosada, made famous by Eva Perón; the Recoleta Cemetery, where Perón and other famous Argentines are buried; and the 18th-century Basílica de Santo Domingo, a historic and architectural wonder. Buenos Aires is a shopper's delight, with some of the finest leather selling at some of the lowest prices; a meateater's fantasy, with restaurants' steak preparations bordering on an art form; and a culture-vulture's haven, with a world-class opera company, a burgeoning dance and music scene, and many fine museums. Furthermore, the city is safe, clean, and easy to get around by foot or taxi (always ask your hotel concierge to call you a cab), making it the perfect urban getaway for a group of girlfriends. Located on the banks of the Plata River, Buenos Aires enjoys pleasant weather year-round—it almost never snows and summers are muggy, but not unbearably so. That said, spring and fall are the most pleasant, with temperatures in the 60s and low 70s.

SHOP TILL YOU DROP

If you can make only one blowout shopping excursion a year, Buenos Aires should be on the top of your list. The city has everything you can find elsewhere (American and international clothing chains) at a fraction of the price, plus fantastic smaller local chains and unique boutiques of its own. For the best of Argentina's boutiques, stroll the pedestrian mall on Calle Florida. Also on Calle Florida is Galerias Pacífico, a sophisticated mall with high-end shops, tea rooms, and a food court. Be sure to look up—the painted murals on the ceiling add an extra touch of elegance to your shopping experience. For the best of the big international chain stores, including Christian Dior and Lancôme, head over to Patio Bullrich in the Recoleta neighborhood (*www.shoppingbullrich.com.ar*). If you buy one item when you're in Buenos Aires, let it be leather: a jacket, a pair of boots, a purse, a wallet. Local chains Lazaro and Prüne, which you'll find both on Calle Florida and in Patio Bullrich, shouldn't be missed.

GO WINE-TASTING

Argentina is the fifth-largest wine producer in the world. Learning about its famous Malbecs, Torrontes, and Tempranillos will only deepen your appreciation for the country. If you sign on for a gal's wine-tasting when you first arrive, you'll prime your palates and be able to choose pairings for your meals during the rest of your stay. Buenos Vinos, staffed by a group of top-notch English-speaking Argentine sommeliers, holds two-hour private tastings at Casa Saltshaker, a restaurant in the Barrio Norte neighborhood ($250 for a group of four; *www.buenos-vinos.com*).

BEST DINING

Prepare yourselves for late lunches and later dinners. Argentines don't usually sit down to eat until nine or ten at night. That might seem late, but if you can embrace their attitude—food and drink are to be savored at a leisurely pace—you'll do just fine. And remember, this is steak country. Unless you're a vegetarian, I recommend letting loose, banning the word "calorie" from your vocabularies, and relishing Argentina's carnivorous cuisine. There's no better place to do that than Cabaña Las Lilas, recognized as one of the top steak restaurants in the world. It's both an international destination (nestled in the Puerto Madero neighborhood) and a favorite with in-the-know locals. It's not your typical U.S. steak house—dark and testosterone-filled. In the bright, elegant dining room, you're as likely to rub shoulders with the elite of Buenos Aires as a family from Kansas. And if you haven't had grass-fed beef before, start sharpening your knives now—you're in for a treat. When you bite into a rib eye, you'll actually taste the grass ($40; *www.laslilas.com.restaurant.php*).

You'll love the scene as much as the food at Sucre, which has an open kitchen and a hip, industrial aesthetic. Sucre offers an excellent blend of modern Argentine fare served with flavorful local wines stored in a giant square cement cellar that dominates the center of the restaurant. The food is out of this world—squid stuffed with braised oxtail, succulent rack of lamb, pork flank, goat sweetbreads flavored with chorizo sauce. Much of it is cooked on a wood-fired grill that sends flames shooting dramatically into the air—ask for a table close to the open kitchen if you're interested in watching the action and feeling the heat. A lounge in the front and a bar that stretches the entire length of the restaurant add energy to an already-buzzing ambience ($50; *www.sucrerestaurant.com.ar*).

CATCH A SHOW
Teatro Colon, which first opened its doors in 1908, is one of the great theaters of the world, staging operas, ballet performances, and orchestral concerts year-round. Every production is world class, so snap up a ticket to whatever's playing there while you're in town. It will be a highlight of your trip. The theater, which has exceptional acoustics and an elegant interior decorated with gilded touches and vibrant frescoes, has hosted the likes of Maria Callas, Arturo Toscanini, and Luciano Pavarotti. It's been closed the last couple of years for renovation, but you're in luck now, it's scheduled to reopen in May 2008 in time to celebrate its centennial (*www.teatrocolon.org.ar*).

BEST ANTIQUES
There are scads of antiques shops to peruse in the historic San Telmo neighborhood every day of the week. On Sundays in San Telmo's Plaza Dorrego, the antiques lovers among you should make a beeline for a fair called Feria de Antiguedades, where you can pick up antiques, handcrafts, jewelry, or scarves.

BEST HISTORICAL STROLL

Cruise the walkways between the 6,400 mausoleums at Recoleta Cemetery and you'll get a history lesson on Argentina's most prominent citizens and families. Presidents, Nobel Prize winners, artists, authors, and perhaps most famous of all, First Lady Eva Perón, are buried here in elaborate tombs dating as far back as 1822. Stretching over 13-plus acres in the tony Recoleta neighborhood, the cemetery is like a mini-city, with tree-lined walkways dividing groups of mausoleums into squares resembling city blocks. You'll also get a glimpse of Argentina's architectural legacy—the tombs range in style from neoclassic to art deco, and several are national historic monuments. It'll be the most fun you'll ever have in a cemetery.

TANGO BEFORE YOU GO

To get a head start on the Argentine tango craze, consider taking a lesson before you go. Two great resources for tango lessons in the U.S. are Makela Tango (*makelatango.com*) in Los Angeles and New York Tango (*www.newyorktango.com*). For musical inspiration, start listening to the tunes of a tango music master like Francisco Canaro; the Tango Catalogue has an extensive collection of CDs to choose from (*www.thetangocatalogue.com*). You probably won't mind that tango dancing requires a little bit of shopping. You'll need comfortable heels and a flowing, below-the-knees dress or skirt. I love the offerings from Tangoleva, which include everything from foxy fishnets to tasteful dresses, skirts, and tops (*www.tangoleva.com*).

HAILING A TAXI IN BUENOS AIRES

In Buenos Aires it is safe to go to restaurants with bars or to nightclubs; however, it is not safe to hail a cab on the street. Ask your hotel or the restaurant to call a reputable taxi for you.

—Marybeth

DANCE THE NIGHT AWAY

You can catch tango dancing any day of the year on the streets of the San Telmo neighborhood, where performers stage surprisingly good shows in Plaza Dorrego, or in the theater at the renowned Piazzolla Tango (shows are $60; *www.piazzollatango.com*). To get in on the tango action yourselves, you can pull on some sexy stockings and a pair of comfortable pumps and take a lesson from one of the masters at Piazzolla Tango (group lessons are just $6).

BEST PUBLIC ART

As you drive between the various neighborhoods in Buenos Aires, you'll no doubt find yourself on Avenida Figueroa Alcorta, one of the city's main arteries. You won't be able to miss the giant, shiny aluminum flower sprouting up in United Nations Park—one of the

MY FAVORITE DAY

☙

My favorite day in Buenos Aires was a Sunday at the San Telmo street fair. We heard the music as soon as we stepped out of the cab and into the Plaza Dorrego. The sultry rhythms of guitar and *bandoneon* (a large, square concertina that is the signature instrument for tango) surrounded us like an acoustic lasso, pulling us through a maze of tented stalls displaying merchandise—antique seltzer bottles, tarnished silver, elaborately carved picture frames, heirloom jewelry, lace baptismal gowns—that ordinarily would have captured our attention for hours.

At a plaza within the plaza, a crowd had gathered to watch a couple dance. She wore billowing red chiffon and matching red stilettos; he sported a black fedora, a jauntily tied silk scarf, and a sultry, come-hither expression. They moved in intricate, sensuous concert, feet flashing, bodies twirling, music coursing like blood through their veins. The audience was held spellbound, as though by a magician pulling an elephant out of his hat.

most splendid pieces of public art you'll ever see. If you keep your eyes peeled, you'll notice that the flower's petals are open during the day and closed at night. That's because the sculpture, which is called "Floralis Genérica" and was designed by local architect Eduardo Catalano, is solar sensitive. For a better look, take a spin around the park, which houses several other sculptures as well. If you can catch it at dusk, the petals glimmer with the orangey-red of the setting sun.

WHERE TO STAY

Recoleta reminds me a lot of Manhattan's Upper East Side—in all the good ways. Elegant apartment buildings, cafés, boutiques, and galleries line streets that inevitably lead to delightful small parks and plazas planted with palm trees and jacarandas whose branches bend with purple blossoms each spring. Caesar Park Hotel is a Recoleta

There was more theater to be observed in the streets surrounding the square: mimes and guitar players, an organ grinder, a contortionist, more mimes, more tango dancers, a man sitting on a stool playing bandoneon with his thoughts somewhere in the clouds.

Buenos Aires feels like a clean, green, European city plunked incongruously into the middle of South America. There are monuments, parks, modern buildings, and gorgeous belle époque edifices. An obelisk resembling the Washington Monument rises from an oval of grass. Nearby I saw a glass office tower with the word "Microsoft" plastered across its top. Wide boulevards are bustling with lots of late-model cars.

Handsome, well-dressed people fill the streets, half of them yakking on cell phones. There are dog walkers with Afghans, boxers, and Yorkies straining at their leashes. Everywhere there are trees, trees, and more trees. Everywhere prosperity is evident and there is very little graffiti.

—Janet Fullwood, 50s, Travel Editor, *Sacramento Bee*,
Sacramento, California

standout, its rooms furnished with plush beds and outfitted with extra-large bathtubs. Its dining room serves one of the best breakfast buffets I've ever had the pleasure of grazing (from $180, including breakfast; *www.caesar-park.com*).

If you want to tap into Buenos Aires's fashion industry, avant-garde art world, and its nexus of innovative restaurants, base your-selves in Palermo. This district consists of several neighborhoods, including Palermo Viejo (old town) and Palermo Soho (its trendy, energetic counterpart). Smack in the middle of Palermo Soho is 1555 Malabia House, a bed-and-breakfast with a sleekly modern design and décor. Rooms are small, with hardwood floors, simple white linens on the beds, and the occasional cow-skin rug. A spacious front living room and a garden courtyard create a more expansive feel. The hotel is a hideaway within a fashionable new neighborhood that you and the girls will delight in exploring (from $139; *www.malabiahouse.com.ar*).

EVENTS TO FLY IN FOR

In the months of February, March, October, and December, interna-tional tango competitions come to town and dance performances are ubiquitous. If you're interested in watching the dramatically elegant dance—or taking lessons—this is the time to come. Or if you're more interested in fine art, the festival known as arteBA might be more up your alley. Each May, contemporary Argentine painters, photographers, and sculptors get their day in the sun during this festival (*www.arteba.org*).

TAKE A TOUR

If you and your girlfriends want an introduction to the fascinat-ing history, architecture, and culture of this great Latin American city—take a tour. Buenos Aires Tours offers a reasonably priced pri-vate, three-hour guided walking tour of the important landmarks around the historic heart of Buenos Aires: Plaza de Mayo, Avenida de Mayo, Buenos Aires Cathedral, and Café Tortoni, the oldest café in Buenos Aires ($40 for one, $90 for three; *www.buenostours .com/buenos-aires-tours*).

ONE CLICK AND YOU'RE OFF

Go to Argentina Tourism at *www.turismo.gov.ar*.

CHAPTER THREE

Wonderful Walks

Karen laced up her first pair of hiking boots as a teenager. While her friends were cruising the malls, she took off with her German shepherd to explore the backcountry and coastal trails of northern California. Her passion for hiking continued through college, into her married life, and into her 50s—family vacations with her husband and two daughters always involved camping and hiking.

But a few years ago, when Karen's trailmate (her husband) suffered a knee injury, she gave it all up for several months. Then she got a call from her sister-in-law, Jane, inviting her on a hiking trip in Switzerland. Karen was ecstatic. It was a chance to pick up her favorite hobby again, to feel herself again, and to hike in the Alps, a dream she had held since she saw *The Sound of Music* as a child.

Karen and Jane immersed themselves in researching the trip,

gobbling up information on hiking trails in Switzerland. It became clear the country has a dizzying number of trails for hikers of all abilities. It was overwhelming; and they didn't want to plan every detail and make every decision themselves. Karen's brother had a friend who owned a women's tour company that specialized in walking trips worldwide, so they contacted her. The owner of the company, also named Karen (I'll call her Karen C.), answered their questions and helped them select a Zermatt-based trip that best suited their level of fitness. Luckily, many of the trails around the ski town of Zermatt are accessed by trams; which means you ride up into the mountains, hike for as long or short a time as you like, and hitch a ride back down. This feature especially appealed to Karen and Jane. And fortunately for them, Karen C. had hiked every inch of every trail, scoured the maps, and explored villages. From her favorite chalets for lunch, restaurants for dinner, and the best areas for wildflower viewing, she created the ultimate trip for her clients.

When they arrived in Zermatt in late June, the two met the other members of their group—a mix of 22 ladies ranging in age from 40 to 80. And every one of them was ready to hit the trails with gusto. Each morning after a hearty Swiss breakfast of freshly baked rolls and local jams, meats, and cheeses, the gals stretched their muscles while Karen C. briefed them on that day's trails and points of interest along the way. The group spent the days meandering through vibrant meadows of wildflowers, walking in the shadow of jagged snowcapped peaks, past grazing sheep, and through tiny hamlets with wooden chalets adorned with flowerboxes of red, pink, and gold geraniums and marigolds. They also encountered European hikers on the trail—all well equipped with walking sticks, backpacks, and smiles. Karen and Jane were delighted that the hiking was fairly easy, and that by being in a group they could become immersed in deep conversations with many of the women and also could escape into their own minds for periods of therapeutic contemplation.

At lunchtime the ladies would stop at little restaurants in stone chalets along the trail to relax, share stories, and sample homemade *raclette*, a traditional melted-cheese dish. They sampled sausages and salads, drank cold beer, and finished it all off with homemade apple strudel for dessert. "It was like having mom cook for you," Karen says. After lunch, their bellies full, they had the option of continuing to hike or taking a tram back down to Zermatt.

For Karen, connecting with these other women who shared her passion for hiking was the most fulfilling part of the trip. A spirited camaraderie blossomed among the ladies. "The women were very inclusive," Karen says. The group would stop in small towns to poke around shops as a break from the trail. "When we left one store, we just called to each other, 'I'm going two doors down to the shoe shop!' " Karen explains. No worries, no stress, no impatient husbands pacing outside. They were a team. Karen and Jane found that one of the greatest perks to traveling with a group is that you're only responsible for your *own* good time: You don't have to worry about what the rest of your family is up to. And with a guide, you don't have to concern yourself with always being the leader of the pack.

In the Alps, Karen tapped back into her lifelong passion—thanks in no small part to this group of old and new friends. And all of her senses were awakened on this trip, returning her home energized. As she strolled through the storybook scenery of the Alps, she smelled freshly baked apple strudel, savored the richness of chocolate, took in the splendor of mountain peaks, touched fuzzy edelweiss flowers, and heard the bees buzzing and the sound of church bells filling a valley. Only hiking could have brought her all of this. And it was just what she had dreamed about as a girl.

Peru

Perched on a mountaintop at nearly 8,000 feet, surrounded by dazzling Andean peaks, the ancient city of Machu Picchu (known as the Lost City of the Incas) belongs on everyone's life list. You may know some of the basics—that the ruins here date back to the 1400s, when Inca architects built an astonishingly intricate system of temples, homes, and enormous stepped terraces, fitting stone blocks together without using mortar. But you must see it to believe it. You can certainly take a train to view the extraordinary ruins, but the exhilaration of hiking the 27-mile Inca Trail—especially with the women in your life—to Machu Picchu will make for a far more rewarding travel experience and accomplishment. One of the world's most classic and spectacular treks, the Inca Trail traverses mountainous terrain, dense jungles, and high desert to the ancient Inca city. Most trekkers complete the journey in four days' time, camping each night along the way. (Don't let the sleeping arrangement dissuade you. You'll be too pleasantly exhausted at night to mind.) And a majority of them go in the summertime, which is why I recommend going in the winter, when the trails are less crowded and the weather is only slightly chillier and wetter. The trek may sound strenuous, but don't concern yourself with that. With one part preparation and another part determination, you'll find it's in your grasp. Plus you'll have your girlfriends to get through it with.

PLAN AHEAD
Before the trip, get in shape the fun way: Grab the gals at least six weeks in advance and do some shorter hikes, carrying a backpack and hitting as many hills as you can. If you're working out in a gym, the Stairmaster and treadmill (on an uphill incline) will become your best friends. The elevation in this region is no joke—after all, you will be huffing up to more than 13,000 feet in the Andes en route to Machu Picchu. Altitude sickness is not uncommon. It's usually limited to symptoms such as fatigue, upset stomach, or dizziness, but it can often be exacerbated by physical exertion.

GET ACCLIMATED
Before you start the trek to Machu Picchu, I recommend spending at least two days in the city of Cusco (11,150 feet) to adjust. Ancient capital of the Inca Empire, this fascinating and friendly town is only an hour's flight from Lima. It is the gateway to the trail and also an excellent spot to treat yourselves to local delicacies like hot corn tamales and *chicha* (a regional drink made of purple corn and fruit). You can experience one of the city's greatest forms of entertainment by parking yourselves on a bench for some people-watching. You'll also want to make a trip to the traditional market town of Pisac, which bursts with local crafts and color. There you can snap up provisions for the hike, including a walking stick and energy-boosting chocolates.

TRAIL ESSENTIALS
The first day you'll hike along a dirt path and up stone staircases to 8,800 feet. The altitude may leave you all gasping, but the astonishing views of saw-toothed snowcapped peaks are what will really take your breath away. On day two you'll hike and explore other Inca ruins along the way, and on the third day—considered the most challenging of the journey—your group might think to form a hiking parade of sorts to cheer each other on as you hike to 14,200 feet and the legendary Dead Woman's Pass. (No need to worry, it wasn't named for a trekker.) This is the very highest point on the Inca Trail, where you'll marvel at your feat (and take some extra sips of water) while you gaze out at the vast scenery all around you

NEIGHBORHOOD MOMS
CRUISE THE AMAZON

჻

Betty and Jan lived on the same street in Akron, Ohio. Their children grew up together in the 1950s, playing in each other's backyards and sleeping over in their family rooms. When their sons were eight years old, Betty and Jan began taking them on short camping trips each summer to nearby state parks. Their husbands would join them on the weekends.

Over the years they discovered that they loved doing the same things: being outdoors, exploring nature, and taking some risks. When the kids grew up and left home, their friendship evolved into travels farther from home. Jan, her husband, and Betty traveled to Africa and Egypt together, and when Jan won a trip to Peru, she asked Betty to be her companion. They cruised the Amazon, explored little villages in the jungle, and learned to observe birds with the avid bird-watchers in the group.

It was their first trip as two married women traveling overseas without their husbands. They were surprised that more than 60 percent of the participants in the group were women, and they weren't all widows. They found out that they all had a lot in common: a love of nature, bird-watching, and exploring new countries and cultures. Jan and Betty felt comfortable in the group and appreciated that women are so inclusive of each other.

with jungle flowers, rushing waterfalls, and smaller ruins. On the fourth day, you'll finish up with an absolutely magical experience: entering the city of Machu Picchu. After what you've accomplished and what you will be seeing with your own eyes, you and your girlfriends may sense a nearly spiritual connection with the absolutely overwhelming natural beauty of the place and the ancient people who once inhabited this land.

BEST TOUR OPERATORS

There's no going it alone on this trail—the law requires you to sign on for an organized tour, which is actually good news for you because a support staff handles the logistics while you hike unencumbered. You'll need to do some advance planning, three months at least, to obtain the necessary government-issued hiking permits. Women's adventure tour company Call of the Wild offers 11-day Peru tours, which include a four-day Inca Trail hike (starting at $2,995; 510-849-9292, *www.call wild.com*). Learn about traditional weaving, agricultural production, and the Quechuan way of life in the Sacred Valley before you trek the classic Inca Trail on an 11-day tour with Adventure Associates, a women's tour company. You'll stay at the Sanctuary Lodge, the closest hotel to the ruins of Machu Picchu, so you'll witness sunset and sunrise and have quiet moments in the ancient city after all the tour buses have left (from $2,499; 888-532-8352, *www.adventure associates.net*). On the higher end of the travel company spectrum, Mountain Travel Sobek runs a ten-day classic Inca Trail and Machu Picchu trip ($9,509 per person, $3,595 for 4-9 members, $3,395 for 10-14; 888-687-6235, *www.mtsobek.com*).

If you prefer to book with a Peruvian outfitter or at the last minute, there are more than 140 accredited trekking companies in Cusco. But take note: Laws protecting the crew's safety were implemented only recently—porters can only carry up to 55 pounds per person (formerly 110 pounds!), and all crew members must be paid at least minimum wage and be provided with food and a comfortable place to sleep. Don't use any tour operator that doesn't comply by these rules.

BEST SPLURGE

There are plenty of ways to reward yourself—and your knees—for all that hiking. At the end of the day, you can kick up your feet, sit back with a pisco sour, and move only to visit a candlelit sauna at the Inkaterra resort, located in Aguas Calientes, down the road from Machu Picchu. Or there's a more leisurely option for experiencing the Inca Trail that some of you may prefer: When you rent a bungalow here you can arrange a day-long Inca Trail excursion with the lodge's own local guides and refuel with a tasty boxed lunch as you sit among the ruins. In your downtime back at Inkaterra, feast your eyes on 372 species of orchids during a stroll through the garden, or join in on the daily tea preparations—leaves are picked, ground up, and roasted in the Tea House (starting at $220 a night, including three meals, transfers and some excursions; 800-442-5042, *www.inkaterra.com*).

EVENT TO FLY IN FOR

If you've been curious about Carnival (the Latin American celebration that precedes Lent each winter), but the massive crowds give you pause, the Inti Raymi Festival is for you. Timed to the summer solstice, June 21, Inti Raymi was long ago considered the most important festival of the Inca Empire. Join the nearly 200,000 locals and visitors who flood Cusco's streets for live Peruvian music, traditional dance performances, and a formal blessing of the sun.

ONE CLICK AND YOU'RE OFF

Visit the Republic of Peru's Tourism Promotion Board at *www.peru.info/perueng.asp*.

England

It's as if you've stepped inside a watercolor painting when you first lay eyes on the Cotswold Hills countryside. Just a hundred miles northwest of the hustle and bustle of London, you'll find a lush, hilly paradise with tranquil villages peppered with golden limestone buildings, thatch-roofed cottages, grand manors, and churches—all interlaced with an astonishing 3,000 miles of footpaths. Cotswold Way National Trail is both the best-marked and gentlest trail of all, stretching more than a hundred miles from the market town of Chipping Campden southwest to the ancient spa town of Bath. The trail is relatively flat, topping out at just 1,066 feet, and to walk the entire route in a week's time, you'll need to average 15 miles per day. But the beauty of the trail is that you can pick it up at any of the 20 or so villages along the way and devise your own girls' inn-to-inn hiking trip. Bite off as much or as little of the trail as you wish, set your own pace, and abandon any stress about navigating: It's very easy to follow. You'll find train and bus schedules accommodating and convenient as a means of transport. Or if you prefer, you can join a tour to take care of all the details. The landed English country folk in the Cotswolds have a dry sense of humor and tend to be amenable to walkers passing through. You and the girls can spend your evenings chatting with villagers over a pint in the pub, and then get up early the next day to peruse local farmers' markets for ingredients for your picnic lunches. After a few hours of hiking, spread your feast out in a meadow of wildflowers and eat while you watch the sheep graze. A quick bit of advice about weather: Late spring and early fall

are the driest times of year, but even so, prepare for drizzle (this is
England, after all). Raincoats are recommended year-round.

TRAIL ESSENTIALS

There are so many different ways to hike the Cotswold Way National
Trail, and so many places to stay along the way, from modest bed-
and-breakfasts and farm-stays to elegant hotels well worth the
splurge, that the best advice I can give you is to study the official
website for the trail, which lists every accommodation along the way
(*www.nationaltrail.co.uk/Cotswold*). Choose the ones that meet your
criteria, and then arrange your itinerary accordingly. A good rule of
thumb is to start in Cheltenham in Gloucestershire, which is roughly
the halfway point of the trail. Trains leave frequently from London
(see *www.cotswoldsaonb.org.uk* for schedules). By cutting the trail in
half and taking a week's time to hike it, you'll have the opportunity
to immerse yourselves in the countryside, but the mileage won't be
so serious that you're dead-tired at the end of each day. When you're
deciding which direction to go, my suggestion is this: For the best
antiques-hunting, head northeast toward Chipping Campden. For
a rewarding thermal soak at trail's end, choose the other direction
to Bath and its perfectly preserved Roman baths (*www.romanbaths
.co.uk*). What better way to celebrate at the end of a hiking trip than
with a muscle-soothing soak?

BEST SPLURGE

After a daylong stroll, indulge yourselves in a rejuvenating spa treatment. At Chapel Spa in Cheltenham you'll find fabulous healing
mineral springs with six treatment rooms that reflect the styles and
spiritualities of various exotic destinations—executed with a mini-
malist elegance and modern comfort. Step into the Hawaii room and
feel yourself transported to the powdery shores of Maui. My favorite
treatments are the Pro-Lifting Booster facial and the Aroma hot-stone
massage, but if you're in need of a good hamstring stretch as an antidote

to all that walking, sign up for a yoga class (from $100 for a 30-minute facial, massage, manicure, or pedicure; *www.chapelspa.co.uk*).

CAN'T-MISS TEAHOUSES

One of the highlights of your trip will be your daily indulgence in teas, an institution in this country that includes scones, cakes, clotted cream, and jams. For a picture-perfect high tea experience that harkens back to the days of English royalty, you and the girls must visit Badgers Hall in Chipping Campden, at the northern end of the trail. Located on High Street, this stone house was built in the 1500s and converted into a teahouse and bed-and-breakfast in 1996. Join hosts Karen and Paul Pinfold for a traditional cream tea that is sure to put some pep in your step. Paul spends the mornings baking, so shelve your diets and savor his crunchy lemon cake, coffee sponge cake, and rich scones slathered in clotted cream (tea from $9, rooms start at $185 for a double, including breakfast and tea; *www.badgershall.com*).

SHOP TILL YOU DROP

The antiques lovers among you will go wild in the Cotswolds. This area has more antiques dealers than almost any other region outside of London. Practically every village boasts at least one shop or a bustling flea market for browsing. A village called Stow on the Wold (in the northern Cotswolds) is one of the best for antiquing, with goodies ranging from affordable old knickknacks to high-end rarities for more serious collectors. My favorite store there is Baggott Antiques, which features two floors of fine English 17th-, 18th-, and 19th-century furniture, precious hardcover books, and exquisite artwork (*www.baggottantiques.com*).

BEST ON-YOUR-OWN OPTION

If you want to strike out on your own and see a different town each day but don't want the hassle of either carrying everything on your back or returning to a bed-and-breakfast simply to pick up luggage, hire British-based Sherpa Van Project to transport your bags. They'll also arrange accommodations and provide you with directions to your destination that evening (starting at $14 per bag, per day, plus a $25 fee to book your accommodations; *www.sherpavan.com*).

BEST TOUR OPERATORS

If you'd rather leave *all* of the logistics to someone else, Going Places Tours, a women's walking travel company out of California, offers a seven-day easy-to-moderate tour (starting at $3,150; 707-935-0595, *www.goingplacestours.com*). Vermont-based Country Walkers offers a seven-day excursion with overnight stays in Chipping Campden and Bath, from where you'll start on walks ranging between four and seven miles per day (starting at $3,398; 800-464-9255, *www.coun trywalkers.com*). The Wayfarers, a walking tour specialist, arrange a six-day guided walk through the Cotswolds and Oxford, with select women's-only programs (starting at $3,495; 800-249-4620, *www.the wayfarers.com*). English outfit Cotswold Walking Holidays provides several options, including a 7- to 11-night self-guided option (there's a luxury version as well) of the Cotswold Way (starting at $780; *www.cotswoldwalks.com*).

ONE CLICK AND YOU'RE OFF

The official tourism site for the Cotswolds provides maps and accommodations information, *www.cotswolds.info*. For additional details, bus and train schedules, and great maps to download, visit the website of the Cotswolds Area of Outstanding Beauty, the English's version of a national park, at *www.cotswoldsaonb.com*.

New Zealand

Hiking, or tramping, as Kiwis call it, is practically a national pastime in New Zealand. And the Routeburn Track, located in the Southern Alps at the very southern tip of the country's gorgeous South Island, is considered to be Down Under's greatest hike for its superlative and untouched alpine beauty—and because it's so easy to access. What makes this world-famous trail among my favorites is that it's so easy to follow and delivers you to some of the planet's most dramatic mountain scenery without requiring you to ascend to exhaustingly high altitudes. In fact, the highest point of the 20-mile route—which connects Mount Aspiring National Park and Fiordland National Park via the Harris Saddle—is only around 5,000 feet. (That's practically at the same altitude as the Denver airport.) Still, you'll want to take the trail slowly, allotting yourselves at least three days to soak in panoramas of out-of-this-world mountains with peaks draped in snow, take time for chatting, and pause for long picnic lunches in the meadows surrounded by waterfalls, lush forests, craggy rock formations, and views of blue-green glacier lakes. But here's the catch: There are no hotels along the way. You can pitch tents at the campgrounds at Routeburn

Y ou can drive for an hour on a New Zealand highway and not see another car! And if you like nature and the outdoors, you will love this tiny country. Although I am not a bird person, I was in awe of their vivid colors—their songs seemed amplified because there is no background noise. With no ozone or pollution in the air, the color of the sky is breathtakingly blue. I now understand what a *blue* sky is. Try to arrange a stay on a working sheep farm. The entire South Island has only one million people, and in lambing season there are over 70 million sheep. The hosts on the sheep farm where we stayed were well traveled and sophisticated. Like most Kiwis we met, they were easy-going and often used some favorite New Zealand expressions, "No worries" and "Mate." We became such good friends that they are planning to visit us in California.

—Wendy Ross, 50s, Bank Executive Vice President,
Berkeley, California

Flats and Lake Mackenzie. Even in the "dry" season from December through March, it can be windy and foggy, so pack your raincoat and some wool socks to pull on at night. And you can count on it raining in these parts during your visit (in fact, the trail is only open between November and April, due to weather). Therefore, you'll appreciate having a real roof over your heads in one of four New Zealand parks department huts. If this sounds unpleasantly close to your idea of really roughing it, trust that any compromises to luxury are made up for by the proximity to a dramatic mountain landscape found nowhere else in the world—and all the bragging rights you'll earn.

TRAIL ESSENTIALS
You can do the trek either from east to west, starting in the spunky adventure-sports town of Queenstown and winding over to

Taking care of my feet on a hiking adventure is my top priority. I know where I usually get a blister and I apply moleskin before I start to hike. I also carry moleskin or duct tape and apply it to a hot spot as soon as I feel any soreness. I wrap the moleskin or duct tape around my trekking poles, just below the handles, so it is always readily available. Wearing specialized hiking socks can make a big difference in your comfort. Also, take hourly breaks and if your socks are wet, change into a dry pair. I've learned to be creative when lacing my boots. I found that if I don't lace them to the very top, my shins are more comfortable, and if I don't lace them at the very bottom, my toes have a little more needed room.

—Marybeth

Te Anau, on Milford Sound, or you can do it in reverse. I like the east–west route because Queenstown's countless sporting goods stores are a great place to stock up on energy bars or any gear you might have forgotten to bring.

If you and your girlfriends plan to follow my lead, you'll start off hiking along the clear, ice-blue Routeburn River, heading mostly uphill through a thick forest of beech trees to the grassy mountain meadow of Routeburn Flats. You'll probably pass people fishing and picnicking beneath a backdrop of snowy peaks. There's a hut you can bunk in for the night, or you can continue an hour or so to the hut by the 600-foot Routeburn Falls. All huts offer indoor plumbing, heat, rustic cooking facilities, and dormitory-style rooms that sleep between four and six. Just be sure to make reservations well in advance ($36 flat fee per person to use the huts or $9 per person to camp; *www.doc.govt.nz*). The next day you'll tackle a seven-mile alpine crossing of Harris Saddle to Lake Mackenzie and the Mackenzie Hut. On day three, you'll continue on a gently sloping five-mile walk to glassy Lake Howden, which shimmers with the reflection of the mountains and alpine flora and is the site of the fourth hut. From here, you're just two miles from the end of the track. Your final reward is a jaw-dropping view of the towering Darran Mountain Range and the Hollyford Valley. That's when you and the gals will want to flock together for a group shot to celebrate your achievement.

BEST SIDE HIKE

If the weather is on your side, count your lucky stars, hoof it an extra one to two hours up from the Harris Saddle shelter to Conical Hill. The trail zigzags its way over wet rocks, grass, and patches of snow up to a stunning 360-degree view of the Hollyford Valley, the Darran Mountain Range, Martins Bay, and all the way to the Tasman Sea.

A QUICKER VERSION

Short on time? You can still soak up the beauty of the Routeburn with a short day hike led by Queenstown-based guiding company Ultimate Hikes. They'll drive you all from Queenstown to Glenorchy, where you'll embark on an easy four-mile walk to Routeburn Flats. Kick back and savor your boxed lunch at the hut before continuing on an optional two-mile climb to Routeburn Falls. You're back in Queenstown by day's end (starting at $135; *www.ultimatehikes.co.nz*).

BEST TOURS

To sample the highlights of the entire South Island, sign on with U.S-based Adventure Associates, which specializes in adventure travel for small groups of women. Their 18-day multisport tour of the island includes hiking part of the Routeburn, sea kayaking, and a visit to Marlborough wine country (starting at $4,755; 888-532-8352, *www.adventureassociates.net*). The active travel gurus at Wilderness Travel offer the three-day Routeburn hike as part of a 16-day South Island tour, with stops at Abel Tasman National Park, Fox Glacier, and an overnight cruise of the Milford Sound (starting at $5,595; 800-368-2794, *www.wildernesstravel.com*).

ONE CLICK AND YOU'RE OFF

Visit Tourism New Zealand at *www.newzealand.com*.

✈ Switzerland ✈

You've seen photographs of the Alps—soaring, snowcapped peaks with adorable villages tucked in the folds of the foothills. They've inspired literature, music, and some of the first adventurers. But you may have thought Alpine towns with horse-drawn sleighs and carriages were simply artifacts from a storied past. In the ski resort town of Zermatt, this history is still alive and well. When your train stops in this town, which is located at the foot of the north side of Europe's most famous mountain, the Matterhorn, you and the girls will board a carriage bound for your chalet and trace the banks of the Vispa River on one of only three paved streets in town. As you ride along, sip in the crisp alpine air and let your worries evaporate. If you lift your eyes up to the mountains, you'll see roads give way to trails and gondolas shuttling visitors up into the Alps. With nearly 250 miles of both walking and hiking paths, Zermatt has the largest collection of navigable trails in all of the Swiss Alps. Here the age-old pastime of hiking remains as unfussy and accessible as it did a century ago. You'll share the trails with friendly European hikers and villagers sporting felt hats with feathers and walking sticks. Rest assured, there's something for every woman here so don't let the scale of these mountains intimidate you. Between June and September (the earlier end of this hiking season means incredible wildflower viewing), venture on gentle day walks with lunches in cute restaurants, embark on a mid-alpine hike past crystalline lakes and waterfalls, or set out to tackle one of the five most challenging trails in the area that take you high up into the towering peaks. No matter your choice, everywhere you turn, you're presented with astonishing mountain views—even from the confines of your hotel room.

TRAIL ESSENTIALS

There are many world-class day hikes in this area. My hope is that you won't limit yourselves to just one, and that you'll strike out on as many as your legs can handle. I recommend that you and the gals warm up with an hour-long easy forest ramble beginning at the historic Papperla Pub. You can breathe easy and gab away as you hike to a lovely promenade above Zermatt, from which you'll catch eyefuls of the Matterhorn before heading back down. One of the most rewarding Zermatt hikes is the three-hour trek up to Höhbalmen, at 9,000-plus feet. Once you catch your breath from this moderately steep climb, you'll be astounded by the beauty of the 14,693-foot Matterhorn soaring above you against a perfect blue sky. If you're feeling incredibly energetic and are fit, consider hiking to the base of the Matterhorn, which is a pretty strenuous four-hour trek from Schwarzsee to the Hörnli Hut.

BEST KEPT SECRET

You can get up close views of the Matterhorn without even putting on your hiking boots. Three smaller peaks in the area—Gornergrat, Klein Matterhorn, and Rothorn—are accessible by train, cable car, or funicular (picture an elevator on a slant). A glass cable car zooms up the Klein Matterhorn (Little Matterhorn); when it stops, ask the lift operators if the Gipfel-lift is open. This elevator goes to the highest summit (12,736 feet) of Klein Matterhorn for an unbelievable panoramic view of Switzerland, Italy, and France. You and the girls should also plan to rise super-early one morning and ride the funicular to the 10,200-foot summit of Rothorn. You'll take in one of the most spectacular sunrises of your life staged over the Matterhorn.

GET THE SCOOP
Your innkeeper could end up being your most valuable source of local information. Most of them take the time to chew the fat and share their best local knowledge with their guests.

BEST DINING
You're in Switzerland, so you'll need to indulge in at least one sinful fondue experience—nothing says best girlfriends like dipping bread into a pot of melted savory cheese. Café du Pont is my favorite for cheese fondue, paired with a deliciously crisp white wine (*www.dupont-zermatt.com*).

GIRLS' NIGHT OUT
GramPi's is a Zermatt institution: A tri-level pub, pizzeria, and dance club (*www.grampis.ch*). Everyone from swanky jet-setters to rambunctious tourists come here. The food and cocktails are reliably good and if the music doesn't move you, you can just soak up the local energy and take part in some prime people-watching.

EVENTS TO FLY IN FOR
July's Zermatt Marathon is one of the most physically grueling foot-races in the world, starting in St. Niklaus, leading up to Zermatt, and

My tried-and-true favorite trekking gear includes ankle-height boots with a sturdy sole, a women's-specific day pack with a waistband (wider at the hip for support) and a sternum strap, a Camelback hydration system (with an easy sipping tube), walking sticks, which take the load off your knees, especially on the downhill portions, and a rain poncho. There's nothing like hiking the foot trails of the world. Your days can be meditative, refreshing, or full of bubbling conversation, as you walk alongside friends. You experience absolute freedom. You can empty out your mind and be carefree. You let go of all your worries. Just follow the trail. As adults, we don't have enough of those moments.

—Sandy Braun, 55, Founder Adventure Associates,
Seattle, Washington

---

culminating in the high mountain town of Riffelberg. This race isn't for novices, but being a spectator is an unforgettable experience in itself. Then Zermatt's Folklore Parade takes place every August, celebrating local dance, music, and brilliantly colored traditional Swiss costumes. Regional food abounds here, so be prepared to overdose on regional cheeses and cured meats—and, dare I forget, chocolate.

BEST TOURS

Going Places Tours for women hosts an annual trip to Zermatt in July, when the wildflowers are at their colorful apex (starting at $2,895; 707-935-0595, *www.goingplacestours.com*). Adventure experts Backroads leads a six-day Swiss Alps tour that includes nights in deluxe accommodations and two days of hiking around Zermatt (starting at $3,898; 800-462-2848 or 510-527-1555, *www.backroads.com*).

READ UP

There are so many trails from Zermatt that it's best to plan which ones to do ahead of time so you can spend more time on them rather than waste time each morning choosing. The comprehensive "Walking Guide to Zermatt" can be downloaded (for about $12) from *www.ski-zermatt.com/walking_guide.html*.

ONE CLICK AND YOU'RE OFF

Visit Switzerland Tourism at *www.myswitzerland.com*.

❧ Nepal ❧

Wedged between India and Tibet in the alluring Himalaya Mountains, Nepal is definitively trekker's nirvana here on Earth. It's home to the world's tallest mountains (including the very tallest, Mount Everest at 29,035 feet), exotic Kathmandu, stone temples adorned with the eyes of Buddha, fun-loving Sherpas with pearly white smiles, and an international community of travelers with minds focused skyward into the thin air. Outdoor enthusiasts, regardless of age or ability, are drawn to Nepal for a once-in-a-lifetime opportunity to walk the ancient trails, hike to monasteries, immerse themselves in an ethnic mosaic of native people and traditions, and become enveloped in the enormous scale of the mountains. In the Himalaya there are few roads; hiking is a necessity for the Nepali. For you it will be a luxury. Girlfriends will share the novelty of hiking along terraced hillsides with local people, crossing rope bridges with them over rushing, glacial streams, and then accepting an invitation for a sweet hot tea in their home (you'll come to know these huts as the local tea-houses). The Nepali have a gaiety and warmth that is contagious. The Sherpas, who live in the Mount Everest area and are expert mountaineers and guides, especially find laughter comes easily to them. The premier trekking area, in my mind, is the Mount Everest region. It's another life-list item to tick off and a very reasonable trip to make if you're with an experienced outfitter, who can take care of all logistics and keep in mind your safety. As for when to go, sum-mertime in Nepal can be hot and humid, so visit in the spring (early March to early May) or the fall (October to mid-December).

THE EVEREST AREA ESSENTIALS

Most hikes in this region begin in Lukla, a small town in the Khumbu region of eastern Nepal (90 minutes by plane from Kathmandu). Treks vary in length from 10 to 20 days and peak at 12,650 to 16,400 feet, with optional day hikes even higher. All the treks pass through ancient Sherpa villages, including Namche Bazaar (where you can shop and acclimatize for a couple of days) and include a visit to the legendary Tengboche Monastery, where 40 monks are in residence. (You may hear them chanting early in the morning.) There are also shorter ten-day treks that leave from the airstrip at Lukla and culminate at Tengboche Monastery. Throughout your journey you'll be surrounded by the most dramatic scenery of your life: The great white mountains swirl with icy mist and reach miles into the clouds. You and the girls will marvel at how you all feel as if you've stepped into a different world.

FEELING FIT?

If you want to take on a longer 20-day trek to the Everest base camp, you'll have the chance to climb the 18,192-foot black rock of Kala Pattar for sensational views of Everest's entire South Face and West Ridge. You will also have the option to hike farther to the Everest base camp, where you'll see clusters of camped-out international climbers and tents strung with brightly colored Tibetan prayer flags.

TEAHOUSES OR TENTS?

Overnight lodges, aka teahouses, are social hubs for trekkers. You and your girlfriends, along with dozens of other adventurers, will bond as you chat and dine in the heart of one of the world's most stunning mountain landscapes. In recent years, the teahouses, which used to be extremely bare bones, have gotten a face-lift. Most now have dormitory-style and private rooms and running water and many even have hot water for bathing. At dinnertime you're in for a nourishing treat: Tibetan fried bread, lentils, meat, yak cheese, and plenty of veggies. Many of the trekking outfitters set up their own comfy camps outside the villages, with sleeping tents, dining areas, and clean toilets, so you can skip the teahouses. You'll dine

I have lived in Nepal for most of the year for 15 years, and I have not heard of a single foreigner who was killed or kidnapped during the 13-year insurgency. All parties to the conflict have bent over backward to avoid harming tourists. There are still many Europeans trekking in Nepal.

You'll be surprised and amazed by the friendly, charming children along the trails. If you want to give something, bring pencils and school supplies and donate them to the headmaster of the local school, who will invite you in for a visit.

Everyone who has been to Nepal returns with a feeling of awe and gratitude—at the friendliness of the Nepalese people, the fabulous scenery, and the joyfulness of Nepalis who have so little, yet give so much in friendship and hospitality.

—Olga Murray, 82, Founder, Nepal Youth Opportunity
Foundation, Kathmandu, Nepal

alfresco while you watch the sun rise over the Himalaya and eat in a cozy dining pavilion at sunset. But don't miss out on the teahouse camaraderie—be sure to stop in for an afternoon hot chai (tea) or a cold beer.

NEPAL'S OTHER WILD SIDE

After all that hiking, you and the gals think you might not have time (or energy) for a Himalayan safari, but think again. You don't want to miss out on a visit to Royal Chitwan National Park, located in south-central Nepal, due west of Kathmandu. Here, you can climb onto the back of a massive elephant and see rhesus monkeys, graceful Asian deer, and one-horned rhinos. If you're really lucky, you'll get a glimpse of the elusive royal Bengal tiger—Chitwan is one of the last refuges for this magnificent cat.

EVEREST FROM THE AIR

Leaving from Kathmandu, an hour-long plane ride will give you a bird's-eye view of the eight majestic mountains that loom over the valley, bringing you closer and closer to your final destination—the mighty Everest, looming more than fives miles into the air (starting at $135; www.mountainflights.com).

BEST TOUR OPERATORS

If you travel with a reputable adventure-travel company, their itinerary will be paced for maximum acclimatization and comfort. You'll have experienced guides and a staff who will prepare tasty (and sanitary) meals. Five-star "teahouse tours" are generally more expensive than camping. The women travel specialists at Adventure Women have organized a deluxe two-week tour that includes seven days of hiking the lower altitude Annapurna foothills, accommodations in luxury teahouses, two days of rafting on the Seti River, and two days at the Royal Chitwan National Park—elephant ride included (starting at $5,695; 800-804-8686, www.adventurewomen.com). Wilderness Travel runs two Everest-area treks: Ultimate Everest is a 25-day expedition to the top of Kala Pattar, and Everest Adventure involves 14 days of touring and hiking at lower elevations departing from the town of Lukla for the Tengboche Monastery at 12,680 feet (starting at $3,595 and $2,695, respectively; 800-368-2794, www.wilderness travel.com). Mountain Travel Sobek operates an 18-day trip to the Everest base camp (starting at $2,745, with an additional $220 for internal air; 888-687-6235, www.mtsobek.com).

Long skirts or pants are appropriate dress for women trekking in Nepal. It is a social faux pas to wear shorts, spaghetti strap shirts, or anything revealing.

—Marybeth

GET READY

To get in shape, I suggest walking a couple of months before your departure for Nepal for at least three hours a day on well-maintained paths with steep inclines and steps to get used to walking uphill. Altitude sickness can happen, even to the fittest athletes. To avoid it, you should select a tour that requires only about five hours of hiking per day over 10 to 20 days. (Don't opt for a cheaper outfitter that covers the same distance in fewer days—there's no sense in saving a few dollars and risking altitude sickness.)

SMART TRAVEL

Trekkers should always travel with a guide or at least with a companion. There have been political uprisings over the past few years; however, no foreign hikers have been injured. The U.S. State Department continues to post updates about the security situation in Nepal (search "Nepal travel advisories" on Google and read news on the country at *www.travel.state.gov*).

ONE CLICK AND YOU'RE OFF

Visit the Nepalese Tourism Board at *www.welcomenepal.com*.

CHAPTER FOUR

Tasteful Travel

In her work as a neonatologist, Mary spends long hours taking care of sick newborn infants. Because it's such an emotionally and physically draining job, she needs a way to restore her sense of balance when she gets home from work—a way to press the restart button. "Cooking always does that for me," Mary says. As she grinds spices, chops vegetables, sautés onions, and marinates meat for her family and friends she unwinds and relaxes.

Mary's mother was a gifted cook, who stuck to basic Southern cuisine, but Mary always dreamed beyond that; she fantasized about creating exotic concoctions full of new tastes and textures. When she happened upon the French recipes from Julia Child's first cookbook, Mary knew she had found the key to finally break into this new world of cooking. As she moved on to other cuisines over the years, she was amazed by how much she learned about different cultures through their recipes.

She had gotten a recommendation about a cooking school in Oaxaca, 300 miles southeast of Mexico City, and she enrolled quicker than she could dice a clove of garlic. The course, which focused on Oaxacan cuisine, was for serious cooks and dabblers alike. It took place over Mexico's famous annual Day of the Dead celebration in early November. It's an animated holiday when Mexican families remember their deceased loved ones by building altars in their homes and adorning them with flowers, treats, and mementos, and by visiting their gravesites. A festive celebration, it's a time when communities across Mexico come together.

Mary enticed two of her physician friends to join her for the weeklong culinary adventure, but when she arrived in Oaxaca, she observed that a cooking school is a good way to make new friendships with women as well. Mary met Eleni, a graduate student who had come to Oaxaca with her mother. Unlike Mary, Eleni wasn't the type of gal who considers dicing vegetables a way to relax in her busy life at home. "I'm single and I live in New York, so I eat out all the time or make myself something simple," she confesses. "A real chef would be appalled." But despite her habits, she adores taking culinary classes on her vacation time. Eleni may not consider herself a chef, but when she has time to spend in the kitchen, she loves the process of creating a new dish. It was women like Eleni and Mary who mostly converged at this cooking school; they take so much joy in the process of cooking that to them it is like practicing an art form such as painting.

Based in a ranch house that also serves as an inn, the students spent part of their days cooking creations and the other part eating them. At night, they went out for dinners in town and took advantage of the local nightlife. "One classmate was passionate about Latin music," Eleni says. "He'd find the hot spot, and we'd hit the town for live shows." They also traveled around the state of Oaxaca to remote villages to visit friends of the school's founder, Susana Trilling. They took part in Susana's friends' lives, sharing food, admiring (and purchasing) works of art, touring the ancient Monte Alban ruins, seeing how native crops are grown and harvested, drinking mescal, and dancing in traditional celebrations.

For Mary, aside from learning a cuisine unlike any she had studied before, getting to know the local people, who shared their homes, their hearts, and their culture was a wonderful part of the experience. The biggest highlight of all was the Day of the Dead celebration.

The students got very involved in preparing for the Day of the Dead by going to a special market to buy sugarcane, calla lilies, marigolds, delicate candy confections (in the shape of skulls and skeletons), chocolate, candied pumpkin, and little carved statues of skeletons dressed to represent men, women, and children to place on family altars to represent their dead loved ones.

The finale for the students was attempting a *mole negro*, a super-complex sauce made with multiple varieties of chilies, chocolate, fruits, nuts, spices, and herbs. It's considered the pinnacle of Oaxacan cuisine, and is an integral part of Day of the Dead celebrations. Mastering the mole negro wasn't easy—but the school's kitchen provided the most inspiring setting imaginable. "Picture a huge kitchen with windows looking out in all directions over the rural landscape," Mary says. "The kitchen walls were decorated with beautiful native pottery, baskets, and rugs, and there were flowers everywhere." The focused cooks charred chilies, raisins, almonds, and avocado leaves on an outside grill heated by a wood fire. They set fire to the chili seeds to produce a special smoky flavor. The sky was blue, and a breeze scented with flowers and smoke blew through the rooms of the house while peaceful music played on the stereo. Mary jokingly equated it to a scene out of the film *Like Water for Chocolate*. The neighbors came with their children to help build the altar at the school, which was draped with sugarcane, traditional flowers, and pictures of the dead. And then everyone sat down for an enormous feast of chicken smothered in the delectable mole sauce.

"We were there to learn how to cook, but using that as a vehicle, we were fortunate to come across people who shared the extraordinary richness of their culture and celebrated life and death with great dignity," Mary says. She also made a new, lifelong friend and cooking comrade in Eleni, the self-declared non-chef. The two of them have since returned to Mexico to attend other culinary classes. "Cooking," Eleni sums it up, "is a great activity that transcends any language barrier and brings women together."

❧ Spain ❧

You may be familiar with the legendary running of the bulls, but you likely know little of the city that serves as its scenic stage. Pamplona, Spain, the capital of Basque Country, is a destination very worth your knowing, especially if you're a foodie, because Basque Country is a gastronomic paradise. The sprawling farmland, seaside resort towns, and mountainous villages of Basque Country straddle the border of northern Spain and France and trickle into the Pyrenees mountains. The jagged, snow-covered peaks and deep, green valleys create a natural boundary between the two countries. Basque culture stands out as singular in Europe—the locals speak their own language, there's a strong feeling of Basque pride, and Basque women have enjoyed equality since the feudal era. For centuries, American chefs were utterly oblivious to the wonders of Basque cooking, which uses ingredients I'd describe as exotic surf and turf: tuna, cod, oysters, eel, and baby squid, along with farm-raised sheep, lamb, pork, and ox. Basque cuisine is dominated by fresh seafood from the coast: clams, anchovies marinated in olive oil, thick cuts of beef, smoked and aged country hams, salt cod, sautéed onions, sweet red peppers, tomatoes, and mild, dried, red Espelette peppers (originally from South America, now cultivated in the Pyrenees). Of course, no Basque meal is complete without the local specialty, Txacoli wine, a golden-colored, light white wine that often has a hint of natural carbonation. In the 1970s, a group of young chefs from San Sebastian, one of the largest Basque cities, began incorporating the lighter flavors of French nouvelle cuisine into their colorful cooking. In their restaurants, they presented their creations with whimsical, artistic flair, textured it with fresh herbs, garden vegetables and legumes, drizzles of olive oil, and smoky, unusual cheeses. And the modern movement known as new Basque cuisine was born.

You and your pals may get lucky and be invited into one of the local Sociedades Gastronomicas—private social clubs where Basque men gather to cook, eat, and drink. Traditionally they admitted males only, but nowadays they admit women, too. Often these private cooking clubs are just a few guys in the back of a bar with a few tables, indulging in their national passion: cooking. At first you may only see a table surrounded by a small group of men playing cards, drinking coffee and wine, but the adjoining kitchen will be alive with a large stockpot simmering on the stove. Here you can learn the secret techniques and ingredients of Basque cuisine from the locals. Let the masters do the cooking for you. Or you can take a formal cooking class (see below). Either way, I recommend renting a car in the city of Bilbao and setting off on a ladies' culinary road trip through the countryside, hitting coastal San Sebastian. The concentration of restaurants and bars throughout the region is staggering as is the amount of food you'll be tempted to eat. The weather in Basque Country is mild year-round, and winter can be rainy, so your best bet is to come from April through October when the days are longer and sunny.

HIT THE MARKET

A visit to La Ribera Market (in English, the River Market), in the city of Bilbao, is sure to be an educational experience even for the farmers'-market aficionados among you. It will also give you an overview of the local ingredients you're about to spend the week making sense of and tasting in regional cooking. Ribera is a three-story food-lover's paradise exploding with more than 180 covered shops selling every local food you can imagine. The first floor is devoted entirely to seafood, and the other two floors are bursting with butchered meats, cheeses, olive oil, vegetables, and fruits.

TINY DISHES, BIG FLAVORS

These days, all types of stateside restaurants are serving tapas: Greek, American, and even Japanese. If you travel around other regions of Spain, you'll certainly notice that tapas are ubiquitous. But it was the Basques who originally created the small-portion dish. The slightly confusing part is that in Basque Country, tapas are known as *pintxos,* pronounced "pinchos." (Spread the word about that to the girls while you're deliberating over the menus.) If you have time, why not spend a whole day going from one bar to the next, sampling plate after plate of hot and cold pintxos? Bar Bergara in San Sebastian serves some of the most the innovative creations. Try the foie gras with apple compote or the cuttlefish with onion. Then wash it all down with *txacoli* (pronounced "chacoli"), the fruity, fizzy white wine that waiters love to pour from high above the table into your glass. They never miss a drop or splash on you (*www.pinchosbergara.com*).

BEST TOTAL-IMMERSION COOKING COURSE

If you're looking to add a few Basque dishes to your repertoire, who better to learn from than one of the founding fathers of new Basque cuisine. Master Chef Luis Irízar is one of the originators of the movement, and if you and your friends speak enough Spanish between you, you can learn from Irízar himself at his San Sebastian school. If your Spanish stops at *"hola,"* his daughter and protégé, Visi, instructs in English during courses in the summer. These immersion courses include six nights of accommodation, breakfasts, and three or four hands-on cooking classes per week along with visits to food markets, historic sites, and local vineyards to choose the best pairings for your meals (starting at $1,100 per week; *www.gourmetsafari.com*).

BEST QUICK COOKING COURSE
The surest way to impress your foodie friends back home is to whip up an airy foam to decorate the plate or a flavorful gelée. A Taste of Spain offers half-day lessons in San Sebastian where you'll study avant-garde cooking under the tutelage of Natalia, a Cordon Bleu– trained chef who specializes in Basque cuisine. After spending the morning in the kitchen, you get to enjoy the fruits of your labor— and wash it down with some lovely Spanish red wines (starting at $322; *www.atasteofspain.com*).

BREAK THE BANK
When it comes to food, one of my mottoes is this: If you encounter a Michelin-starred restaurant, drop whatever you're doing and beg (if necessary) for a reservation. San Sebastian's Arzak is a place worth groveling for: It's one of only three restaurants in Spain with three Michelin stars. Owner Jean Mari Arzak is a living legend in these parts and a founding member of new Basque cuisine. The cozy seaside res- taurant is housed in a small wine tavern built by Arzak's grandparents in 1897; today Jean Mari works side by side with his daughter Elena, an esteemed Basque chef in her own right. Basque cuisine can be sur- prisingly light, which means you and each of your friends can order everything that sounds good, do some sharing, and definitely not leave the table feeling stuffed to the gills. At Arzak, you'll adore the grilled eggplant purée with yogurt mouse, the avocado soup, the anchovy filet served with a fried egg white and a "yolk" of puréed orange bell peppers, and the lamb prepared with beer malt. After all of that, you'll probably still even have room for dessert. Although the Basques aren't known for their sweet tooth, Arzak's Chocolate Hamburger will provide both a sugar fix and a giggle. It's made with a dark chocolate mousse—the burger—and dried fruits and white chocolate—the bun (dinners aver- age $195 per person, not including wine; *www.arzak.info*).

MUST-SEE MUSEUM
When you need a break and to get your head off the topic of food, head to Frank Gehry's architectural masterpiece, the Guggenheim Museum Bilbao. The enormous structure, which helped put Bilbao on the map, is made of limestone blocks, curved titanium, and glass walls housing a wide array of modern art. You won't be able to resist

the iconic "Puppy," a 43-foot-tall sculpture of a dog covered with flowers and greenery ($15 per person; *www.guggenheim-bilbao.es/ingles*).

WHERE TO STAY

Ladies who love exploring Europe's urban centers should use cosmopolitan Bilbao as a home base. There's everything you might expect of a city—window-shopping, people-watching, cafés—you get the picture. But it's the subtle variations of these details that we love discovering country by country, city by city, isn't it? As for a place to rest your heads at night in Bilbao, the aesthetic of the sleek Gran Hotel Domine Bilbao is heavily influenced by its neighbor, the Guggenheim (starting at $275 for doubles, including tickets to the museum; *www.hoteles-silken.com*). But for laid-back gals hungering for the Basque countryside, you may prefer the casual atmosphere, proximity to the sea, and spectacular dining of the town of San Sebastian. The Ondarreta Apartment, just two blocks from the beach, sleeps six people and comes with a fully equipped kitchen and a private terrace (starting at $220 for doubles; *www.friend lyrentals.com*). There are plenty of lower-priced options near Ondarreta beach in San Sebastian, notably Isabella B&B, a lovely smoke-free inn with four bedrooms and two separate apartments (starting at $80 for doubles, and $36 for an apartment; *www.roomsisabella.com*).

EVENT TO FLY IN FOR

Don't be self-conscious about sticking earplugs in your ears before heading out to the Tamborrada festival. It's one of the loudest food festivals you'll ever attend. Starting at midnight on January 19, members of the region's Gastronomic Societies parade through the streets dressed as cooks and soldiers, pounding heavily on drums and barrels. If you and the gals aren't night owls, not to worry. You can watch the parade anytime the following day—participants march for a full 24 hours, stopping occasionally for hearty meals at the Gastronomic Societies.

ONE CLICK AND YOU'RE OFF

Visit Tourism in Spain at *www.spain.info*.

❧ Mexico ❧

Oaxaca is known as the land of the seven *moles*. The most famous mole sauce is *mole negro*, a rich concoction made of the seemingly impossible combination of dry chili peppers and Mexican chocolate traditionally served over chicken, turkey, or pork. Learning to make mole is a feather in the cap for any gal with an interest in cooking, and eating it is one of the great pleasures of a visit to Mexico. Located about 300 miles southeast of Mexico City, the state of Oaxaca is tucked between the Sierra Madre del Sur and Sierra Madre Oriental mountain ranges. Oaxaca City, in the heart of the state, is the central point for tourists (and is served by an international airport). With all this talk about mole, you might think Oaxaca is a culinary one-trick pony, but that's not so. There's a near-endless variety of cuisines in this region, and that's because it has an amazing cultural diversity. No fewer than 17 different ethnic groups live here, and while each has its own distinctive culinary traditions and flair, you'll invariably find bold textures balanced by delicately refined flavors, locally grown produce, farm-raised meat and savory garden spices and herbs. Visiting the city of Oaxaca provides a fascinating look at Mexican colonial archi-tecture: Its baroque-style Santo Domingo temple is one of the most beautiful in all of Mexico, with a domed ceiling and an intricate gold altar. The weather is sunny and dry here year-round, which makes it a wonderful place for you and the gals to gather for strolls down the cobblestone streets, gaze up at brightly colored colonial buildings, stop in at museums and, of course, eat your hearts out (literally). The town square, called the Zócalo, serves as the bustling hub of restaurants and street stalls selling Mexican treats such as tamales, chorizo, pickled mangoes, and homemade ice creams. If you're interested in taking a cooking class, there are several world-class cooking schools within walking distance of the Zócalo—or just a short bus ride away. Let Oaxaca City be the starting line to what is bound to the Mexican-food adventure of your lives.

BEST TOTAL-IMMERSION COOKING COURSE
Cooking, eating, and sleeping—what else do we *really* need to do in life? I would argue, not much. If you agree, you'll be thrilled to learn that you can do all three at Seasons of My Heart, which is both a bed-and-breakfast and a culinary school. Seasons of My Heart is run by expatriate chef Susana Trilling, who has shared the secrets of Oaxacan cuisine with Americans through her travel cookbooks and a PBS cooking series. The school is located at Rancho Aurora, the home of Susana and her family. This quaint bed-and-breakfast is situ-ated on a hillside, nestled among the palm fronds and desert cactuses of the Etla Valley just outside of Oaxaca City. If you'd rather stay in bustling Oaxaca, you can arrange to be picked up and dropped off in

the city each day. Susanna offers afternoon, weekend, and weeklong cooking courses in which she introduces students to the sensuality of Oaxacan cooking. You'll savor the smooth, rich texture of your own mole negro spooned over spicy pork and fresh cilantro, and you'll roll your eyes in ecstasy at the dense, sweet flavors of traditional Oaxacan chocolate pudding. Strolls through the market and visits with various local artisans, including potters, weavers, and wood-carvers, will round out this cultural immersion experience (from $50 for a half-day class to $1,995 for a weeklong class; *www.seasonsofmyheart.com*).

BEST QUICK COOKING COURSE

For ladies who are short on time, a half-day cooking class in the heart of Oaxaca City is the way to go. At Casa Crespo (also a bed-and-breakfast), Chef Oscar Carrizosa holds four-hour courses every morning, and on Friday he teaches in the afternoon as well. As Carrizosa's students, you'll walk to the district market, Sánchez Pascuas, to gather ingredients, and then return to prepare your afternoon *comida*. Gather around the sunny courtyard with the gals to enjoy the fruits of your labor, and wash it all down with a shot of *mezcal*, a potent local spirit made from the agave plant, before giggling your way back to your room for a long siesta (half-day classes are $60; *www.casacrespo.com*).

A MARKET FOR EVERYONE AND EVERYTHING

You can find an authentic Mexican market every day of the week somewhere in the state of Oaxaca, but be sure you coordinate your visit with a stop at the Etla Market on a Wednesday morning (located nine miles northwest of the city and accessible by bus). This is the largest market in the Etla Valley and is the best spot to find the most authentic Oaxacan cheese, a string cheese called *quesillo*, or *queso Oaxaca*. Once there, you and your friends can huddle around to watch Etla's local cheese expert, a woman named Silvia, as she demonstrates the complex process of stretching and kneading the curds and winding them into balls. Pull the thin strings apart and fill up a warm tortilla for a tasty snack.

Looking for pottery? Fried crickets? A donkey? Mercado de Abastos has it all. Located about ten blocks west of the Zócalo, the market is open daily, but Saturdays are the liveliest, with local villagers stopping in to shop and Indian craftspeople setting up their work. You'll feel like a part of the Oaxacan community as you get lost in the brilliant colors, buzzing crowds, and scents of roasting corn and sweet spices. Save up your appetites one day for a buffet meal of sorts from the dozens of food stands at the Mercado 20 de Noviembre, an indoor market packed with food stalls located about two blocks south of the Zócalo. As you stroll, you can either pick up a single snack or go from vendor to vendor creating your own multicourse lunch. Be sure to try *tlayudas*, a traditional Oaxacan tortilla covered with beans, meat, and cheese. Just across the street is Mercado Benito Juarez, the original town market of Oaxaca. Dairy stands proudly showcase locally made cheeses, and stalls brim with meat, produce, and round loaves of bread. These markets are open every day, but try to visit on a Wednesday or Saturday, the traditional market days for locals.

WHAT TO COME HOME WITH

If you're looking for a special keepsake platter or bowl to serve your new Oaxacan culinary creations in when you get home, the famous black pottery of Oaxaca should be on your shopping list. You can find choice pieces of the pottery in the town where it was invented—San Bartolo Coyotepec (accessible by taxi). In 1953, a female potter named Doña Rosa discovered (entirely by accident) that if she rubbed quartz against the clay before she fired it, she got a glossy finish. You can visit Doña Rosa's shop, where her son, Valentin, continues making her signature black pottery and frequently demonstrates the method for visitors. Valentin sells pots, plates, vases, jugs—even Christmas tree ornaments. They make for impressive, yet inexpensive, gifts.

WHERE TO STAY

The Seasons of My Heart bed-and-breakfast, surrounded by climbing flowers and wild foliage, provides a tranquil spot to gather for a week with your friends. If you're seeking more of an electric town vibe, the Hotel Aitana, a 23-room colonial-style hotel with spectacular views of the city, is located just a few blocks from the Zócalo (starting at $58; *www.hotelaitanaoaxaca.com*). Meanwhile Casa Colonia is a serene, 15-room getaway located just eight blocks from the Zócalo. This old-world, elegant house boasts a lush courtyard and is hosted by a wonderfully gracious American couple, with superb meals created by a cook who has been with them since 1977 (starting at $95; *www.mexonline.com/colonial.htm*).

EVENTS TO FLY IN FOR

There are dozens of festivals in Oaxaca, and one of the best is Guelaguetza, a statewide celebration that takes place in late July.

All of Oaxaca's indigenous groups come together in a brilliant flurry of colorful costumes, sprays of flowers, traditional dance performances, and lantern-lit parades. Día de Los Muertos (Day of the Dead), right after Halloween, is a major national holiday in which Mexicans believe the dead return to the mortal world for two days to visit their loved ones. They're honored with brilliantly colored altars, bright, skull-shaped candies, and mounds of food. A Taste of Oaxaca (formerly known as Foods of the Gods Festival) is a culinary extravaganza in October and December that's geared toward tourists, with renowned Oaxacan chefs giving cooking demonstrations (*www.taste-of-oaxaca.com*).

ONE CLICK AND YOU'RE OFF

Find the Mexico Tourism Board online at *www.visitmexico.com*; Oaxaca's tourist guide offers information on the state's attractions, history, and culture (*www.oaxaca-travel.com*).

～ Italy ～

The passion of Italy and the Italians is most alive in its cuisine, and nowhere is that passion more evident than in Tuscany, a region of central Italy where women devote hours (even days) of loving attention to developing the intense flavors that go into recipes passed down for generations. Pasta, pizza, thick breads, bruschettas, and truffle oil all hail from Tuscany. You can learn the centuries-old culinary secrets of this region in its kitchens—or just sample them at the table with your best friends each night. Either way, a trip to Tuscany will have you sipping robust Chianti, treating yourselves to gelato (one a day is my policy), taking in views of sunflower-dotted fields, plucking luscious bunches of sun-warmed grapes straight from the vines, and dining on pillowy pasta and plump, ripe figs. Women can't help but find contagious the Italian fervor for food, wine, and beauty, and it won't be long before you're swept up in it. Even after you return home, a simple whiff of lavender or the taste of a vine-ripened tomato will bring back a whirlwind of memories. A trip to the city of Florence is a must for its historic role in art, but don't miss out on the breathtaking beauty of Tuscan towns. Much of the Tuscan countryside is accessible by rail or bus from Florence, including the famed towns of Siena, Pisa, and Lucca. To visit smaller villages and really get onto the backroads of the countryside, you'll want to rent a car.

My favorite time to visit Tuscany is during the months of September and October, when the harvest season is just beginning. April and May are also pleasant, with warm, sunny days and cooler nights.

BEST OFF-THE-BEATEN-PATH FINE DINING

You'll have a lifetime of bragging rights once you've traveled deep into the heart of Tuscany in search of the perfect meal. Nestled in the hills of Montefollonico is La Chiusa, a quintessential Tuscan restaurant, cooking school, and inn. La Chiusa operates out of a converted farmhouse serving Tuscan hearth cuisine with a twist of modern elegance. Traditionalists devour plates of handmade *pici*, the classic pasta of Tuscany, while more adventurous eaters may opt for lamb liver in wine sauce. None of you will be able to resist their exquisite cheese plate, which includes three types of Parmesan, or the wine—the list is 120 choices strong (from $105 per person per night, including lunch and dinner; *www.lachiusa.com*).

BEST TOTAL-IMMERSION COOKING COURSE

At Tuscan Women Cook, you'll learn the traditions of four generations of Italian women in the tiny hill town of Montefollonico, a province of Siena located one hour south of Florence, near the Montepulciano.

Several of my friends and I have studied or traveled in Tuscany in the past year. We learned that you should always check a menu for the word "*coperto*" which is the fee or service charge for the clean napkin, silverware, and tablecloth. We were careful not to factor that charge into our tipping. When you get into a taxi, make sure they start the meter. If not, they will try to take advantage of you. At night, when a flower-seller approaches your dinner table, be aware that if you touch a rose, you buy a rose. Italian men can be referred to as eye candy and they love American women, so be ready to flirt! Heels are cute and they make our bottoms look perky and our calves look muscular, but in Italy, wearing heels is like asking for a broken ankle. Even if you master walking on cobblestones with heels, your favorite heel will end up looking like it lost a fight with wild dogs.

—Caitlin Coakley, 21, and Morgan Aibinder, 22, Students, University of Washington, Seattle

Montefollonico brings to life everything you imagine of an old Tuscan village, with crumbling walls surrounding a town that was built on ancient Etruscan and Roman ruins. As a student at the school, you'll cook in a villa and in the kitchens of local restaurants, studying under a different woman every day for five days—82-year-old Iolanda, for one, rules the kitchen with a steel knife and a heart of gold. Elbow-deep in floury pasta dough, you'll inhale the scent of garlic simmering in extra-virgin olive oil and beg for seconds of your very own rum-soaked tiramisu. You can also opt to immerse yourselves in local culture by visiting markets, spending a day in Florence, and tasting wine at a 750-year-old cellar. Lodging is at the nearby four-star La Costa hotel ($3,750 for a week; *www.TuscanWomenCook.com*).

BEST SHORT COOKING COURSE

Ladies who would rather stick to the hustle and bustle of cosmopolitan Florence and stick close to its museums can still learn a thing or two about rural Tuscan cooking at the city's Divina Cucina's day-long course, hosted by American expat chef Judy Witt. You'll start your day at the San Lorenzo market, designing your own four-course menu using seasonal ingredients—popular dishes include stuffed zucchini-blossom risotto, handmade pasta, and *panna cotta*. A local sommelier will pair the appropriate wines with your personalized menu ($420; *www.divinacucina.com*).

SHOPPING SECRETS

After all that food, you may need a whole new wardrobe—or use that as your excuse to get a little chic European flare into your closets. Skip the cheap knockoffs that are sold along Florence's touristy streets. Florence's Mall Outlet Center is the place where savvy women go shopping: Droolworthy labels like Armani, Gucci, and Fendi are sold at tolerable prices, making this one of Florence's best-kept secrets. Don't miss the Prada outlet shop, which also carries labels like Miu Miu and Jil Sander. You'll be the envy of your friends back home when you return wearing a buttery-soft leather coat you picked up in Florence for a fraction of the retail price in the States (Via Europa 8, Leccio Reggello, Florence; *www.outlet-firenze.com*).

FOR CULTURE VULTURES

Among a staggering number of historic and artistic claims to fame, Florence is the hometown of the great Italian Renaissance artist Michelangelo. You can do a self-guided tour of his work, starting at the

Academy of Fine Arts, where you can marvel over his "David" sculpture, and continuing to the Medici Chapel, which he designed for the Medici family in the 1500s. To download a Michelangelo-themed itinerary—or one that incorporates other Florentine museums, palaces, and cathedrals—visit *www.aboutflorence.com*.

WHERE TO STAY

If you opt to base yourselves in Florence, one of my favorite stays is Hotel David, a villa in the heart of the city with homey rooms and a surprisingly good continental breakfast (starting at $119 for doubles; *www.davidhotel.it/en*). The appeal of a smaller Tuscan town may be more up your alley. The town of Greve, in Chianti, is speckled with wineries offering charming accommodations. A standout is Villa San Andrea, a 1,300-acre winery with a bed-and-breakfast and three converted-farmhouse apartments (starting at $150 for doubles, $190 for a two-bedroom apartment; *www.villa-sant-andrea.com*). In the small city of Siena, the ultra-luxurious Grand Hotel Continental has an array of frescoes plus top-notch service and a lovely garden wine bar and restaurant (starting at $565 for doubles; *www.ghcs.it*).

EVENTS TO FLY IN FOR

Montepulciano's annual wine-barrel-rolling competition, the Bravio delle Botti, was made famous in the film *Under the Tuscan Sun*, but its origins go back to the 14th century. On the last Sunday in August, eight *contrade* (village districts) challenge each other in an uphill rolling competition; in the week leading up to the contest, each contrade has its own evening party, welcoming visitors to enjoy food, games, music, and free-flowing wine. Think strong men, strong wine, and book your tickets!

There's a wine festival in Tuscany literally every weekend in September. One of the best is the Chianti Classico Wine Festival, which takes place in the market town of Greve (about 50 miles south of Florence) during harvest season in early September. Upon arrival, you and the girls will buy a glass and float your way from winery to winery, breaking for a late lunch at an outdoor trattoria on the piazza. Greve is accessible by train or bus from Florence (*www.greve-in-chianti.com*).

BEST FAMILY TUSCAN TOUR

If you and your mom, grandma, or daughters want "a little cooking" along with a guided tour to see the highlights of Tuscany, join the

Last summer I did the "eat your way through Italy" tour and this is my advice: Wear expandable clothes! Every tension evaporates when you step off the bus in Tuscany. Life doesn't get much better than sitting with a glass of wine or a cup of tea watching the sun go down over the vineyards in the Tuscan valley. In terms of the cuisine, I became a pizza snob because the Italian pizzas are so good and yet so simple. The crust is very thin, like a tortilla. The margarita pizza is just crust, olive oil, and tomatoes—it's absolutely delicious. The olive oil is to die for, too. You'll get used to seasoning it with salt and pepper and dunking your bread in it before a meal.

—Virginia Peart, 35, Participant in "Taste of Tuscany," Adventures by Disney, Orlando, Florida

Adventures by Disney "Taste of Tuscany" tour. It lasts seven days, and includes Rome, Orvieto, a Tuscan villa, San Gimignano, Siena, and Florence (from $1,990, early booking; 877-728-7282, *www.AdventuresByDisney.com*).

ONE CLICK AND YOU'RE OFF
The Italian Tourism Board can be found at *www.italiantourism.com*; Tourism in Tuscany is a one-stop resource for events, transportation information, and accommodations at *www.tourism-in-tuscany.com*.

☞ Thailand ☜

Capital of Thailand and one of the financial centers of Southeast Asia, Bangkok is two parts sophisticated metropolis and one part traditional-culture hub. It's a dynamic environment where (nearly) anything goes. On most streets you'll find sandal-clad European backpackers mingling with harried business folk, all of them navigating their way through the city's nonstop hustle and bustle. The city center of modern Bangkok is choked with high-rise steel-and-glass office buildings, massive shopping complexes, and gridlocked traffic of cars and *tuk-tuks* (motorized tri shaws). Much of Bangkok's history has evolved along the bustling banks of the Chao Phraya River, and this is the place to book a hotel, so you can travel by ferry to the opulent temples and palaces. You may glimpse an elephant wandering through back alleys, and everywhere you'll see tranquil monks in bright orange robes. Many small canals *(klongs)* snake through the city and are bordered by wooden homes built on stilts with open porches. Look carefully for the intricately carved "spirit houses" (don't mistake them for bird feeders), where the family places incense, flowers, and food as an offering to guardian spirits. Some of your girlfriends will adore combing the rustic market stalls for old-world handicrafts, while others will flock to the upscale malls to score designer duds. There's something for everyone in Bangkok, but as far as I'm concerned, foodies have it the best. The city is brimming with a dizzying variety of cheap eats with exotic flavors like spicy red and green chiles, lemongrass, coconut, Thai basil, and kaffir leaves. Thai food uses the exotic flavors of mango, curry, chilis, and peanuts. While you're here, you'll have a hoot learning to maneuver chopsticks around tangy *pad Thai* (noodles served with chicken or shrimp and peanut sauce) and how to use sticky rice patties to pull chunks of chicken off a stick. After a few days, you may find yourself feeling particularly adventurous—if so, sample some deep-fried grasshoppers or beetles.

COOK YOUR OWN DARN LUNCH

The Oriental Bangkok Hotel, located near the city center on the banks of the Chao Phraya River, offers a world-renowned half-day cooking course. You'll learn techniques from master Thai chefs, starting with the basics of Thailand's mouthwatering spices and herbs, and moving on to grinding, chopping, and frying techniques—and, of course, taste-testing along the way. On any given day, you may learn how to roll up fresh veggies for frying up tantalizing spring rolls; pound spicy chili paste to toss into stir-fried squid; simmer a tangy coconut milk soup, or slowly stir thick, warm Thai custard to serve atop sticky rice. The courses are open each morning to anyone, not just guests of the hotel, and are followed by a multicourse lunch of your handiwork (starting at $140; *www.mandarinoriental.com*).

BEST DAY TRIP

Traditionally, Thai villagers bought their produce at floating markets, flat boats cruising canals selling fresh fruits and vegetables, blooming flowers, and even fully cooked meals made from onboard kitchens. The Damnoen Saduak floating market, located about 35 miles from Bangkok, is among the most popular of the remaining floating markets. You and the girls can rent your own guided boat and indulge in near sensory overload as you squeeze against hordes of tourists and locals sailing alongside you, while munching on an endless array of traditional Thai treats. The market gets increasingly hectic as the day goes on, so make sure to get there in the wee hours of the morning, between 6 a.m. and 8 a.m. (for information on boat rentals, visit *www.tourismthailand.org*).

BEST LEAST-EXPENSIVE, EXPENSIVE THAI MEAL
The Blue Elephant is an ideal stop for ladies looking for a celebratory setting and menu for an evening. It's a splurge, but that's relative to Thai prices, which are rock-bottom cheap to start with. It's a chain restaurant that hasn't hit the U.S. yet, but has outposts in Europe, Russia, and the Middle East. Although it's a chain, this is a culinary exception. The Bangkok branch is an intimate, colonial-style building—two floors are dedicated to fine dining, and on the top floor is yet another fabulous cooking school. The menu showcases traditional Thai cuisine with more modern variations, such as salmon *laab* instead of typical minced chicken, foie gras with Thai tamarind sauce, buffalo *satay* (versus chicken), and crocodile with chili and basil (from $40 per person for the prix-fixe menu; *www.blueelephant.com/bangkok*). Many Thai people eat outdoors at street food stalls, which are dirt cheap and often offer fabulous food, but the sanitation can be questionable. Restaurants vary in quality, but are more hygienic than street stalls.

MUST-SEE COOKING EXHIBITION
At Bangkok's enormous Seafood Market and Restaurant, dozens of chefs work their magic in full view of 1,500 guests and a 160-foot display counter filled with literally every kind of seafood you can imagine.

Traffic in Bangkok is legendary. Traffic lights aren't timed, and drivers tend to ignore them anyway. Getting around Bangkok by car, taxi, or *tuk tuk* can be a nightmare, so book a hotel on the Chao Phraya River and travel by public (inexpensive) river taxis or longtail boats along this historic waterway to visit the Grand Palace and temples along the river. From your hotel window or the outdoor patio, you'll watch barges, ferries, and wooden boats ply the river day and night.

—Marybeth

If you wish to visit a temple or a palace in Bangkok, you must have your shoulders, knees, and heels covered to show respect. If you are wearing a tank top, shorts, or sandals, you won't be allowed in unless you rent clothes made available at the entrance.

—Marybeth

Ordering your meal is an experience in itself: You choose your seafood from the tank and then pick out the produce you want to accompany it, such as garlic, ginger, chilies, beans, mushrooms. At your table, you can specify exactly how you'd like the food prepared, for instance, steamed fish with chilies and black bean sauce, lobster with drawn butter, fried shrimp balls, or stir-fried veggies with clam sauce. It's a deep-sea experience you'll never forget (*www.seafood.co.th*).

BEST BARGAIN SHOPPING

In the Chatuchak Weekend Market you may feel like you're in a sea of leather handbags, antiques, and jewelry. The market reigns as the largest in all of Bangkok and is a must-do for all women with a yen for accessories. You can spend an entire day stopping at every stall you see, and still not see them all. That's because its 15,000 shops and stalls are spread over 35 acres. You'll very likely find yourself lugging home more gifts than you can carry, and since prices are already rock bottom, you don't have to worry about breaking the bank. But in my opinion, part of the fun of this shopping experience is haggling with the vendors, some of whom you can negotiate down by 50 percent. Most stalls open at 7 a.m. on Saturday and Sunday.

SAFETY TIP

The in-your-face attitudes toward sexuality in Bangkok can be rather shocking (as demonstrated by the plethora of "massage parlors," strip clubs, and dance shows by "ladyboys"). But rest assured, Bangkok is so tourist-friendly that women can feel perfectly safe. Just follow your common sense. When I visited Bangkok with my 13-year-old daughter, we stayed at a hotel along the Chao Phraya River, traveled effortlessly by ferry to visit the temples and Grand Palace, and even got a massage at the reputable Thai School of Traditional Massage in Wat Pho (Temple of the Reclining Buddha). You can avoid the seedy side of the city—we did.

WHEN TO GO

To save yourselves from heat exhaustion, I suggest planning your Bangkok eating-and-shopping extravaganza for the period from November to February, which is the coolest time of year (daytime temps are in the low 80s). August and December are peak tourist months.

ONE CLICK AND YOU'RE OFF

Visit Bangkok Tourism Division online at *www.bangkoktourist.com*; the website for the Tourism Authority of Thailand can be found at *www.TourismThailand.org*.

⇗ Provence ⇖

Savory spices, olive groves, tangles of winding grape vines, fields of lavender, and the glistening coastline give Provence a distinctly Mediterranean feel—and taste. Located in the southeastern region of France, wedged between the Italian border, the Alps, the Rhône River, and the Mediterranean Sea, Provence enjoys a near perfect climate, magnificent mountain views, and sloping vineyards. Conjure up images of a Paul Cezanne or Vincent van Gogh painting (both of these artists lived in and painted Provence's landscape). In fact, one of van Gogh's most celebrated masterpieces, "Starry Night," was painted near the Provençal town of Arles. Like its scenery, Provence's food is guaranteed to captivate, charm, and delight. Dishes like ratatouille and bouillabaisse prevail in the dozens of culinary tours and cooking schools scattered throughout the region. With so many cities, towns, and villages clustered together, Provence is an ideal destination for girls-on-the-go who like the idea of renting a car and a road trip through the countryside. But it also appeals to more laid-back types who prefer to stay in one place, take their time, lounge in the sun, and sip wine. Whereas the major southern cities of Avignon, Nice, and Marseille are accessible by train or bus, it's far more convenient to rent a car to visit smaller villages. The best time to go is spring or fall. Summers are crowded and hot.

GO TRUFFLE HUNTING

A stop at Annie's Kitchen is like visiting an old friend. Annie Jacquet-Bentley welcomes pupils into her private residence in the village of Murs-en-Provence. And she's got a thing for exotic black truffles—those pungent tubers that cost more than a week's worth of groceries. During truffle season in January, when she arranges truffle-centered cooking classes, be sure to pass through her doors. That means getting down and dirty with Roxy, the truffle-hunting dog, and learning how to infuse meals with this flavorful delicacy. Small-group classes are conducted entirely in English; accommodations are not included, but they will be provided in a nearby hotel for an extra fee ($2,950; *www.annieskitcheninprovence.com*).

BREAK THE BANK

Provence is teeming with—my favorite—Michelin-starred restaurants. If there ever was a time to pull out your credit cards and worry about it later, dining at Le Grand Pré (The Big Pasture) is it. Located in Roaix, a short drive north of Avignon, this culinary gem is owned by Belgian-born chef Raoul Reichrath and his wife, Flora, who's from Mexico. You gals can settle in and get cozy in what will seem like a friend's home; it's housed in a traditional Provençal cottage in Roaix with a dining space in a courtyard surrounded by an aromatic herb garden. Raoul is an ambitious chef who creates elegant dishes like summer truffle salad, tender roasted lamb, and goat cheese ice cream. Flora, a professional sommelier, can guide you toward the best pairings with lovely Côte du Rhônes, rosés, and other regional wines (from $75 for a four-course dinner, wine not included; *www.legrandpre.com*).

DESSERT TIME

Chocolate, chocolate, and more chocolate. That's the theme of renowned chocolatier Joel Durand's tiny shop in St. Remy (11 miles south of Avignon). Here, Joel graciously works with visitors to create luscious bite-size chocolates and fruit confits. Try the ganache filled with distilled Provençal lavender, roll your tongue around the sweetness of honey-filled truffles, and surprise your palate with chocolate spiced with unusual flavors like basil and thyme (call ahead to arrange visits and for prices; *www.chocolat-durand.com*).

BEST CULINARY SCHOOL

The school, A Week in Provence, offers a true immersion in Provençal cuisine for budding chefs. If you get enough friends together you can take over their entire five-bedroom, 18th-century farmhouse just outside the village of Condorcet (20 minutes northeast of Nyons). Girls who share a passion for cooking (and becoming even better chefs) will learn side by side how to perfect classic Provençal dishes like roasted duck and grilled lamb from master chef Daniel Bonnot. You'll incorporate fresh "herbs du Provence" (marjoram, rosemary, and thyme) picked from the garden behind the house and meet with local artisans to blend and bottle your own wine, visit a generations-old olive mill, and learn how to choose your fish from a trout farm (starting at $2,950 per person for a week; *www.frenchcookingclasses.com*).

BEST MARKETS

There are weekly markets in almost every city and village throughout Provence, and you could potentially go shopping every day of the week within a 20-mile radius. The best of the best, Les Halles, Avignon's most famous covered market, is open daily except for Sunday. You and the girls should carve out a couple of hours to peruse the 40-plus stalls looking for farm-fresh produce for picnics or meals you prepare back at your villa, accompanied by pressed olive oil, jars of honey, and freshly baked baguettes. An afternoon at the St. Remy market, which takes place on Wednesday just south of Avignon, is like being at a carnival. Let yourselves be entertained and charmed by the street entertainers performing amid the brightly colored booths.

WHERE TO STAY

If you and your girlfriends are celebrating a reunion or birthday gathering, consider renting out your own villa in Avignon, one of Provence's larger hubs. The 18th-century Avignon Mansion can accommodate up to eight ladies, with elegant décor and all the modern amenities you could possibly need (starting at $4,949 per week; 800-726-6702, *www.rentvillas.com*). The centrally located Avignon Grand Hotel offers elegant standard rooms, suites, and apartments (from $299 for doubles, book online for large discounts; *www.the grandhotelavignon.com*). There are also many hotel bargains throughout Provence: In St. Remy, five minutes by foot from the city

Once on the back roads of Provence, I thought I would have to spend the night in my car because I was almost out of gas and couldn't find an open station. Now when driving in a foreign country, I make sure to know what time the gas stations close for the night and I refill the gas tank when it reaches the halfway mark. Then I don't have to worry.

—Marybeth

center, Hotel du Soleil is a comfortable, 24-room hotel in a converted single-family house (from $85 for doubles; *www.hotelsoleil.com*).

ONE CLICK AND YOU'RE OFF

For more information, contact the French Government Tourist Office at *www.franceguide.com*.

CHAPTER FIVE

Spectacular Spas

∂ **MARISA'S STORY** ∾

Traveling doesn't always mean relaxing—in fact, it can be rather exhausting. There are times when we all need to go somewhere, or to take a break in our travels, to relax, let go of all responsibilities, and be nurtured. A spa visit can also be a time of feminine renewal in the company of other women. Some women, like Marisa, believe that every trip should include time for healing and pampering ourselves. Marisa has a long tradition of going away to spas with girlfriends. Whenever she can get away she heads for a health retreat to bask in the silence of nature and soak in the mineral hot tubs overlooking green meadows or valleys of wildflowers.

Five years ago she finagled a one-year sabbatical from her job, in human resources for the state of California, to travel around the world, visiting girlfriends and spas along the way. During her adventures on four continents, "I sought out resorts and health spas," she says, "and submerged my travel-weary body in healing waters from Thailand to New Zealand."

Although Marisa didn't design her travel itinerary based on health spas, she naturally gravitated toward them, even in the most unlikely places. In France, where she started her trip, she learned about La Mosque, a spa right in the center of historic Paris, in the Latin Quarter. The exotic Turkish baths with rose-colored marble pillars and mosaics offered a welcome respite. After a shower, she lathered herself with the traditional black soap, which naturally exfoliated her skin. Then she soaked in the baths, sipped a pot of steaming Moroccan mint tea and waited for her massage. She lay on a platform built around a large steamy room. Two women administered massages to a succession of languid bodies that rose from the platform to the massage table for their turn. "We looked like lounging queens in the *1,001 Arabian Nights*—minus the clothing," Marisa says. Visiting the Turkish baths in Paris was just the beginning of her spa escapades worldwide.

When she eventually reached Thailand, she headed for Ko Samui, an island renowned for spas, for an unforgettable seven-day cleanse at Spa Samui. Her Thai massages came in many flavors including wild mint oil, lemongrass skin toner, and tangerine oil. Five or six smiling masseurs ministered to her body with precision and softness on a long wood deck shaded by fruit trees. They pulled, stretched, and pressured points in her body and then applied her choice of oil to suit her skin. Thai massage is both relaxing and energizing. "It's a bit like doing yoga," Marisa says, "without putting forth any effort while getting acupressure treatments."

After spending two weeks touring around New Zealand, schlepping her bags, hiking, taking buses and flights, she collapsed into the healing waters of Rotorua. "I was in my element in Rotorua," she says. "I dipped in the 27 hot mineral bath pools at the Polynesian Spa." The Aix massage, done under jets of water with plenty of coconut oil

Schedule spa appointments in advance to ensure the time slot, therapist preference, and treatment you desire. If you wait until the last minute they may not have a female therapist available, or you many get the last appointment of the day at 9 p.m. when everyone is tired and in a hurry to go home.

—Marybeth

spread on her skin, helped her to recuperate from her intense travels.

In more than two decades of frequenting spas and hot springs worldwide, Marisa has found that "spas and soaking tubs often create a deep sense of belonging and a time of feminine renewal in the company of other women."

⤜ Bali ⤛

Gorgeous beaches, surfing, and a tropical landscape of jungle-cloaked volcanoes and rice terraces reserve Bali a special place in the hearts of international jet-setters. But this island province, located in Southeast Asia's Indonesian archipelago, is also an idyllic spa haven if you're in need of help dropping that heavy baggage we all carry in our lives. I don't know of many places more perfect for this than the town of Ubud, the epicenter of Bali's art, music, and traditional dance scenes, to alternately expand your cultural horizons and get the least expensive, most relaxing massages of your life. The women in your life who share that intrinsic need to be pampered and would dedicate an entire vacation to "getting centered" at a spa will think Ubud was put here on Earth for them. Girlfriends love the inner exploration Ubud encourages through its many spas as well as the discovery of its breathtaking scenery. Surrounded by rice paddies and rivers, the town is a quiet oasis—except at night, when the chorus of croaking frogs starts up. It is thought to be a spiritual balancing point, equidistant between Bali's sea and a sacred mountain. And dozens of spas have opened here to feed off that vibe—my favorite is Ubud Sari Health Resort. Its supremely relaxing "Zen village," comprised of airy private bungalows that serve as guest quarters, was designed using a Balinese principle similar to feng shui. Your stylish private villa will be surrounded by tropical gardens, with the sounds of a waterfall nearby. As you stroll the streets of Ubud (no need to rent a car here), you'll encounter Hindu temples, palaces, and views of the surrounding rice paddies. Ubud couldn't be more conveniently located for day trips to other parts of the island. A quick geography lesson: Bali is a tiny island (about 90 miles long by 50 miles wide), so the fact that Ubud is near Bali's geographical center means nearly every corner of the island is a short drive away. Minibuses are the safe and easy mode of transport for side trips here—you can hail them on the street. As for the delightful sultry weather, Bali's dry season extends from April to October—the rest of the year brings more rain and humidity.

LAY OF THE LAND

At Ubud Sari, you'll find a spa treatment center, sauna and whirlpool baths, beauty salon, alternative health treatment center, outdoor amphitheater, vegetarian restaurant, health store, and private villas scattered throughout its jungle property.

WHAT'S INCLUDED

The accommodations at the Ubud Sari Health Resort are wrapped into the prices of most packages, along with the use of spa facilities. Most meals are not. To design your own spa-and-stay program, book a room and order up as many treatments as you'd like. If it's your first time in Bali, this is a good way to familiarize yourselves with the local style of treatments; next time, when you and the gals are planning your Bali reunion trip, you can sign up for a specific package (from $45 nightly, $60 for double occupancy, with breakfast; *www.ubudsari.com*).

THE SPA

Inside the world of the Ubud Sari Health Resort, the biggest decision to make will be whether to get a massage ($15) or a mud bath ($25). You'll soon get used to simply lying back and turning yourself over to someone else during à la carte spa treatment or join their head-to-toe, inside-and-out detox program. If you choose the latter, the helpful staff will tailor a program to your needs as part of the Ubud Sari Health Resort's intensive weeklong health program, which involves a long list of cleansing, fasting, daily yoga, and detoxifying treatments. And when what you need is a moment alone, you can stroll through nearby rice paddies as the sun rises.

DON'T-MISS TREATMENTS

During the 1.5-hour-long Javanese Lulur, your body gets the full attention of a therapist, who scrubs you with an herb-and-rice powder mixture to slough off dead skin ($25). Then you'll slip into a flower-and-herb-filled tub for a warm soak. If your skin is crying out for a detox, try the Volcanic Mud Bath with ash from Mount Agung (a volcanic Balinese peak), followed by an hour-long massage ($25).

COME HOME NEW

If eating a less-than-healthy diet lately has caught up with you and you'd like to order a helping of detoxification with your spa-treatment entrée, Ubud Sari gives you the option of following a day-long to a weeklong juice fast or raw-food diet, or a combination of the

In tropical locations, ask if treatment rooms are open-air or air-conditioned. Some people are more sensitive to heat and humidity than others—I personally prefer not to sweat while I'm having a spa treatment. I also enjoy getting a massage from a local woman, while partially clothed, on a platform on the beach. It is a less expensive and less private experience than at a resort, but if there is a breeze, it can be heavenly. It's true: Too much of a good thing *can* be wonderful.

—Marybeth

two. (Those of you who aren't cleansing can still reap the benefits of the vegetarian restaurant on the property.) If you're up for an intense recharge, the Two Week Total Revitalization Retreat incorporates colonics, juice fasting, and a raw-food diet—along with classes on raw-food cooking and healthy lifestyle pointers. On top of all of this, you'll get ten massages, a range of beauty treatments, private health consultations, meditation classes, and daily yoga sessions ($2,700).

SPECIAL PACKAGES

The Two Week Total Revitalization Retreat (mentioned above) is the most extensive of the packages—I'd recommend it for those of you searching to seriously recalibrate your body and curb bad eating habits. For those with limited time or an aversion to colonics (I can't say I blame you), Ubud Sari offers loads of different choices. I find it hard to resist the weeklong Body, Mind, and Spirit Rejuvenation Program, which includes treatments from craniosacral therapy to reflexology, plus beauty boosters such as facials and body scrubs, daily colonics and juice fasting, and daily yoga and meditation sessions ($1,000).

FOR ANOTHER TREAT

If you've ever fantasized about splurging on a Four Seasons vacation, Bali is the place to do it. Where else in the world would you have—or need—a "Personalized Paradise Planner" at your beck and call? Located 15 minutes from Ubud, this spectacular oasis has lush tropical plants, a lotus pond, and views of the Ayung River. Its luxurious suites and villas are decorated with Indonesian furnishings and handmade fabrics. Don't leave this place without trying their Balinese massage, which uses long, kneading strokes, skin rolling, and foot massage (combined with a luscious-smelling coconut oil infused with fennel, ginger, and vetiver). You should also seriously consider getting a synchronized massage, where two therapists work out your aches and pains simultaneously—that's four hands on you. (Enlist your friends to carry you back to your room afterward.) In the Four Seasons' spa pavilions, you'll even enjoy the background noise: the soothing trickle of the nearby Ayung River. If you ask me, heaven must be something like this. The three-night Sayan Spa Experience, which includes a floral bath on arrival, one 60-minute massage session for two, and daily breakfast, starts at $770. Nightly rates are from $460 (800-332-3442, *www.fourseasons.com/sayan*).

EVENTS TO FLY IN FOR
The bookworms among you can combine a spa trip with the Ubud Writers and Readers Festival, held in September or October. Published authors, renowned playwrights, and poets gather here from around the world for workshops and discussions. Recruit your girlfriends and sign up early for their popular Yoga and Writing Workshop; hear masters speak about their work in cooking and travel; and learn the basics of batik-making or writing a memoir (*www.ubudwritersfestival.com*).

FOR SPA-AHOLICS
If you want to learn more about different spas and spa-based programs in Bali (yoga retreats, surfing classes, and more) visit the Bali Spirit website (*www.balispirit.com*). One tip: Ask spas if treatment rooms are open-air or air-conditioned. Some people are more sensitive to heat and humidity than others—I personally prefer not to sweat while I'm having a spa treatment.

ONE CLICK AND YOU'RE OFF
For more information about Bali, visit *www.bali-tourism-board.com*.

❧ Czech Republic ❧

Join the ranks of Beethoven and Bach, Goethe and Mark Twain, and Freud and Thomas Edison, all of whom spent time in the healing waters of spa towns in the Czech Republic. In the early 1990s, after the fall of communism, Czech spas received a much needed face-lift, and soon began throwing open their doors to a new crop of visitors. The spas here are a different breed from what we're used to in the United States. First of all, they're a lot less expensive, which is reason enough to make the trip to Eastern Europe. They aren't all-inclusive spa resorts, but rather hotels with in-house spas. And also, many Eastern European spas cater to medical treatments rather than relaxation (some even provide dental care, believe it or not). If you've got general aches and pains, like most of us, or if you're suffering from a specific ailment like arthritis, the spas here can be just the ticket. Or perhaps you're just in search of relaxation and discovering a new country. You and your girlfriends will love coming to Carlsbad, a quaint and quiet spa town where you can take a bath fit for a queen. More than a hundred springs gurgle to the surface in this spa town (known in the Czech Republic as Karlovy Vary), about a two-hour bus ride west from the Czech Republic's capital of Prague. Twelve of them are captured in pools that hot-spring savvy Europeans flock to, and Americans in the know are starting to catch on. Carlsbad is the kind of place where you can immerse yourselves in old-world elegance, in a small town of pergolas, pavilions, and colonnades, without having to pay exorbitant prices.

All of the hotels here are centered around the mineral springs and have spas that incorporate soothing soaks in them. Stay in a centrally located hotel and fill your days visiting the mineral bath and sights in town. Even if you don't stay here, visit the belle-époque-style Grandhotel Pupp—when you book a treatment at this hotel spa, you'll receive a complimentary two-hour soak in the springs. In between spa treatments and soaking in the bubbling water together, you can go for group walks over the footbridges and along the Teplá River, amid pastel-colored baroque buildings, or gather in a café for a glass of wine, or do some people-watching. Nestled in a valley, surrounded by forests, the town is a quiet respite. While I adore the festive atmosphere at these spas in the summertime, availability is limited this time of year, so you should be sure to book treatments well in advance. You'll get better rates (and the beautiful sight of the Eastern European architecture coated in snow) if you bundle up and travel during non-holiday winter months.

THE SPA

The Castle Baths are the main attraction in Carlsbad—and lucky for you, they're just a five-minute walk from Grandhotel Pupp. At the Castle Baths, there's a thermal pool fed by two natural springs. The bubbling and warm water here makes up a two-part cure.

Leave your jewelry and valuables in the room safe. Not all spas offer lockers with a key.

—Marybeth

You and the gals can sit in a mineral spring bath and watch the water fizz around you, leaving your skin soft and supple. If you're feeling daring, sip directly from the mineral springs using the provided porcelain cup—don't be afraid, this is what the locals have done for years. You too will soon believe in the mineral water's restorative powers. To spend more time here, consider their three-hour program, which includes two treatments (with various styles of massage) and starts at $48. Robes and towels are complimentary, but don't forget your swimsuits (*http://english.edenhotels.cz/castle-spa-karlovy-vary*). The Spa Clinic Harp offers beauty and spa treatments that incorporate soaks at the Castle Baths (from $60 for the Anti-Aging Treatment, including a spine, foot, and head massage, an oxygen therapy, and a carbonated or mineral bath; *www.harfa.cz*).

WHERE TO STAY

You may recognize the ornate Grandhotel Pupp from the recent Bond flick, *Casino Royale*. The main façade has gorgeous ornamental balconies, and when you step inside, you'll see 19th-century oil paintings, serene statues, twinkling chandeliers, and stuccowork. The Pupp was built in 1701 and owned for more than a hundred years by the Pupp family (from $260; *www.pupp.cz*). Centrally located Hotel Promenade, with 16 large rooms, offers excellent service at a reasonable price (from $76; *www.hotel-promenada.cz*).

SPECIAL PACKAGES

If you're a history buff, golfer, hiker—or even if you want to get a little crazy and take an small-plane acrobatic flight over the valley—there's a package to suit any gal's interests at Grandhotel Pupp. The Touch at Tenderness package for women includes three nights' accommodation, breakfasts, an aromatherapy massage, reflexology, a mud pack, and a facial massage, among other treatments (from $480; *www.pupp .cz*). The Hotel Promenada's special Christmas Package offers four nights' accommodation, breakfasts, a Gala Christmas dinner, herb baths, a classical massage, daily use of the swimming pool and sauna, and homemade cookies (from $425; *www.hotel-promenada.cz*).

CURATIVE CUISINE

At the elegant Grandhotel Pupp, you'll dine in a mirrored, ballroom-style restaurant under huge chandeliers. You can order a range of Czech and international cuisine, along with many seasonal dishes. Look for bright green asparagus in springtime, black truffles in summer. Try Czech favorites such as goulash and beef tenderloin in cream sauce (main courses $15-30). The snack that this and other Czech spa towns are best known for is the spa wafer, or *oplatky*. The custom is to alternate between sips of the bubbling water and bites of these sweet biscuits. If you're thirsty for a stronger beverage, try Becherovka, an herbal liqueur created here, reputed by the locals to have medical healing properties. Another great dining option is The Embassy, one of the oldest restaurants in town, located in The Embassy Hotel. Try the Czech specialties: spicy goulash, soup with liver dumplings, sauerkraut, roasted porkchops, or goose (main courses $10-40).

INTO THE WILD

You can stretch your legs in between treatments on one of Carlsbad's many paths along the Teplá River or the steep trails leading into the forest. From the Grandhotel Pupp, you can hike to a hilltop viewpoint or take a two-hour walk along the Ohre River to the charming town of Loket.

RETAIL REMEDY

Shopping is therapy, too, and in Carlsbad, you can get your dose at the 150-year-old Moser Glass Factory. Take a tour for a glimpse at their glassblowing and the museum. Then, of course, buy some treats to take home. Most women are partial to the elegant stemware, the likes of which was used by kings and ambassadors in the 19th century, and the colorful crystal bowls and vases (*www.moser-glass.com*).

BEST SIDE TRIP

Girlfriends find no spa pilgrimage here complete without a stop in Marienbad, about 25 miles southwest of Carlsbad. Marienbad is a smaller spa town, with a must-do spa experience: a soak in the mineral springs at the New Spa, or Nové Lázn. It was popular with composers, from Strauss, Chopin, and Mahler to Wagner. Britain's Edward VII fell in love with the place (he visited as many as nine times), and you will, too. You'll understand his infatuation when you and the girls slip into the tile-decorated antique Royal Bath, built for the king himself, with stained-glass windows all around (*www.marienbad.cz*).

EVENTS TO FLY IN FOR

Film junkies should plan a July trip for the Karlovy Vary International Film Festival, a celebration of the cinema that began during World War II (*www.kviff.com/en*). Big names show up here, and some notable films in the competition have gone on to much worldwide acclaim, among them *Amélie* and *Ma Vie en Rose*. The sounds of classical music take over Marienbad in August at the Chopin Festival, which orchestrates an extensive schedule of piano, symphony, and vocal performances in homage to the Polish maestro (*www.chopinfestival.cz*).

ONE CLICK AND YOU'RE OFF

To learn more about the Czech Republics's spa towns, visit *www.spa.czecot.com* or *www.czechspavacations.com*. The official Czech Republic Tourism website can be found at *www.czechtourism.com*.

❧ New Zealand ❧

No doubt you've seen New Zealand's stunning scenery in the *Lord of the Rings* trilogy (even if you were only *really* watching Viggo Mortensen). If your idea of the perfect girlfriends getaway combines a classic road trip with good old-fashioned exercise, stunning scenery, and a spa, you can't beat what this two-island nation offers. The Kiwis (aka New Zealanders) have devised a mind-boggling number of adventurous ways to explore their two islands and all the mountains, fjords, and rivers. There are helicopter rides, bike trips, sailing excursions, treks, kayaking trips, and even bungee jumping. Rent a car in the capital city, Auckland, located on New Zealand's North Island, and set off on a whirlwind adventure road trip with the girls. As you explore the island, gradually make your way to Rotorua, the heartland of Maori culture and a small city bubbling with geothermal activity (there's a hint of sulphur from them in the air) in the center of the North Island. Surrounded by mountains and forests and resting on the shore of dazzling Lake Rotorua, this place is a hot spot for travelers who play hard—and relax just as hard. Here, natural thermal springs and volcanic mud baths will soothe your aching muscles. My pick for a girls' spa getaway Kiwi-style is Rotorua's Polynesian Spa. It has an airy, tropical feel and 26 hot mineral pools heated by two springs. The Polynesian Spa isn't a destination spa in the traditional sense, which means it doesn't have hotel rooms. But as far as I'm concerned, that's a bonus: You'll have your choice of lodging in Rotorua, from budget motels to five-star splurges. Be sure to catch a Maori cultural performance, in which stories are relayed through beautiful song and dance. And since you've come all this way, you might as well see the South Island, too (see Chapter Four: Wonderful Walks). New Zealand has a temperate climate with mild temperatures, moderately high rainfall, and many hours of sunshine throughout most of the country. Because New Zealand lies in the Southern Hemisphere, the average temperature decreases as you travel south. The north of New Zealand is subtropical, and the south is cooler. The warmest months are December, January, and February, and the coldest June, July, and August. The busiest times are late December and January, when many Kiwis take their summer holidays (and overseas travelers flock to take advantage of the plentiful sunshine). If you come during New Zealand's winter, you'll have more elbow room and, often, lower prices.

THE SPA

The Polynesian Spa is divided into four compounds: deluxe, adult, private, and family. You and the girls will want to head to the Lake Spa Retreat, the deluxe section, where four steaming pools landscaped with natural rock give way to views of a garden and Lake Rotorua ($27 day fee, including towels and lockers). You'll also find a lounge with full bar service to relax in when you need to cool off. For some privacy, reserve your own lake-view pool ($15 per person, per half hour; *www.polynesianspa.co.nz*).

SIGNATURE TREATMENTS

Treatments here use the best of New Zealand's natural resources. The body wrap starts with a full body treatment using either Rotorua's thermal mud or New Zealand manuka honey and concludes with a scalp massage ($107 for an hour). The Kiwi Soufflé Wrap, an hour-and-a-half treatment, combines a salt scrub, a full-body wrap with the detox powers of kiwifruit enzyme, and a full body massage ($146).

When you make your spa appointment, ask about the cost, including tax, to avoid surprises. Also ask if they accept credit cards and whether you can add the tip to the credit card charge, or do they prefer cash? You leave the tip at the checkout desk when you pay your bill.

—Marybeth

WHERE TO STAY

One place to put at the top of your list for a splurge is Treetops Lodge, about 9 miles from Rotorua, located on a 2,500-acre wilderness sanctuary with spring-fed streams, ancient trees, native birds and animals, and 43 miles of trails for hiking, mountain biking, or horseback riding. Depending on what you're in the mood for, you and the girls can agree on your own room in the main lodge, bunk up in a villa on the property, or rent out the entire three-bedroom Pheasant House. Dine in the main dining room or fireside in the library, on game, fish, and locally grown produce, complemented by an array of the finest New Zealand wines (rates include accommodation, breakfast, pre-dinner cocktails, dinner, and selected lodge activities, from $397 per person; *www.treetops.co.nz*).

If proximity to spas and town life are your priority, try the Millennium Hotel Rotorua. It's right next door to the Polynesian Spa and a short walk to downtown Rotorua's shops, pubs, and cafés (from $120; *www .millenniumhotels.com*). The hotel also has its own spa, featuring tempting treatments like the *Taitama puawai*, which includes an echinacea, kelp, and *kawakawa* body mask and a foot or scalp massage. Many rooms have balconies that overlook the lake and the Polynesian Spa.

GET WILD

It would be almost impossible *not* to have a wilderness experience here. Rotorua is located smack in the middle of beautiful lakes and mountains. You can get out onto the calm water of Lake Rotorua with Clearwater Cruises' chartered boats, which ferry you to the hot-water pools in Te Rata Bay. Bring the champagne! Clearwater Cruises can also arrange for a flight-seeing trip through this volcanic region (*www .clearwater.co.nz*). And if you've come here to mark a special occasion (a big birthday or retirement), there's no better way to immortalize this trip than by skydiving with your closest girlfriends (*www.nzone.biz*).

A sarong comes to the rescue in many situations. I've used my colorful, washable, lightweight-cotton sarongs as a picnic cloth (on a beach in Bali), as a swimsuit cover-up, as a temporary skirt (to cover my legs over shorts in a Bangkok temple), as a towel (after an impromptu waterfall shower in Costa Rica), and as a shawl on cool evenings in New Zealand.

—Marybeth

BEST DINING

You may equate the cuisine of New Zealand—once a British outpost—with your memories of dreary English cuisine. But trust me when I say that you'll be swept off your feet by New Zealand's wonderful fresh produce, fish, and meats—and flavor. On the town in Rotorua, check out Bistro 1284 (from $24; *www.bistro1284.co.nz*) for oven-roasted lamb shanks with kumara and plum cakes, or Aorangi Peak (from $25; *www. aorangipesk.co.nz*) for spectacular views and French and Japanese cuisine. At the Polynesian Spa's Hot Springs Café, you can sip on fantastic smoothies and sample healthy meals. Another thing to try in Rotorua: a Maori cultural performance with a traditional Maori *hangi* feast (similar to a Hawaiian luau), with various types of meats, sweet potatoes, and vegetables wrapped in leaves and cooked in the ground on hot stones.

FARTHER AFIELD

Hawkes Bay, about three hours away on the North Island's eastern coast, is celebrated for its award-winning wines, art, and cuisine. Long Island Tours will take you from Rotorua for an all-day gourmand's tour of sprawling vineyards, orchards, farmers' markets, cafés, and restaurants, and can also arrange a tour of an artist's studio and visits with the Maori (half-day tours from $160 and $180, respectively, full day each from $340; *www.longislandtoursnz.com*). There's also the option of a self-guided tour of the Wine Country Food Trail and its 85 stops (download an illustrated map at *www.hawkesbaynz.com*).

PUB CRAWL

You may be here for your health, but a dose of Kiwi friendliness found in its pub scene can be good medicine, too. Plan with the girls a night out at Rotorua's Pig and Whistle Historic Pub, where you'll find New Zealand's finest brew on tap, along with a healthy dose of naughty bar food (*www.pigandwhistle.co.nz*).

ON THE ROAD

Rent a small RV—or camper van, as they're called here—and take a spa road trip up a notch. Accommodations will be taken care of, and you'll drive in comfort while you cover a lot of ground in this diminutive country. It's also a great way to bond, especially over the difficulties of driving on the left side of the road! Try Kea Campers (*www.keacampers.com*) or Britz (*www.britz.com*) to find a camper that will set you on a road trip to remember (from $450 for a week).

ONE CLICK AND YOU'RE OFF

To learn more about Rotorua, try *www.rotoruanz.com*; for more on adventures in New Zealand, visit *www.newzealand.com*.

➶ Costa Rica ᔖ

Close your eyes and think about immersing your body in rainwater-fed natural hot springs, with views of waterfalls, lush tropical plants, and, at night, gushing red-orange lava. Tabacón Grand Spa Thermal Resort, at the base of Costa Rica's most active volcano, Arenal, offers spa treatments and soaking in this exact setting. Costa Rica, located between Nicaragua and Panama in Central America, is renowned for both its friendliness and eco-friendliness. This full-service resort, 90 minutes north of capital city San José, underwent a recent $2.5 million upgrade, which included the addition of the fantastic Grand Spa, located just across the street from the resort's guest rooms. (If you're too blissed-out to walk back home after your soak or massage, you can hop a shuttle you to your room.) With a group of four friends, you can reserve one of the junior suites—perfect for late-night dips in your private outdoor Jacuzzi, or for curling up in your comfy cotton robes to watch DVDs. Don't forget to partake of one of the simplest pleasures of all: sipping piña coladas at the swim-up bar in the pool. Costa Rica's high (dry) season runs from late November through April, so if you're trying to escape a dreary winter, this is the time to come. Christmas and Easter can be especially festive—and busy. But if you and the gals can only coordinate a trip in the summer, you've got it made, too. During the rainy season, there's usually a downpour in mid-afternoon and clear skies the rest of the day. It just means you'll get in an afternoon nap—along with low-season deals and bright-green landscapes.

LAY OF THE LAND

Tabacón Grand Spa Thermal Resort offers 11 private open-air treatment bungalows, each with a Jacuzzi. There's also an open-air yoga studio, a fitness center, restaurant, and bar. Hot springs dot the property via a steamy river running through; cool baths, waterfalls, gardens, and walking paths are there for your discovery as well.

SIGNATURE TREATMENTS

Massage therapists help regulate your body's energy flow by stretching you out during the Tabacón massage and then following up with a vigorous, volcanic-mud massage ($145 for 80 minutes). The three-hour fire package includes a hot-stone massage with essential oils, a volcanic mud wrap, and a balneotherapy session ($315). Tabacón originated the Huey Temazcal Aahuatlan, a sweat lodge treatment used in native cultures for cleansing both body and spirit. The spa has a resident shaman to guide you through the process—chanting and building up heat to release toxins. Share this intense physical and spiritual experience with your girlfriends (but if some of your group are claustrophobic, they should meet up with you afterward—the sweat lodge is small and dark). The session ends with fruit juices and teas ($65 for a group session, private groups $145 per person; *www.tabacon.com*).

CUISINE
You'll have enough dining options that your taste buds won't get bored. There's the open-air Los Tucanes restaurant, which serves international favorites with a Latin flair. You might order *risotto al funghi* or a roasted chicken breast with guava. The El Palenque Bar specializes in BBQ with views of Arenal Volcano. Girlfriends swoon over the dinner prepared for them in a private rain-forest bungalow by a personal chef and waiter; it's the resort's customized Gala Dinner and a must for girlfriends in a celebratory mood.

BEST ADVENTURES
The resort will keep you ladies busy with a variety of full- and half-day guided trips. Sky Trek, an adventure through the rain-forest canopy, will give you a bird's-eye view of the rain forest (and possibly a glimpse of many resident species), and an adrenaline rush as you soar on a zip line. If you're more interested in seeing Costa Rica's bounty at a less heart-pounding pace, a boat tour in the Caño Negro Wildlife Refuge affords a glimpse of sloths, caimans, turtles, or monkeys, as well as dozens of colorful bird species. There's also the option of hiking around Arenal Volcano National Park with a guide.

WHAT'S INCLUDED
Room rates include lodging and unlimited access to Tabacón's thermal springs throughout your stay (meals are not included).

RATES AND PACKAGES
Rates start at $230 with a two-night minimum stay. The Tropical Hideaway Package includes two nights' lodging, thermal springs access, daily breakfast buffet, a Gala Dinner, a massage for two, and

two additional 50-minute spa treatments, a sweat lodge ritual, a half-day tour, and transfers to San José or other destinations (starts at $1,700; 877-277-8291, *www.tabacon.com*).

ANOTHER WAY

If you'd prefer to be a hot springs day-tripper, you can spend one night at the Arenal Observatory Lodge and buy an unlimited all-day pass for Tabacón's thermal springs ($55). At the lodge, you'll get up close and personal with the lava-spewing volcano, and you easily access the five miles of winding trails (look for brightly colored toucans in the trees). The Smithsonian rooms feature picture windows framing Arenal's glory; if you've got a big group, take the White Hawk Villa (rooms from $55 with breakfast, villas are $425 nightly; *www.arenal-observatory.co.cr*).

ONE CLICK AND YOU'RE OFF

For more about Costa Rica, go to *www.visitcostarica.com*.

❧ Thailand ❧

Thailand can't help but be a spa destination. The Southeast Asian country has no choice but to soothe, with a Buddhist culture setting the tone for mindful living; a fragrant, light cuisine that goes easy on your body; massage and yoga integrated into the lifestyle; and silky beaches and friendly people. Ko Samui, an island in the Gulf of Thailand about an hour's flight from Bangkok, is a peaceful retreat that will lull you and the girls into a state of complete relaxation, Thai-style. Girlfriends love the calm, warm seawater, inexpensive massages at the water's edge, soft breezes, fresh fruit and fish, and the friendly Thai people. You'll get a rubdown in an outdoor *sala* (pavilion) or read and nap on a white-sand beach. Tropical Ko Samui has no shortage of spas, and it's easy to get around. Your options are unlimited: Stay at one spa for a week of luxurious treatments and accommodations, hop from spa to spa, or base yourselves at a hotel and sample the island's day spas. You really can't go wrong with whatever plans you and your girlfriends agree on. Ko Samui is a particularly ideal spa destination for hot-weather-loving gals; for maximum sunshine, visit between December and August. Just be sure to get plenty of hydration when you're there—especially after spa treatments. And of course, if you want to go out and dance the night away while you're here, the nightlife awaits—you can always recover with a massage the next morning!

BEST SPA SPLURGE

The Sila Evason Hideaway and Spa at Samui, on the northern tip of Ko Samui, stands as the crème de la crème for spa vacations on the island. Even the pickiest and most well traveled among you will be charmed by the infinity pools, the two-story villas with sea views, and the surrounding 20 acres of native vegetation. Relax under an umbrella at the beach or lounge on the sundeck of your villa and let your personal butler quench your thirst with fruit juice. In the Hideaway Spa, you can opt to take your treatments in one of five indoor villas or four salas (with fans and mosquito netting). What better place to try a Thai massage than the place where the technique got started? Kick off your trip with the country's signature massage style—a traditional Thai Royal massage, which uses yoga-like stretching and compression to release tension ($83). The Hideaway Retreat treatment combines Thai and Western massage techniques and closes with a Thai herbal compress ($108 for 90 minutes). If you fall for Thai massage as much as most guests do, there's a chance to pick up some of the techniques from an experienced therapist in a two-hour class (from $140). Then you can round out your health kick all week long with yoga, tai chi, and Pilates classes, at no charge.

The Weekend Escape packages for two at Sila Evason Hideaway and Spa at Samui include accommodation, breakfast, airport transfers, a massage for each person, one dinner at the resort's signature restaurant, and a welcome drink and fresh fruit in your villa (starting at $1,470). For yoginis, the two-and-a-half day Yoga and Vitality Retreat includes two daily yoga sessions, meditation, a lifestyle evaluation and personal consultation, two massages, and additional treatments (starting at $1,560 without accommodation). Room-only rates fluctuate by season and by villa type; a stay in a Hideaway Villa starts at $530 (*www.sixsenses.com/hideaway-samui*).

SPA HOPPING

To get a better sense of the island and its beaches—as well as to get spoiled in many different ways—consider spa hopping. Sample the Spa Resorts: Spa Beach and Ban Sabai Sunset Beach. At the former, you'll find an affordable health program. It is known for its cleansing fasts, yoga, meditation, and vegetarian menu. The resort

AROMATHERAPY HERBAL OILS

❧

Aromatherapy herbal oils are used extensively in traditional Thai massage. Before your treatment you may be asked to select one. These are the most common oils and their reputed benefits.

Nutmeg – a warming herbal oil, for deep tissue massage

Wild mint – refreshing and invigorating, especially on a hot day

Tangerine – a sweet herbal oil, stimulating to the skin and very relaxing

Prai – a ginger root famous for its skin-conditioning qualities

Ylang-ylang – a sweet herbal oil that's relaxing and often used as a base oil in perfumes

Lemongrass – invigorating, a natural mosquito repellant, enhances breathing

—Marybeth

has ten newly built A-frames with decks, air-conditioning, and easy access to the beach, pool, and tropical gardens; there are also standard rooms, villas, and studio apartments. Iyengar yoga, meditation, Chi Gung, and even Reiki and Thai massage classes are just some of the goodies offered here. And of course, even if you're taking massage classes, don't miss out on receiving an hour-long session ($10). The Spa Resorts: Spa Beach room rates are from $40 for an A-frame bungalow (*www.spasamui.com*).

On the island's southwest side, the Ban Sabai Sunset Beach offers its guests privacy and a menu of spa treatments perfect for those who can't have too many choices. Air-conditioned suites and villas have whirlpool tubs. But you want to hear about the treatments: Well, from the traditional Thai massage ($74 for two hours) to a sauna treatment with four different saunas (steam cave, ice cave, hot and dry pine room, aroma room), followed by a plunge in the ice pond—Ban Sabai has a little of everything. Try the Jasmine package ($305), which includes a body scrub, a trip to the steam room, Thai massage, an aroma bath, and a foot massage over a deliciously long five hours. The resort's L'Ananas Restaurant features light Thai salads and fresh seafood dishes, such as grilled fish wrapped in banana leaves. You can also arrange a private sunset BBQ on the beach, with your own chef and waiter ($117 for two). You'll have many packages to choose from. One worth pointing out: The five-day Sapphire package includes airport transfers, ten treatments, breakfast, and accommodation (starting at about $1,670; *www.ban-sabai.com*).

BEST SPA BY DAY

Stopping in for treatments at one or more day spas is a smart approach for mix-and-match spa goers who'd like the flexibility to stay and spa where they want. This makes sense particularly if you're on a tighter budget. You pay for one treatment at a time rather than going the all-inclusive route. One of my favorites is the Tamarind Retreat, an unpretentious, natural spa located up a hillside in a coconut grove. Treatments begin with a steam bath, built between two huge prehistoric boulders. You'll inhale steam vapor made from turmeric, ginger, lemongrass, bergamot lime, leaves of the camphor

Every time I visit Bangkok, tired and jet-lagged, I head for the Traditional School of Thai Massage in Wat Pho (Temple of the Reclining Buddha). No reservations necessary. I recommend you try the massage with the hot pack—a steaming herbal poultice filled with aromatic herbs and spices. It is applied in a kneading action to aching muscles to alleviate pain or inflammation along the energy lines. The poultice treatment dates to Thailand's Ayutthaya period (14th to 18th century) when a fragrant hot pack was applied to war-weary soldiers returning home with bruises and muscle aches. It's a perfect treatment for my ravaged body after hours of inactivity and discomfort aboard an airplane, and it helps alleviate my symptoms of jet lag. Traditional Thai massage costs $12 for an hour, or splurge for the herbal massage for $15.

—Marybeth

tree and the tamarind tree, then you'll shower in a natural waterfall flowing over the huge boulders and dip in the shallow pool beneath the rocks. Then your massage will be given in a large and breezy Balinese-style open pavilion with a thatched roof. Soothing music blends perfectly with the natural sounds of the birds and frogs living in the surrounding coconut grove (from $83, *www.tamarindretreat.com*). Check out the Samui Spa Guide for reviews and information about day spas and spa programs (*www.siamspaguide.com*).   .

CHAPTER SIX

Castles Fit for a Queen

You can make your girlhood fairy-tale dreams come true by staying in a castle, and you won't even have to suffer the cold and drafty cobblestoned palaces of yore. There are dozens of castles-turned-hotels in locations from Ireland to India that come equipped with stunning antiques and architecture plus modern amenities like spas, fine dining, and high-speed Internet. These are luxury hideaways, perfect for indulging any lingering fantasies of running off with Prince Charming. If you're with a group, staying at a castle doesn't have to blow the bank. Yes, it's a splurge of a lifetime to stay in most of these castles, but when you split the cost with a girlfriend, they're not that much more expensive than a deluxe hotel in the United States. In so many world-class destinations, castles can also be a good excuse to explore a nook of the world. And many castles act like destinations in themselves—places you and friends will want to be immersed in fully, spending days on their grounds, in their stately halls and regal bedrooms, and finding their secret corners. I have selected authentic castles that are beautifully preserved, renovated with state-of-the-art plumbing and comfortable beds, and furnished with antiques. They also serve fabulous food and are easily accessible by rental car or public transportation. They are all located in spectacular settings, near other attractions. I included more than one castle in some countries, like Ireland, which are better set up for road trips and multiple nights in different castles. Even if you are unable to spend the night, due to time or budget constraints, consider stopping in for afternoon tea, a flute of champagne on the terrace, or a royal meal.

ॐ CHERYL'S STORY ॐ

For several years Cheryl, a marketing entrepreneur in Sausalito, California, went to all her closest friends' 50th-birthday parties. Some were small, intimate dinners; others were elaborate trips to wine country or the Bahamas. As her own big birthday approached, she decided to plan a big bash for herself. "I didn't have a big wedding or baby showers to mark the major passages in my life. In fact, I've been single most of my adult life so I'm accustomed to making great things happen for myself," Cheryl says. She wanted a grand, once-in-a-lifetime birthday party, something that would make her feel like a fairy-tale princess. To fulfill her dream, she concluded that a castle in Europe would be the perfect venue for a big blowout celebration, marking a major passage in her life and allowing her to reconnect with all her girlfriends.

With the help of her girlfriend in London she located and rented a regal castle in Scotland, just outside Edinburgh, only 15 minutes from the airport, but light-years away from the real world. Dundas Castle, nestled into acres of rolling lawns in the peaceful Scottish countryside, was built in 1818 and extensively renovated in 1995. It is grand enough to "wow" anyone, yet small enough to be intimate, and modern enough to be very comfortable.

The first night everyone sipped champagne in the 15th-century Auld Keep Armory beneath weapons and swords dating back to the days of Braveheart, followed by a candlelight dinner in the dark stone-walled Stag Chamber amid hunting trophies and mounted stag's heads.

Twenty of Cheryl's close friends from all periods of her life, including her Florida "YaYa Girlfriends" and her parents, flew into Edinburgh from all around the world for the celebration. Although her birthday falls on January 2, the weather was perfect—cold days, with frost on the forest floor, and brilliant blue skies—perfect for wintry walks and long talks, wandering the grounds in snuggly fur coats, or strolling to the boathouse to see the swans on the loch. Everyone climbed the 14th-century stone tower for a panoramic view of Edinburgh and the River Forth. After exploring the vast property, guests curled up with a cozy cup of afternoon tea in front of a roaring log fire in the drawing room, played a game in the Billiards Room, or sipped sherry with a good book in the library.

A hearty Scottish breakfast was served every morning to get the group going for forays into town to visit local abbeys and to shop in the nearby village of South Queensferry. One afternoon, Cheryl invited a world-class Scotch master to the castle who conducted (in full kilt, of course) a scotch-whiskey tasting for her guests. On another day, a shuttle bus arrived and they toured the countryside, pub-hopping along the way. John, the houseman, was always waiting to greet them at the castle door upon their return and served them a fine old Scotch or hot tea and biscuits.

Lord and Lady Stewart-Clark, the owners, lived discreetly out of sight in the South Wing, but framed family photos displayed on the grand piano reminded guests that they were in a family home and not an impersonal hotel.

Cheryl's 50th-birthday dinner—celebrated on New Year's Eve, or Hogmanay as the Scots call it—was a black-tie, sit-down affair in the castle's formal Georgian dining room. "Everyone was dressed to the nines in evening gowns, glamorous tartan, and dinner jackets—including me in my Princess tiara," she laughs. A kilt-clad bagpiper entertained the guests and piped them into the dining room announcing the arrival of the traditional haggis feast—a stuffed sheep stomach that looks a bit like a castrated bagpipe. "It looks and sounds as if it would be hideous—but it's actually delicious; rather like sausage," she explains. The Scots joke that eating haggis is how Braveheart really got his name.

After many more toasts and roasts and much fine wine, the guests adjourned to the grand hall foyer for dancing and many rounds of "Auld Lang Syne." They toasted the New Year from the castle porch as fireworks exploded from all seven hills of Edinburgh in a crystal-clear midnight sky.

Cheryl fondly remembers driving onto the property for the first time down a long, winding, tree-lined lane. "We turned a corner and there the castle loomed—a majestic edifice set in a pristine sea of green grass," she says. "The pictures didn't begin to do it justice.

In fact, the whole celebration was beyond my wildest expectations."

Dream big, she urges us; a castle is a great venue for a once-in-a-lifetime, "special passage" type of party, not just for one woman, but for all girlfriends.

⁊ Ireland ⁊

Ireland's emerald landscapes are dotted with hundreds of castles; some are medieval ruins, others are palace hotels. You'll see them as you drive down corkscrew lanes aflame with red fuchsia and yellow gorse, through frog-green hills crisscrossed with ancient stone walls and grazed by baaing sheep. I've been to Ireland four times; biking, hiking, and tooling around by car. And there's no memory quite like strolling around the castle grounds after an exquisite dinner, smelling the freshly cut grass, watching the moonlight dance on the ancient stone walls, and picking out the lights glowing from your window in the turret room of "your" castle for the night. Especially if you've got Irish roots, staying in a castle is a great way to start exploring your heritage and begin to appreciate Ireland. But for women of all backgrounds, Ireland is an escape to another era, to a land of myths and a pastoral existence. And if you're a group of gals who take golf trips every year together, this is a good one for your list. In western Ireland, castles are conveniently strung along the countryside, allowing you to customize your own road trip with friends, taking in the country's best sites by day—and the occasional golf course—and retiring to your own room in a castle by night. Giving yourselves a week in the west for this castle tour lends a nice pace to the road trip and the chance to really get into all the niches of these palaces. Fly into the airport in Shannon, in County Clare on Ireland's west coast, to start a three-castle tour that explores western Ireland's towering seaside cliffs, gorgeous countryside, and renowned hospitality. In Shannon, rent a car (if you can get an automatic, it will be one less thing to think about as you navigate on the left side of the road) for an easy castle-to-castle itinerary along this magical coast. First up, Dromoland Castle, just an eight-mile drive from the airport. After relaxing here for a few days, travel northward about 50 miles to the vibrant university town of Galway, and then another 30 or so miles northwest to the rugged enchantment of Connemara, a barren, treeless area with tall jagged mountains and green lakes, and its Ballynahinch Castle. When you've fallen under this castle's charms, it's time to make the hour's drive eastward to elegant Ashford Castle. From here, it's less than two hours back to Shannon airport. Note that all those beautiful green fields come with a price: rain, even in summer. May to October is the best time to visit: Expect rain, rainbows, patches of sun, and more clouds.

⤳ DROMOLAND CASTLE ⤳

Dromoland Castle, Newmarket on Fergus, County Clare, might be just eight miles from the Shannon airport, but once you begin driving through the rolling pastures and secluded woodlands surrounding it, you and your girlfriends will be completely enveloped in the world of the royal O'Brien clan. In the 11th century, the land belonged to Brian Boru, High King of Ireland. The castle you'll see today has been enhanced throughout the ages: Look for the gorgeous Queen Anne–period residence and the stone walls of the Gothic main castle. The castle was converted into a luxury hotel in 1962, and it couldn't be better equipped to soothe your jet lag. The 85 guest rooms and 13 deluxe suites will charm you with their damask wall coverings and antiques. The 18th Baron of Inchiquin, a descendant of Brian Boru, still lives on the property in the Georgian-style Thomond House. So, in a sense, you and the girls will be guests of royalty.

CASTLE ATTIRE

⤳

What's the dress code for fine dining in a castle? My rule of thumb is: Dress as you would for a fine restaurant at home. For castle dining, I have worn a simple black dress with pearls and a pashmina shawl; a cocktail dress; black slacks with a tailored blazer, black heels, and understated jewelry. T-shirts, shorts, halter tops, and jeans are not appropriate.

—Marybeth

PALACE LIVING

Life on this 410-acre estate can be filled with as much—or as little—activity as you'd like. Explore the grounds, which include an extensive series of gardens that are based on the designs of a Versailles garden planner, spotting the occasional deer and pheasant (be sure not to miss the formal rose garden). After all that walking, an afternoon at the Dromoland's spa will remind you that you are the royalty when you're a guest. (My treatment pick: the Sligo seaweed wrap.) If you're not too useless after that indulgence, attend Mrs. White's afternoon tea in the drawing room. The expression "to eat like a king" won't be lost on your group when you sit down to a dinner of Irish and French cuisine, such as a lamb fillet with foie gras or a hearty Irish stew, accompanied by soothing music from a harpist. If the plush beds in your rooms and the novel you're hooked on don't tempt you to retire early, retreat to the Library Bar for a nightcap and the partaking of hearty Irish songs by candlelight.

IRISH GREENS

Maintaining another Irish tradition, Dromoland has been voted one of the world's best golf resorts. The golfers in your group can tee off on the estate's 18-hole, par-72 course. And there are plenty of more sporty options: Take lessons from the resort's pro, whack balls at the ten automated driving bays, or work out in the clubhouse's fitness center, the 17-meter pool, the tennis courts, or mountain biking trails.

RATES AND PACKAGES

Rates vary seasonally, and range from about $280 to $2,000. The hotel offers specials for winter weekends, which run about $600 per person for two nights, including full Irish breakfasts and one dinner (800-346-7007, *www.dromoland.ie*).

BETWEEN THE CASTLES

As you head north along the Irish coast, make sure to allot some time to take in the Cliffs of Moher, a meeting place of sorts, where wave-carved cliffs and rolling hills fend off a moody, restless ocean, and the memories of sea battles merge with the scent of wildflowers. In the quaint town of Doolin, known for its traditional music, you can take a break from driving and find a welcoming pub in which to share lively conversation and music over a pint of nut-brown Guinness. Take a seat, call for a drink, and listen as the tune is handed on from fiddle to flute, from strings to pipe. Toe tapping begins and you'll feel the rhythm deepen as it goes around, strengthening and gaining in confidence. You'll find yourself lost in the melodic verses and lyrics that are personal yet sublimely universal. The gaiety in Irish pubs is a force you can't resist. As you journey to the next castle for the night, you'll be passing right by Ireland's cultural hub, Galway. Chances are you'll be able to catch one of its many festivals, such as the summer arts festival or the October beer festival. And this is one of your best bets for shopping in this country: You'll come across traditional Claddagh friendship rings as well as classic Irish linens and crystal. You may even hear the lyrical language of Gaelic spoken as you wander through the streets.

❧ BALLYNAHINCH CASTLE ❧

In the heart of Connemara's wild landscape, Ballynahinch Castle has long been a haven for those who don't play by the rules. Grace O'Malley, the Pirate Queen of Connemara, lived here during the 1500s; Richard Martin, who fought for human and animal rights, was a 17th-century resident of the grounds. Today, you'll find the peaceful seclusion of one of the castle's 40 rooms the perfect escape for a group of adventurous ladies—without having to pay a king's ransom.

PALACE LIVING
Surrounded by the Twelve Bens Mountains and overlooking the Ballynahinch River, this castle's greatest amenity is its views. Each room looks out onto the courtyard, river, or mountains, so it's hard not to find yourself stopping in your tracks to take in the scenery. And the inside of your room is just as picturesque—many have four-poster beds and furnishings reflecting the castle's history. You and the girls will immediately want to get out into that lovely landscape on paths to the terraced gardens, where you'll find a labyrinth and a tennis court, and then continue through the castle's 450-acre grounds and along the river. Back at the castle, you can curl up in front of a log fire before dining on fresh local fish at the Owenmore Restaurant with views of the river. Desert is a plate of creamy Irish farmhouse cheeses.

WILD IRELAND
Ballynahinch puts you in range to explore the rugged allure best associated with the region. In Connemara National Park, you can hike through bogs and heathlands while skylarks and wrens swoop through the air. If you're visiting during the fishing season (from

Diet before you go! The thrill of Ireland is to wander from county to county and discover fabulous regional cuisines based on the local produce in each area. You may be surprised that on the culinary front, times have changed in Ireland. The current economic success has led to a burgeoning food culture. No longer are the best chefs with culinary talent hurrying abroad, they are staying at home and creating a distinctive Irish style of newfound sophistication. Ireland has products that are undeniably equal to and often superior to those of most other countries. Try the fresh oysters, organic lamb, local grass-fed beef, and super-fresh seafood—salmon, trout, and mussels from the Atlantic shores. I discovered that select local pubs now serve a salad with a vast array of locally produced chesses, including goat's, ewe's, and cow's milk cheeses. Ask a local where the best pub dining is. My advice: take slacks with an expandable waist and don't look at a scale until you've been home for a month.

—Marybeth

February to September), you'll witness the Ballynahinch River busy with famous salmon and trout and the fishermen casting for them from the banks. In addition to trying your hand at fishing, there's hiking, sailing, and pony trekking offered in the area, as well as a ferry ride to the Aran Islands, 30 miles off the coast (and the legendary hand-knit Aran sweaters). The isolated Aran Islands, a stronghold of traditional Gaelic customs, language, and culture, are dotted with small stone cottages and pony-drawn carts. Ballynahinch Castle can arrange tours and guides for whatever activity suits your fancy.

RATES AND PACKAGES
Prices vary seasonally with summer rates starting at $183 for a standard room and $293 for a riverside suite, including breakfast. Check with Ballynahinch for specials and their calendar: The castle closes during some parts of the winter months (*www.ballynahinch-castle.com*).

❧ ASHFORD CASTLE ❧

From Ballynahinch, it's a short drive eastward, skirting the shores of Lough Corrib, to the luxuries of Ashford Castle, a beautifully crenellated castle that blends elegance and countryside charm 30 minutes outside Galway. First built in the 13th century as a monastery, the castle was so special to renowned Dublin brewer Benjamin Guinness that he bought it in 1855 and converted it to a family residence. Since becoming a hotel in 1939, Ashford Castle and its 350-acre grounds have attracted notables including Ronald Reagan, the band U2, Pierce Brosnan (who got married here)—and now, of course, you and your friends.

PALACE LIVING
When you check into one of Ashford's 83 guest rooms (including six staterooms and five suites) you're welcomed with either a decanter of sherry or an Irish liqueur. Put your feet up, take a few sips of your welcome drink, and gaze at the panorama of the castle's extensive gardens from your window, or at vistas of the River Cong or Lough Corrib (Ireland's second largest lake) from your room. After you settle in, reconvene with the girls and wander the Woodland Walk, lined with oaks, beeches, and chestnuts. You'll quickly learn that this castle caters to sportswomen (see below), which, in addition to getting you into the outdoors, means you have an excuse to soothe your muscles with a spa treatment or time in the sauna, Jacuzzi, and steam room. Continue winding down over dinner with the girls at the cozy Connaught Room, with its intricately hand-carved fireplace and eyeful of Lough Corrib. The night owls in your group can make their way down to the Dungeon Bar, which can get festive with Irish toasts after dark.

DO AS THE NATIVES DO
Ashford is the place to try your hand at the old-fashioned pastimes of royalty. If you've always marveled at the outstretched wings of a falcon flying overhead, learn more about these magnificent birds in a falconry class. Try archery or clay-pigeon shooting. Or cast a line with a local fly-fishing guide. You may think this sounds like a more appropriate venue for a guys' weekend, but just wait until you see your best girlfriend reel in her first salmon. You can't beat that kind of exhilaration, girls.

BEAT THE CHILL
The best ways to stay warm in the Irish countryside, you'll learn, are a hot-stone massage, an Irish coffee, and a book in front of one of the Ashford's many fireplaces. Head farther afield and take a day trip to the decadent Celtic Seaweed Baths, about two hours north of

Ashford Castle, and restore your road-trip-tired body with a soothing dip in their hot baths (about $30 for bath, about $80 for an aromatherapy massage; *www.celticseaweedbaths.com*).

RATES AND PACKAGES

Rates at Ashford Castle vary seasonally from $183. Ashford's summer spa packages, which include two nights' accommodation, Irish breakfast, one dinner, and a massage, starting at about $790 per person for a river-view room (800-346-7007, *www.ashford.ie*).

ONE CLICK AND YOU'RE OFF

If you can't get enough of Ireland's castles and would like to see the full roster of their finest palaces for an extended road trip, inquire with Celtic Castles (*www.celticcastles.com*). You'll find a helpful listing of castles in Ireland and elsewhere in Europe. For general information about traveling in Ireland, try *www.discoverireland.ie*.

❧ France ❧

There's no denying it, nothing says "over the top" better than a castle in France. Along with all the wonderful things the country tempts girlfriends planning a trip together with—Paris, fabulous wine, cheese, sauces, breads, pastries, shopping, and on and on—you can add castles in the countryside. Mind you, by countryside, I mean wine country. Two of the best examples of regal castle hotels happen to reside in the world-famous Beaujolais and Loire Valley regions. I recommend you select one area and visit it in depth, using a castle as your home base. Unless you have lots of time, a road trip between these two castles in France is not feasible. Château de Marçay, located in the Loire Valley, is an easy one-and-a-half-hour drive south of Paris, whereas Château de Bagnols, in the Beaujolais area near Lyon, is located in the south. I recommend you fly, drive, or take the train from Paris to Lyon.

Although summer can be warm, it also ushers in fields of yellow sunflowers in bloom, gardens of aromatic lavender, fairs, and festivals. In Lyon, you'll find music and theater festivals all summer, along with a busy riverside café scene. But don't rule out winter: The Loire Valley and the Beaujolais area are less crowded, and one of Lyon's most renowned events, the Festival of Lights, takes place every December 8. Winters in France are rainy and cold and the days are quite short—all the better for sipping wine next to a cozy fire in a castle.

CHÂTEAU DE BAGNOLS

The impressive towers and honey-colored stone walls of Château de Bagnols dominate the landscape in the heart of the Beaujolais region and its vineyard-rich terrain. Nestled among green hills, vineyards, and forests, the castle is 17 miles from Lyon in southeast France. You may fly into Lyon from the U.S. or Paris, or there's the option of the TGV, a high-speed train, from Paris. From here, rent a car and delve into the French countryside on your way to this 13th-century castle. Soon after you get settled in, you and the girls will get the first history lesson of your stay: In the 1400s, when Charles VIII visited here, a coat of arms was carved in the dining room in the Salle des Gardes stone fireplace to celebrate. During the French Revolution, the Salle des Gardes became a meeting place for revolutionaries, and throughout World War II, the château's cellar hid stained-glass windows and artwork to protect Lyon's treasures from looters. In its near past, in 1992, after four years of restoration, all of this history was channeled into transforming this castle into an elegant vineyard hotel, with a courtyard tiled in golden paving stones and Renaissance wall paintings (revealed by happy accident during the renovation), all surrounded by bountiful grape vines.

PALACE LIVING
Château de Bagnols is relatively small and therefore very intimate; with only 12 rooms, 8 suites, and an apartment. If you're traveling with a big group, look into taking over the entire place: It's the ultimate spot for a celebration among girlfriends. Rooms brim with 17th- and 18th-century antiques, column and four-poster antique beds with fine linens and silks from Lyon. Mornings will be spent trying to get lost on the verdant grounds, where you'll happen across a French garden with a fountain, a cherry orchard, a vegetable and flower garden, and hundred-year-old lime trees. Rocking chairs are scattered throughout these charming surroundings so that you can stop to savor this spectacular land.

FRENCH FARE
The château's Salle des Gardes restaurant alone is worth making the overseas trek to France. With dishes like blue lobster dressed up in butter and champagne, or slow-roasted chicken breast for two with truffled Parmentier (a popular dish of mashed potatoes and minced beef), you don't have to be an expert foodie to know you're eating a

work of art. Make sure you take a seat at one of the bay windows to listen to the crackle of the fire in the enormous stone fireplace. In summer, you can dine under the shade of the terrace's lime trees. A sommelier is on hand to steer you toward the perfect pairings for your meal.

WINE BUFFS
You and the girls will want to save some time to fully experience the hillside vineyards heavy with grapes. Beaujolais may even be France's most beautiful wine region, worth visiting for its summer green and fall purple-and-gold landscapes even more than its wines. Hundreds of little wineries' owners want you to taste their wares. You'll never forget the flower-lined paths leading to tiny stone wine cellars where you'll sit and sip among gigantic oak casks. And Vine Park and its museum, located 45 minutes from Lyon, can give you a primer on the history and lore of France's favorite beverage (*www.hameauduvin .com*). Back at Bagnols, arrange a private feast just for your group among the casks and centuries-old wine presses in the Cuvage (a large winemaking barn), with the resident oenologist on hand.

SHOPPING, ANYONE?
You are only 17 miles from Lyon, a friendly city packed with boutiques. Savvy shoppers will adore exploring the 650 shops in and around Lyon to get your shoe fix (stylish French and Italian models) or silk blouses (and there are plenty of seasonal flea markets for those in search of French treasures at bargain prices). And two hours away by TGV lies Paris, of course (see Chapter Two: Cosmopolitan Cities, to find more information about Paris).

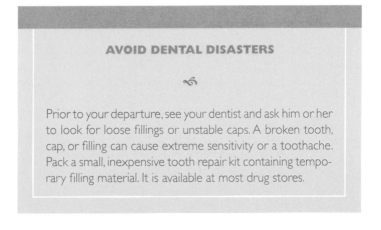

AVOID DENTAL DISASTERS

∽

Prior to your departure, see your dentist and ask him or her to look for loose fillings or unstable caps. A broken tooth, cap, or filling can cause extreme sensitivity or a toothache. Pack a small, inexpensive tooth repair kit containing temporary filling material. It is available at most drug stores.

RATES AND PACKAGES

Traditional rooms at Bagnols start at $700 nightly. Several packages, focusing on holidays and the wine harvest, are available throughout the year, such as the Discover Beaujolais package, which includes accommodation for two, wine, and fresh fruit on arrival, continental breakfast, dinner at the Salle des Gardes, and a half-day wine-tasting tour with a private guide from $1,195 (*www.bagnols.com*).

⁂ CHÂTEAU DE MARÇAY ⁂

The lush, green Loire Valley, home of the royal castles of the French nobility, lies 180 miles southwest of Paris. The best way to see the region is by car. Château de Marçay was built in 1150 as a fortress with secret underground passages. Some parts were destroyed over the years, yet like any sturdy castle, it has weathered the ages and now stands resplendent in its restored beauty.

PALACE LIVING

Ladies, as guests in this 34-room citadel, you will appreciate being shielded from the stress and demands beyond its stalwart walls. You'll find yourselves easily distracted from life at home with ventures into the surrounding scenery: Rent a bike and cycle through the countryside or take a canoe down the Vienne River. Perhaps a tennis round robin with the girls, a friendly game of lawn bowling, or a dip in the outdoor swimming pool will rid you of the last of your stress—as will the wine cellar's 700 choices of Loire Valley varietals served at the castle restaurant. In the evening, you'll sit down to beautifully orchestrated dishes of the region's delectable lamb, veal, and seafood, and Loire Valley strawberries with homemade brioche and licorice.

RATES AND PACKAGES

Rooms start at $171 nightly and run to about $431. The Gastronomic Package, which includes a room for two, continental breakfast, and a four-course meal for two, begins at $740. The hotel closes during the last few weeks of November, and again between mid-January and mid-March (*www.chateaudemarcay.com*).

ONCE CLICK AND YOU'RE OFF

For more detailed information about traveling in France, visit *www .franceguide.com*.

ᚽ Scotland ᚼ

The castles of Scotland do not disappoint those mesmerized by the lonesome notes of a bagpiper, those with a fondness for golf (the world's most historic courses are here), men in skirts, or those who like the idea of curling up with friends and a glass of single malt scotch in front of the fireplace after a foggy day in the bright green moorland. From traditional music to theater, art to architecture, culture to fabulous shopping, walks in green glens to rambles along the savage coast, there's so much to enjoy in Scotland. You have the option of selecting a single castle for your vacation or lining up a tour of several on a Scottish driving adventure with the lassies. Rent a car, but be sure to designate a quick-thinking driver for navigating on the left side of the road through the Scottish countryside. If you'd all rather sit back and watch the scenery, you can also arrange a taxi or private car through any castle you have a reservation with. For a wonderful three-castle tour that I recommend to girlfriends (which can also be used à la carte), you'll want to fly into Edinburgh—get your first taste of Scottish royalty with a glimpse of the iconic Edinburgh Castle, perched atop Castle Rock, before heading less than an hour south to a spa-castle extraordinaire, Stobo Castle Health Spa. After easing aching muscles and minds, take an hour-and-a-half northward trip, past Edinburgh, into the kingdom of Fife, the ancient home of Scotland's monarchs, to Myres Castle. And from there begin your biggest adventure yet—a three-hour drive northwest into the lochs, mountains, and waterfalls of the Scottish Highlands. You'll near gape at the dramatic scenery in this part of the world. The cameras will never be put away, and you'll feel the otherworldliness of the place start to peel back your own defenses. Upon arrival at the Inverlochy Castle Hotel, a favorite of Queen Victoria herself in the 19th century, you'll see what the Highlands of Scotland are famous for: green lochs (or lakes), cloud-veiled mountains, thick forests, and moorlands.

ᚽ STOBO CASTLE HEALTH SPA ᚼ

Stobo Castle Health Spa looms over the countryside 25 miles south of Edinburgh. Nestled in the Scottish Borders region, known for its green rolling hills, serene moorlands, and flowering valleys, it's a movie-set perfect destination for your Scottish holiday with girlfriends.

PALACE LIVING

Stobo gets plenty of attention for its renowned spa, with a 25-meter pool, hydrotherapy, and 40 treatment rooms (with a menu of 70 incredible treatments). And here, your home really is your castle—feel free to lounge around in your bathrobes. The Cashmere Suite, perfect for girlfriends looking to really indulge themselves, comes equipped with a magnificent limestone bathtub and plasma screens everywhere.

GET ACTIVE

On the castle grounds, you can soak up the soothing sounds of the Japanese water garden. Improve your backhand with a tennis pro, your downward dog in a yoga class, or Pilate's breath work with a personal coach. But its best perk is the scenery, to which you must dedicate at least an afternoon pedaling through or wandering on foot; the hotel provides bikes and maps of suggested routes.

RATES AND PACKAGES

A castle lodge room, including all meals, use of all facilities, and the exercise and well-being program, starts at $145 per person based on double occupancy. The Cashmere Suite, where chocolate and Bollinger champagne will greet you on arrival, is well worth the investment (starting at $380). The So Indulgent for Ladies spa package, which includes a deluxe manicure, an aromatherapy massage, and rebalancing facial is $240 (*www.stobocastle.co.uk*).

☞ MYRES CASTLE ☜

Myres Castle began simply as a fortress in 1530 and has been developed over the centuries into something far from humble (the striking square tower, made of gray stone blocks, was added in 1616). Located deep in the Scottish countryside near the village of Auchtermuchty, the castle is less than an hour's drive north of Edinburgh. With only nine rooms, Myres is ideal for those gathering for a reunion or birthday extravaganza with 6 to 18 girlfriends. The 44-acre estate is wrapped by an old stone wall and hidden behind trees, for a truly private retreat with friends.

PALACE LIVING

You might have to fight over the bedrooms. Each has its own charms, but all provide a brilliant special touch: heated towels. Among the most notable rooms, the Schoolroom has children's books and a mahogany bed; Joanna's Room offers a glimpse of the Rose Garden walk from the bath; while the Queen's Room is decked out in sumptuous blues and golds with an heirloom tapestry wedding quilt dating back to the 19th century hanging on the wall.

A ROYAL CELEBRATION

Before dinner, see who's the pool shark in your group at the billiards table. Then, looking out on the garden's formal pond, gather for an exquisite meal at the elegant mahogany dining-room table. There's always time for sipping cocktails under the crystal Baccarat chandelier in the lovely drawing room. And there may be a night or two when you'll want to settle into the library's couches with popcorn and in your PJs. You'll find a collection of 200-plus CDs and DVDs.

DINE LIKE A QUEEN

The menu at Myres Castle changes with the seasons. In summer, you'll probably find the berries you spotted on your afternoon stroll in a to-die-for *panna cotta* that evening, or maybe impeccably prepared venison raised right in Auchtermuchty. The castle's chef, Christopher Trotter, who was trained at the Savoy in London and worked in France and Switzerland, also hosts cooking classes throughout the year.

GET ACTIVE

If you can tear yourselves away from the rooms at Myres, treat yourselves to the fresh country air beyond its walls. Walking Lomond Hills, which you can see from the castle, will reinvigorate you. There's also the option of an afternoon game of croquet on the lawn, golf at one of the hundred golf courses within an easy drive, or a game of tennis on the courts at Myres, topped off with a cocktail of Pimms.

RATES AND PACKAGES

The castle has a two-night minimum stay, and booking must be for six guests or more, for $730 per person per night. This package includes all meals (full breakfast, lunch, afternoon tea, and a five-course dinner) and exclusive use of the grounds. Bed-and-breakfast rates are available if you stay more than two nights. Rates are lower if you have a larger group (*www.myrescastle.com*).

BEST SIDE TRIP

If you're traveling castle-to-castle, be sure to take a detour to St. Andrews, north along the coast, and see the historic Old Course golf course. If you wish to play, reserve well in advance, or just walk the beach and watch golfers tee off. Give yourselves enough time to meander through the spaghetti maze of streets and narrow alleyways that make up the old city center, or simply sit on a bench in the shade of the ivy-covered walls of the 15th-century university.

∽ INVERLOCHY CASTLE HOTEL ∽

Queen Victoria traveled to Inverlochy in 1873 to sketch and paint. She said she'd never seen a lovelier spot, and I think you'll agree. In the Scottish Highlands, Inverlochy (two and a half hours north of Glasgow or three hours from Edinburgh) has the good fortune of proximity to the country's most famed scenery. Ben Nevis, Britain's highest mountain, makes up the castle's backdrop; Loch Ness and a host of gorgeous glens, lakes, and mountains are nearby. Built in 1863 near the site of a 13th-century fortress, the castle was a private residence until 1969, when it was converted into a hotel that has gone on to win a constant stream of accolades for its service, cuisine, and overall ambience.

PALACE LIVING

Each of the castle's 17 rooms comes decorated in its own unique décor. The expansive Queen's Suite, with its four-poster bed, presents a view of a small loch and the surrounding mountains. The Venetian crystal chandeliers throughout the castle will make you stare, as will the three dining rooms brimming with ornate furniture, a gift from a king of Norway.

DINE LIKE A QUEEN

It's not just good food that is served at the tables of Inverlochy's restaurants: This is Michelin-starred cuisine. You can sample some of Scotland's finest fare, such as Isle of Skye crabs with a green apple salad or carpaccio of black pudding with white truffle, scrambled eggs, and roast veal sweetbreads.

GET OUTDOORS

A worthwhile day's outing, Glencoe (about a 30-minute drive away from Inverlochy) presents nature (and movie) lovers alike with idyllic rivers and the dramatic mountain scenery found on-screen in *Braveheart*. For sporty gals, have your pick here of mountain biking and rafting. But no trip to Scotland can be considered complete without a stop at Ben Nevis, a 4,406-foot mountain just a four-mile drive from Inverlochy. The views from the top are spectacular, and the experience of ascending it makes for a lasting bond between friends.

EVENTS TO FLY IN FOR

Scotland, and Edinburgh in particular, gets lively during the long summer days. The film buffs in your group might want to combine a castle tour with the Edinburgh Film Festival in summer (*www .edfilmfest.org.uk*). The Edinburgh International Festival is held over a three-week period in late summer each year (usually in August), and you'll see classical music, theater, opera, and dance performed in theaters, concert halls, and on stages in the streets (*www.eif .co.uk*). But holiday celebrations in Scotland make winter a prime time for a castle vacation: At Inverlochy Castle, the New Year's Eve celebration of Hogmanay starts with a black-tie dinner, continues with a ceilidh band with traditional Scottish dancing. At midnight a traditional piper, in his formal tartan, closes the evening.

RATES AND PACKAGES

Special packages for dinner, bed-and-breakfast, November to March, holidays excluded, are $370 per person. Rates in off-season from around $600 (888-424-0106, *www.inverlochycastlehotel.com*).

ONE CLICK AND YOU'RE OFF

The Scottish Tourist Board can help you plan this castle trip; start out by visiting them at *www.visitscotland.com*. And for detailed information on stopping in at as well as staying overnight in many of Scotland's castles, go to *www.clansandcastles.com*.

Italy

Close your eyes and imagine pastel Renaissance villas framed by symmetric Cyprus trees hovering over a blue lake with snowy Alpine peaks in the distance. Add rich, hearty Italian cuisine, the clink of glasses brimming with wine, and long afternoons of sunshine—all with your own group of girls—it will feel like heaven. Lake Como, tucked among the Alps near the Italian-Swiss border, is renowned for the string of glamorous towns and wedding cake villas that line its shores—and you and the girls will visit or stay in one of the finest.

VILLA D'ESTE

The Villa d'Este, Cernobbio, is more than a historic palace hotel, it is a secluded world—enjoyed by the privileged few—of gardens (35 acres), opulent suites, and a jasmine-scented terrace overlooking the lake. Considered by many to be the grandest hotel in Europe, its guest rooms resemble museum galleries. Home of princes, cardinals, and dukes in the 16th century, the hotel retains the luxury and magnificence of a bygone era. Villa d'Este is renowned for its elegance and privacy, attracting celebrities from Woody Allen to George Clooney.

To feel like royalty—or its modern-day Hollywood equivalent—fly into Milan's international airport and have the villa arrange for a chauffeur to escort you and the ladies (and all of your luggage) directly to your superior dwelling for the next few nights, less than an hour to the north. (Also see Chapter Nine: Glorious Gardens for more information about the Lake Como region.)

Villa d'Este is closed from mid-November to March 1, so you'll want to plan accordingly. For a retreat feel, pick the quieter spring and fall; festive gals will want to come in the summer, when warm days and balmy nights fill with jazz during the Lake Como Festival (*www.comolakefestival.com*).

PALACE LIVING

No two of the 152 antique-filled guest rooms are alike, but if you can, try to get rooms in the main villa that face the lake's sparkling waters. The Cardinal Suite is the indulgence of a lifetime, with a private terrace for soaking up the rays and simply gazing out at Como's sapphire waters. The cavernous walk-in closet will likely blow your mind. Another of its decadent amenities are the three swimming pools on the property. Nothing will make you feel more like a superstar than basking with a Campari and soda around the pool that looks as if it's floating on Lake Como's surface.

ITALIAN CUISINE
You don't have to go far to experience authentic Italian fare. Villa d'Este, after all, is looking after all of your senses. And their dining room, Veranda, overlooks the lake and classical gardens and orchestrates meals of handmade fresh pasta, risotto, and fish. For more casual meals, make your way over to the Grill. You and the girls can pick up some skills to re-create these dishes back at home. Villa d'Este's longtime executive chef, Luciano Parolari, will instruct you in making one of his fabulous risottos.

There are lots of fine restaurants for every budget all around the lake, many with terraces and drop-dead views.

GET ACTIVE
Fortunately, you'll be able to burn off some of that pasta and cheese with a match of tennis on one of eight courts, a round of golf at one of six nearby courses, windsurfing and water skiing on the lake, or the biggest adventure Lake Como has to offer: dancing at local nightclubs.

Or put on your hiking boots and take the funicular from Como to the village of Brunate, 2,160 feet high for hiking trails and beautiful views of the lake and the Alps.

HIGH-FASHION FANTASY

A ten-minute boat ride will take you into the town of Como, a silk-savvy town, with many silk factories and outlets. Prices are low on designer fashion fabrics. Como also has a Silk Museum where you can see the entire silk-making process (*www.museosetacomo.com*) and then splurge on scarves, shawls, and blouses.

LA SPA

Villa d'Este won't have let you down yet, and it will continue to knock your socks off with its extensive and expensive spa menu. Try the new collagen and aloe total rejuvenation mask for the face (about $160), or get an all-over recovery from your travels with the jet-lag treatment (about $345).

CRUISE THE LAKE

Magical Lake Como has served as muse to poets and composers. You and the gals can channel this inspiration on an all-day cruise, which provides a spectacular perspective of the lake's shoreline villas. Boats leave constantly throughout the day to various ports. Dignified boatmen in starched uniforms greet you and escort you onto the dock. Stop in the ritzy village of Bellagio on a promontory in the lake's center; sit at one of the hotel cafés that line the shore; have a drink and watch the steamers go by (the boats have electric motors which are very quiet, so they're never a nuisance). Or hike up the cobbled alleys and paths from the lakefront to the center of town adorned with pots of impatiens and geraniums. Hop another boat to Varenna, with its pleasant mix of multihued houses, restaurants, hotels, and stores.

In the evening it is fun to go to the walled town of Como, the largest and most visited town along the lake, and walk along the narrow streets, window shop or stroll down the lakefront boulevard to see the town lights reflected against the water. At dusk, nicely dressed locals also promenade (For more about Lake Como's gorgeous gardens and shopping see Chapter Nine).

FARTHER AFIELD

The Villa is an exquisite home base for a tour of Italy, especially for those of you who will be visiting the country for the first time. You can drive or ask a chauffeur to escort you and the girls to nearby wineries or high-fashion Milan. Whether it's tickets to the opera at La Scala or a viewing of Leonardo da Vinci's "The Last Supper" in

Milan, the concierge at Villa d'Este can keep art lovers, shoppers, or any group of gals satisfied.

BEFORE YOU GO
Get in the mood; watch the movie *A Month By The Lake*, starring Vanessa Redgrave, Uma Thurman, and Edward Fox.

WHEN TO GO
Lake Como is a popular weekend destination for people from Milan, so try to plan your trip for during the week. Spring or fall are less crowded and the weather is pleasant.

EVENTS TO FLY IN FOR
The town of Como ignites with activity during the Sagra di San Giovanni Festival. On the first night children and their parents float hundreds of tiny lamps in the lake, and there's a big fireworks display in the evening. The next morning there's a boat parade with traditional vessels decorated with flowers followed by folk dancing and flag-throwing competitions. The festival occurs on the weekend closest to St. John's Day in late June.

RATES AND PACKAGES
Rates vary seasonally; single rooms start around $400, and a double deluxe room with a lake view starts from about $840. The Beauty and Relax package includes a three-night stay in an executive room, two three-course meals, three spa treatments, and use of the fitness center (starting around $1,420; *www.villadeste.it*).

ONE CLICK AND YOU'RE OFF
For information on traveling in Italy, try *www.enit.it*.

India

Many images come to mind when thinking about India. In the company of your thoughts on richly colored saris, elephants, gold bangles, swirls of spices, and long sultry nights, add to it a picture of the decadent palaces of the maharajas. Two of them in particular have a special place in my heart. In India, every woman can fulfill her fantasy of being a princess, living in sheer opulence, comfort, and grandeur. A visit to the palace hotels was the closest I'll ever come to being royalty. The Taj Lake Palace resides on an island in the utterly romantic city of Udaipur in the vibrant region of Rajasthan. The Rambagh Palace, located in Jaipur, south of New Delhi, once home for the maharaja of Jaipur, now operates as 85-room luxury hotel. I recommend these two palaces because they are both "over the top" examples of India's legendary past, and you can visit both of them on a loop trip around the colorful region of Rajasthan .

To make sure your sultry royal days don't turn too steamy, opt for traveling to India's palaces between October and March. Spring is also a terrific time to visit for those in search of lively festivals; during Udaipur's Gangaur Festival, you'll find women with henna-painted hands sending off springtime prayers to find a mate (if you're single, it can't hurt, right?) or for the health and longevity of their husbands (if married, some of us need all the prayers we can get). And then there's the coinciding Mewar Festival, which brims with traditional and vibrant processions, songs, dances, and fireworks. (See Chapter One: Exotic Escapes for more about this region).

☞ TAJ LAKE PALACE ☜

The memories you'll take home with you from the Taj Lake Palace will include the strain of sitar music, floating on a royal barge, gardens chock-full of hibiscus and fountains, and the twinkling lights along the shoreline that emerge as the sun sets on this lovely island estate. Built in 1746 by Maharaja Jagat Singh II, this oasis was rumored to be the maharaja's pleasure hideaway in Lake Pichola after his father forbade him from throwing moonlight picnics at nearby Jag Mandir. Now, this elegant white marble spectacle (which was the setting for much of the James Bond movie *Octopussy*) welcomes you with 83 rooms, including 18 opulent suites. After flying into Udaipur, you can have a chauffeur drive you through the city for a glimpse of its markets, forts, and city museum, or have him sweep past the city's other lakeside palaces. Once you arrive at Taj Lake Palace, the descendants of the royal butlers await you, ready to do anything they can to help you, too, feel like queens.

PALACE LIVING

Perched on a four-acre island, the Taj Lake Palace rewards guests with 360-degree views of the lake (or maybe it's 355-degree). Their suites, especially, which offer amenities like in-room Jacuzzis, vivid silks, and intricately carved wood furniture, even marble bathrooms, are an ultimate escape for those of you who have been in the country for a while roughing it a bit. Guests can opt for personalized yoga instruction, be the audience for traditional puppet shows, exercise in the pool and fitness center, or join a wide range of sightseeing tours in and around Udaipur.

BEST LAKE CRUISES

Historically, the palace's residents held decadent feasts and intimate gatherings on Lake Pichola. You and your girlfriends can re-create this tradition with a dinner cruise on the royal barge, complete with sitar music, traditionally dressed oarsmen, candlelit laughter among friends, and a fireworks grand finale. You'll enjoy authentic Indian food: fresh *chappatis* from a tandoor oven, chicken or lamb kebabs, spicy curries, and fresh vegetable dishes. Or, if a more intimate tête-à-tête with a girlfriend seems better, try a *shikara,* a narrow boat with cushions and bolsters, perfect for sipping champagne and dishing the real dirt. At night, you can lie back and gaze at the stars, smell the jasmine in the warm air, and hear the temple bells ringing.

SPA SPLURGE

Every extravagant treatment at the palace begins with a welcome foot-bath and a cool drink of coconut water. One specialty goes far back in time to bring you comfort in today's world: the Mewar Kas, a ritual that royalty used to prepare themselves for their wedding day. What better occasion than a special girls' trip to do the same. The session commences with a sandalwood and turmeric rice-grain scrub to exfoliate, then ends with an hour-long massage using ayurvedic oils tuned to your needs. Everyone finds something to meet her taste: coconut scrubs, pedicures, an Indian head massage. You might just have to spend the whole day here learning which one is your favorite.

ROLL IN STYLE

Ladies, hire one of the Taj Palace's vintage cars and have the chauffeur escort you around the streets of Udaipur to visit leather shops with handmade shoes, fabric stores with silk bedspreads, and art galleries with tiny Mogul miniature paintings, stationery, or handmade puppets.

HISTORY LESSONS

The Taj Lake Palace's more than 250-year past opens up like a book in the company of a hotel tour guide, who will take you through the historic buildings making up the complex. You can also get recommendations for educational walks throughout Udaipur—plus you can typically extract from them directions and clever tips to navigating its best markets. (For more about Udaipur, flip back to Chapter One: Exotic Escapes.)

DINE LIKE A QUEEN
Prior to what will be a feast, visit the palace's Amrit Sagar, the "sea of nectar" bar, which pours fine French, Australian, California, and New Zealand wines, as well as an Indian wine. Yes, you read correctly—Indian wine is produced in vineyards near Bombay. Try it! Each night you'll choose from one of several restaurants—the Neel Kamal is known for its Rajasthani cuisine in an elegant setting filled with gilded arches, crystal, and sumptuous upholstery. The Indian food is fabulous, and the chef will invite you into the kitchen to observe the preparation of meat marinades from local spices and the grilling of tandoori meats. I'll never forget the lemongrass crème brulée for dessert. A group of you will want to request at least once that the royal butlers set you up with your own personal feast by the lily pond, in your room, or nearly anywhere else you can imagine on these gorgeous grounds.

RATES AND PACKAGES
Rates vary depending on the season: during low season from $355, during high season from $533, which is May to October. There are special summertime packages, available from Taj Hotels, which include breakfast and discounts at the spa. Summer is hot but not humid, and it's also a great time to visit (*www.tajhotels.com*).

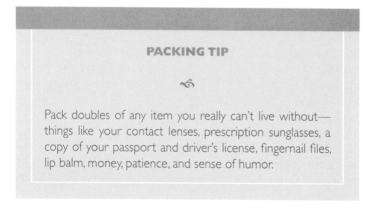

PACKING TIP

Pack doubles of any item you really can't live without—things like your contact lenses, prescription sunglasses, a copy of your passport and driver's license, fingernail files, lip balm, money, patience, and sense of humor.

Known as the Jewel of Jaipur, the 85-room Rambagh Palace, located in Rajasthan, was once the home of the maharaja of Jaipur. In fact it was the home of the royal family until 1957. A flight or private car will carry you the 200-plus miles northeast from Udaipur, or you can travel four hours by car from Delhi.

PALACE LIVING

Rooms in the palace vary, but they are all sumptuously appointed, with thick silk drapes, marble bathrooms, and comfortable beds. Highlights of the palace are its 47 acres of lush Mughal Gardens and the Chandni Chowk courtyard, with its beautiful fountain. If you're lucky, you may spot brightly colored peacocks strutting through the grounds.

DO AS THE ROYALS DID

Also a wonder is the Suvarna Mahal, Rambagh Palace's dining hall, where you'll be swept through the long, mirrored hall by liveried waiters to your table beneath frescoes and crystal chandeliers. You'll indulge on selections from the original menus of several of India's royal houses. Immerse yourselves in another regal hobby: Polo, which is pretty popular in this former Commonwealth country. Over cocktails at the swanky Polo Bar, you'll be surrounded by the maharaja's polo memorabilia.

SPA TREATS

The Rambagh's spa opened in April 2007 and is the perfect place to cool off during those famously hot Indian days. If you're feeling like you've gotten more than your share of India's golden sun, try a Chandana treatment. The sandalwood and aloe will cool your skin under an organic linen wrap. Other refreshing options: the indoor and outdoor pools, both with intricate blue tiling, or the copper tubs, showers, and air-conditioned lounge area in your own spa hideaway.

RATES AND PACKAGES

The Rambagh Palace offers three-night spa packages, including several treatments, starting at $680 per night between June and September. During high season, October to April, a luxury room starts at $585 (*www.tajhotels.com*).

ONE CLICK AND YOU'RE OFF

For more about India, refer to my recommendations in Chapter One: Exotic Escapes and the information found at *www.incredibleindia.org*.

CHAPTER SEVEN

Expand Your Mind

It's not always easy to go out on a limb in your daily life, to enter-tain a fantasy, or to learn something entirely new. But traveling to another country can free you up or give you the impetus to do these things. Through learning trips and adult education pro-grams, you can become intimately acquainted with a country, learn a new language, hone your artistic skills, or pick up a new sport (sea kayaking, perhaps?). Invite your girlfriends to join you for a class on the other side of the world. After all, learning is always more fun when you're doing it in an uncompetitive environment, laughing with your girlfriends, and sharing the experience with them. There are tons of programs all over the world to choose from, programs that last anywhere from a day to a month. And when you return from these immersions, you and your girlfriends will share skills and knowledge that you can bring with you on your next group journey.

For the past ten years, Sandra has painted her passion, in summer classes from Edinburgh to Glasgow, and Assisi to Salzburg. She selects a city, finds a class, and dives into the experience for a week or more. "I'm not a tour person," she says, "and I greatly prefer a vacation where I learn something and get a new perspective on myself, my painting, and the world. I like to stay in dorms, get to know the locals, and take classes that aren't taught by Americans."

Sandra isn't a novice European traveler. In her 20s, she lived in Germany for six years, first as a student, then working abroad, and finally marrying and living there. For many years after, she returned to the Continent for her vacation. "Prague was on my list for a long, long time," she says. "Last year, I searched online and found an 'arts immersion vacation' offered by Artbreak and started to email the director, a Ph.D. sociologist. This was exactly what I had been looking for. And I took off for Prague six months later."

Students began each day at the studio working in different media with local artists. Sandra sculpted a clay figurine of a woman, another day she created a collage, and many days she painted with oils—not the usual watercolors she uses at home. These artistic exercises with different media—getting her out of her comfort zone—and the instruction from seasoned local artists, helped Sandra bring to her painting a fresh perspective and a renewed confidence.

In the afternoon, they visited museums with art historians and toured the historic and architectural highlights of Prague with a local expert. Late in the afternoon they would visit a private art gallery, go wine- or sherry-tasting, and then have dinner, often at a traditional Czech tavern. After dinner, for six nights, they attended a symphony, a modern dance performance, a concert at Prague's art-deco masterpiece Municipal House, a ballet, an opera, and a jazz club. "We walked to classes and went everywhere with public transportation," Sandra explains. "It was so easy in Prague."

What might sound to some like a pretty demanding schedule was actually just what Sandra was hoping for. And she wasn't alone. "Like me, the other students were well traveled and open to new experiences, and they weren't professional artists," says Sandra. They, too, signed on for the class to jump-start their creativity and to get to know Prague's art world.

"Prague is now on my list of absolute favorite cities," adds Sandra. "The people are so friendly. In the week I studied in Prague, I had absolutely no bad experiences, and I came home with my painting having evolved. The talented instructors and the rich art scene there have gone on to inspire me back at home to approach my art in new ways. I'd like to return with my daughter and granddaughter, because it's such a magical city in that way."

❧ England ❧

If you wish you'd had a classic Ivy League college experience—or you're feeling nostalgic for the one you did have—a fix may be a summer at England's fabled University of Cambridge, which hosts International Summer Schools. Cambridge, about 60 miles north of London, is one of the oldest and most respected universities in the world, having taught the likes of Sir Isaac Newton and John Milton. It operates under the college system, which breaks the large university down into 31 smaller colleges. The ivy-strewn walls, gorgeous architecture (such as the Gothic chapel of King's College), expansive lawns, and medieval bridges and turrets are an inspiring backdrop for those seeking knowledge. And who better to recruit for this higher learning mission than your closest girlfriends? You'll boost each other's confidence and be there as support while you settle into being students again. Summer courses range from interdisciplinary programs combining arts and sciences to concentrated art, history, and literature classes. With about 160 classes to choose from, you and the girls will each find something you love—and then get together for a pint at the end of each day and swap stories and fun facts. On warm days, students swarm the green lawns along the banks of the River Cam, picnicking under droopy weeping willows and kissing on benches in the shade. A great way to pass the afternoon is to rent a boat called a "cam" and try to navigate your way up and down the shallow river using a long pole to push against the bottom, while you stand upright balancing in the middle of the flat-bottomed, narrow, unsteady boat. The school also does a good job of keeping you busy with field trips in the surrounding area. When you're at Cambridge, you won't need a car—you can easily navigate by foot and public transport, and taxis are readily available. On your own, you'll discover the area's used bookstores and welcoming taverns. And the train ride to London is about an hour; to the city of Bath, and its famed hot springs, it's about three and a half hours; and to visit your new rivals at Oxford, it's less than three hours.

In college, I was always overwhelmed with the number of course choices—it's the same feeling as being at a wonderful restaurant where every dish on the menu looks equally delicious. Here's a hint to help you narrow down your options if you're considering summer school. You have two options for summer school at Cambridge: two weeks in July at the Cambridge Summer Study Programme, and the more rigorous ten-day to three-week sessions at the International Summer School, which are geared to serious students who want to concentrate their studies on two or three courses.

A LIGHT CLASS SCHEDULE

The two-week Cambridge Summer Study Programme (CSSP), held in Downing College each July, is mainly made up of middle-age international professionals from 20 to 30 countries. Here you can hand-pick courses that steep you in British literature, history, and art. This program keeps drawing people back—nearly half are return students. And dorm life will be much better than you remember: Peaceful Downing College, with a grand neoclassic forecourt and expansive lawns, immerses CSSP students in an elegant scholarly setting.

CSSP classes are composed of small group seminars (a maximum of 15) with classes in the mornings and the occasional afternoon. Among your course selections is a program on British World War I literature—you'll study fiction, letters, diaries, and films by and about those on the battlefields and the home front as well. Another course delves into myth, magic, and medicine in Anglo-Saxon England. Or perhaps you'd like to study revolutions from 1678 to 1759—a fascinating perspective on political upheaval in the British Isles. Architecture buffs will be thrilled by the course on castles and churches of the Middle Ages. No matter what you choose, field trips go hand-in-hand with classroom time. And while the program will provide a reading list for you to polish up on your chosen subject before you arrive, homework while you're at Cambridge is nonexistent. Which means you'll never have to forego a night in the pub to cram. Classes, lodging, breakfasts, and dinners are included in the CSSP program cost (starting at $4,828 per person; *www.cont-ed.cam .ac.uk/intsummer/cssp*).

A HEAVY CLASS SCHEDULE

International Summer School (ISS) is designed for students who would like to get credit for their studies, are willing to attend four to seven hours of class each day, do homework and write papers in the

Avoid overweight charges. Two pieces of luggage are permitted on overseas flights. The weight limit is calculated per bag, and most international airlines now charge extra for suitcases weighing more than 50 pounds. Always check with your specific airline to find out the exact weight limit before your flight. If you are traveling with only one bag, and you fear it might be overweight, pack a small duffel bag in the outside pocket of your suitcase. At the airport, if you've exceeded the weight limit, you can pull out the duffel and shift some of your heaviest items to it, and then check both bags.

—Marybeth

---

subjects of history, Shakespeare, literature, science, art history, and medieval studies. The term ranges from ten days to three weeks; you may combine different classes, and you may opt out of taking courses for credit. For those not staying on campus, academic studies only range from $1,217 to $2,446. Accommodation, meal, and tuition fees range from $2,048 to $5,988 (*www.cont-ed.cam.ac.uk/intsummer*).

TGIF

You're not really going to study all weekend, are you? Not in a classroom, anyway. School-led excursions can take you deeper into England—past trips have included Kew Gardens, performances of Shakespeare at The Globe, Windsor Castle, and the Queen's Estate at Sandringham. You and the girls will also want to plan your own trips to London's museums and theaters as well as to the Roman spas of Bath.

CAMPUS TOUR

Download a walking tour of the campus onto your iPod; plug in and get an introduction to the grounds of your new school and the city (*www.stridedesign.net/shapewalks*).

EXTRACURRICULAR ACTIVITIES

Don't miss punting on the River Cam—a ride in a stable, flat-bottomed boat. This is a sport without paddles or oars. Everyone on the shore watches the neophytes do their best impression of a gondolier in anticipation of a boat tipping and sending its load into the river. It's not as easy as it looks. So I suggest you hire a good-looking young Cambridge student to take you and your girlfriends down a mile-long stretch known as the Backs. You'll glide past eight of Cambridge's colleges and row beneath nine bridges for a unique architectural tour of the campus—be sure to pause by the King's College chapel, completed in 1547, and the covered Bridge of Sighs (for more on self-hire punts, *www.scudamores.co.uk*). Another afternoon treat: English tea at the university's Madingley Hall, a lovely 16th-century country house three miles west of Cambridge surrounded by flowers, meadows, and topiary gardens.

SCHOOL SUPPLIES
Browse the bookshops on Trinity Street. With new, rare, and used bookshops, you'll likely find exactly what you're looking for or stumble on the perfect summer reading. You and your friends can shop together and then trade books among yourselves as you finish them.

EVENTS TO FLY IN FOR
One thing you're sure to appreciate about being in a college town is the arts scene. In July and early August, the Cambridge Summer Music Festival sets the night to music, with evening chamber concerts, quartets, and soloists appearing in several venues (tickets from $16; *www.cambridgesummermusic.com*). At the Cambridge Shakespeare Festival, outdoor performances of the bard's best plays are staged in July and August—you might be able to catch *A Midsummer's Night Dream* outdoors on a midsummer's night (*www .cambridgeshakespeare.com*). Movie buffs will want to plan their trip around July's 11-day Cambridge Film Festival, which screens new flicks indoors and out, holds Q&As with actors and directors, plus lectures and workshops (*www.cambridgefilmfestival.org.uk*).

BEST DINING
Throughout your stay, you'll get breakfast and dinner daily in the historic dining halls; the college Buttery is a hit with hungry students at lunchtime. Off-campus, Cambridge—or much of England, for that

---

Create your own first-class amenity kit for long-haul flights. In a Ziploc bag, pack earplugs, an eye mask, a pair of socks, lip balm, a small bottle of fragrant hand cream, a travel toothbrush, toothpaste, and your favorite chocolate bar.

—Marybeth

matter—isn't exactly known for its cuisine, but a few high-end spots are worth the splurge for a superlative meal. If you've got a special occasion to celebrate, make a reservation at Midsummer House, a French-Mediterranean restaurant spread across a lovely Victorian villa and an airy conservatory. It's one of only a handful of British restaurants to garner two Michelin stars and their "taste of midsummer" tasting menu lives up to the honor, which includes plates of artisanal cheeses, sautéed scallops, and foie gras (three-course prix-fixe lunch for $52, three-course prix-fixe dinner for $99; *www.midsummerhouse.co.uk*). For cuisine that's easier on the wallet, try newcomer Alimentum—featuring French cuisine with a touch of Italian and Spanish flair, all with fresh, seasonal ingredients. It serves a wonderful prix-fixe lunch and dinner, along with à la carte options (prix fixe about $35; *www.restaurantalimentum.co.uk*). If you're in need of some hearty food after walking all over campus or returning from a day trip, the Conservatory Brasserie in the Arundel House Hotel serves tasty sausages, Yorkshire pudding, and thick-crusted breads (*www.arundelhousehotels.co.uk*).

ONE CLICK AND YOU'RE OFF

For information on the University of Cambridge's International Summer Schools, visit *www.cont-ed.cam.ac.uk/intsummer*; Cambridge tourism is at *www.visitcambridge.org*.

The Baltic Countries

Considered by many sophisticated travelers as the most dynamic tourist destination in Europe today, the Baltic countries of Estonia, Poland, and Russia promise a hands-on European history lesson. You and your girlfriends will enjoy learning about the history as well as the phenomenal and rapid changes in these countries in the past decade. The occupying Russian military forces are gone; the long lines at poorly stocked groceries and bureaucratic banks have disappeared, replaced by fresh produce at outdoor markets and ATM machines. And instead of silent, somber people shuffling down streets, laughter, music, and excited conversations on cell phones are heard in every city. Most of all, you will feel like you're experiencing the social and political evolution of the Baltic countries as it takes place. Elderhostel is renowned for its learning and traveling trips around the globe for folks over 55 years of age. On their Northern Capitals program, you'll take a spin through the capital cities of the countries lining the shores of the Baltic Sea, including Copenhagen, Stockholm, St. Petersburg, and ports in Estonia and Poland. Your home base for this 17-night tour is the cruise ship M.V. *Discovery*. Some days you'll be at sea, and some days disembark in a city. On the mornings before you enter a port, you'll have "classroom time," during which an Elderhostel tour leader (retired Cambridge professors, British Broadcast Company [BBC] lecturers, and international archaeologists and Viking experts) will fill you in on the history of your destination. That afternoon, a local guide will introduce you to historic sites as well as modern daily life. To make the most of the Baltic region's long summer nights, this Elderhostel trip runs in May, late June, and early July. The light-sky nights and warm weather encourage plenty of open-air festivals, alfresco dining, and people-watching late into the evening. And there's music everywhere.

YOUR SHIP
You may feel an instant kinship with the M.V. *Discovery*—its sister ship was the *Pacific Princess* (aka *The Love Boat*). But don't worry, you won't

CRUISING THE BALTIC

∽

I selected a study cruise to the Baltic Sea because it's an area of Europe I didn't know much about; Estonia, Russia, Sweden, Denmark, Poland, and northern Germany. I wanted to learn more about my Swedish ancestry, Viking history, and the Hanseatic League—the largest trade organization in northern Europe in the 1400s.

The Baltic is a wonderful place to visit in the summer because it's relatively cool, dry, and not crowded. Best of all are the long, long days—it is light until after 11 p.m. One evening we went to see *Swan Lake* at the St. Petersburg Ballet, and then returned to the ship for an open-air Russian Buffet accompanied by an orchestra playing Russian folksongs and Russian classic music.

—Judy Sanford, 70s, History Buff, Northern California

be stuck in out-of-date digs. The recently refurbished cruise ship, which can hold 650 passengers, mixes modern amenities like art galleries and Internet access with old-world charm like wooden decks.

SEA SCHOOL

Your on-board professor, Poul Erik Kandrup, was once a member of the Danish National Commission for UNESCO, and he attracts quite a following—past shipmates have said they'd follow him anywhere in the world. He'll give you a crash course on Baltic countries and cultures, from the early days of the Vikings to the modern Russian economy to Lutheran, Jewish, and Russian Orthodox religions. In-class discussion is welcome. The ship's crew conducts separate lectures that you're more than welcome to attend as well. If you miss one, you can always catch the rebroadcast on your in-room TV.

A BOATLOAD OF FUN

You and the gals will have a ball during your days at sea on the M.V. *Discovery*. Only about 40 of the 650 or so passengers are part of the Elderhostel program, so you'll get the best of the small group in personalized lectures and city tours, plus socializing with *all* your shipmates over Swedish meatballs and crepes in the Seven Continents Restaurant. On board, immerse yourself in the ongoing bridge competitions (and instruction, if you need tips) or catch a flick with the gals in the movie theater. Check out the well-stocked library for additional research into your destination or the perfect summer page-turner. If you want solitude, slip on your starlet sunglasses and soak in one of two open-air Jacuzzis, or indulge in a massage and facial. In the evenings, take in a shipboard show and dance the night away in the cruise ship's Night Club (or in front of the orchestra in the Carousel Lounge).

SCANDINAVIAN SIGHTS

Your first three stops take you to the capital cities of Denmark, Sweden, and Finland (in that order). All three are water's-edge and walkable cities. In Copenhagen, Scandinavia's largest capital, which sits on the island of Sealand and is known for its architectural diversity, you'll see charming 17th-century gabled houses along Nyhavn Canal, as well as the remains of a tower built in the 1200s abutting the latest in modern architecture. You'll start the day with a stroll around the cathedral, university, and synagogue of this charming, pedestrian-friendly city. At night, you'll hit Tivoli Gardens, a small, clean, old-fashioned amusement park with floral displays, theaters, symphony music, and fireworks. The wooden roller coaster actually employs a brakeman. Then in Stockholm, a city built on 14 islands, you'll explore glorious swaths of green parks and neighborhoods, learn about medieval architecture, and join the city's fashionistas in shopping and dining in the trendy Södermalm District. For a brush with genius, you'll stop in to peer at the golden mosaics at City Hall, where the Nobel Prize banquet is held each year. Your next stop, Helsinki, is a youngster by European standards (the city was founded in the mid-16th century, whereas Copenhagen and Stockholm date back to 1167 and 1252, respectively). The city, with its prime view of the Gulf of Finland and surrounding islands, will impress you with its neoclassic architecture and also its attractive parks and squares. Market Square is a good place to buy gifts for your family back home; vendors sell souvenirs, produce, and silvery fish from the Baltic Sea.

NEXT STOP, RUSSIA

When you arrive in the seaside city of St. Petersburg, the ornate churches and the white domes with glowing gold, greens, and yellows will take your breath away. One of the highlights of your three-day visit to St. Petersburg is The Hermitage, an enormous museum with more than three million works of art from the Stone Age to the present. During your stay, you'll also attend the ballet and explore St. Petersburg's residential areas on the underground Metro; experience traditional Russian music and dancing over a multicourse lunch at Podvorje, a renowned restaurant, and visit the stately palaces and parks of Tsarskoye Selo, once the summer residence of Russian royals.

SMALLER PORT TOWNS

After St. Petersburg, you'll delve deeper into Europe and have the chance to explore cities that many visitors to Europe don't see. In Tallinn, the capital of Estonia (which only gained independence from Russia in 1991), you'll learn about the country's tumultuous history while eating lunch on a onetime collective farm. You'll visit the Estonian and Estonian-Russian suburbs, where you can even meet with local students to learn more about daily life. In Poland's Gdansk, you'll find a beautiful Old Town, a fascinating Solidarity Museum (former Polish president Lech Walesa began his activism here), and great food—you won't want to miss the 15-plus varieties of pierogi (potato dumplings) at Pierogarnia u Dzika. You'll also visit

Lübeck, Germany, where you can stroll narrow, cobblestone streets while sampling marzipan, one of the city's sweet specialties.

END OF THE LINE
Your ship docks in Harwich, England, but that doesn't mean your journey must end. You'll be whisked off to London to stay at the City Inn Westminster, near the banks of the River Thames and next door to the Tate Britain museum (art lovers, rejoice!). You and your group can plan ahead to catch the latest show in the West End's theaters.

WHAT'S INCLUDED
Classes, ship accommodations, and meals ($5,684 for 16 days; 800-454-5768, *www.elderhostel.org*).

ONE CLICK AND YOU'RE OFF
For travel planning tips and more information about each country, visit *www.cruisebaltic.com*.

❧ Czech Republic ❧

Have you secretly always wanted to drop everything, jet off to Europe, and live the artist's life? Or are you an experienced painter interested in refining your technique? Wherever you fit in the spectrum, art school in Prague, one of Europe's most beautiful cities, will provide the inspiration for your artistic pursuits. The painters, sculptors, and potters in your circle of friends will come to see Prague as their muse. The capital of the Czech Republic and the heart of Bohemia, Prague inspires you on first sight: The skyline has a fascinating blend of architectural styles and lovingly restored buildings, from Gothic to ornate baroque to striking art nouveau. The winding cobblestone streets connect cafés, antiques shops, and bookstores. City vistas from the Charles Bridge and the impressive Prague Castle alone might stir a new work of art in you. Prague is a city for pedestrians, and it is best explored on foot, at a slow pace. Central Prague is small and manageable by foot or trolley car. I stayed just below the castle, and about six minutes' walk from Charles Bridge. My daughters and I walked through elegant neighborhoods of baroque buildings to the river, across the spectacular Charles Bridge to all the major sites in the Old Town. At night, we took note of the warm light of the old gas lamps along the moon-silvered river, and discerned the old

As a teacher, I had summers off, so I have studied history, creative writing, music, dance, and languages in Rome, Prague, and Havana. I did the program in Rome through Loyola University in Chicago, and the one in Prague was through West Michigan University. Educational programs give you a reason to dig into a culture, put down roots, and discover a place at a slower pace. I also liked the safety and social aspects of living in a dorm with other international students.

—Kelly Westhoff, 31, Former Teacher, Writer,
Plymouth, Minnesota

timbered beer halls, the shimmering slate towers, and pastel-colored baroque buildings. I closed my eyes and thought Prague could almost be Paris—Paris in the 1920s.

To aid in your artistic transformation, sign on with Artbreak, an all-women's arts immersion program that offers daily art classes, private gallery tours, nights on the town, and lodging in a hotel decked with modern art. Fittingly, Prague's weather acts like a temperamental artist with serious mood swings: Spring and summer tend to be the sunniest months but the period between May and August is the rainiest, so be prepared for sunny days interspersed with rain. Snow is rare in Prague during the winter.

TAKE YOUR PICK

Artbreak's immersion vacations are all about women—participants in their 40s and 50s from across the globe. Students meet for three-hour art classes in the mornings from Monday through Friday at Muddum Art Space, a gallery, workshop, and café. Choose from plein air painting, ceramics, collage, sculpture, and more. The classes are small, and usually four teachers are on hand to guide you. There's no need to come with any previous experience—or even paintbrushes.

LEARN FROM THE BEST

Your guides on this artistic immersion are all talents in their respective fields—and all women. Prague native Klara Dodds, who founded the Muddum Art Space in 2004, will escort you into the world of ceramics and collage. Russian artist Tatiana Irbis has produced 40 theatrical performances as a stage producer and designer; at Artbreak she teaches painting and life drawing. A college-level art-history instructor,

British instructor Natasha Sutta, will guide you through Prague's galleries. She's not only an authority on 19th-century Czech painting, but a master of Chinese brush painting as well.

AFTERNOONS ON THE TOWN

As part of the Artbreak experience, you'll visit private galleries and attend wine tastings under the wing of a guide—a fantastic way to explore the city with a little inside help. Your guide will also take you on a shopping excursion and an informative tour through Prague's Old Jewish Quarter and the Old Town area. Come evening, you may break off from the group to sip sherry with some of your fellow artists in cafés or bars.

SMART DINING

Your meals are not included in your program fee, but Artbreak happily recommends local restaurants to their students. That said, I'll go ahead and make my own suggestion as well. Since 1902, Café Louvre has been a meeting ground for high minds—both Albert Einstein and Franz Kafka patronized this traditional Prague coffeehouse. Hold your own intellectual debates over coffee and warm apple strudel, and when the topics get too heated, share a Chateaubriand steak for two, with three sauces, for $27 (*www.cafelouvre.cz/en*). Café Louvre can get smoky; be sure to ask for a table in the nonsmoking area.

BEST BEER BREAK

Beer lovers and history buffs converge at the Strahov Monastery Brewery. This former monastery was founded in 1140 by King Vladislav, and its monks may have started brewing as early as the 13th century. In the brewpub and restaurant, sample local light and dark beers while filling up on traditional, hearty fare—beer cheese on toast, Bohemian potato soup, and goulash (*www.klasterni-pivovar.cz*).

CULTURAL HIGHLIGHTS

Artbreak's evening activities include nights at the symphony, ballet, opera, and jazz clubs. You and the girls can sign on for as many of these outings as you have the energy for. The Czech Philharmonic Orchestra has played around the world, from Carnegie Hall to Tokyo, and made award-winning classical recordings. It will be a real treat for you and your friends to be able to listen to them play at their home theater. The orchestra's long tradition of fine music has been with it from the beginning—composer Antonín Dvořák conducted the orchestra's first performance in 1896. Starting around nine at night, groove to live music at the legendary Reduta Jazz Club. It's one of Prague's oldest jazz clubs, and since 1958 it's been the place to hear incredible musicians and see familiar faces—Bill Clinton once played the sax here, so who knows who you might see.

YOUR LODGING

The program includes lodging at the Art Hotel, a four-star hotel in the residential Letna district, a short walk from Old Town Square and the Prague Castle. To help keep you inspired while you're outside of the studio, Czech modern art from the owners' private collection decorates the wall. If you and the gals are thinking of staying in Prague for longer than a week, a short-term apartment rental is your best bet (from $100 a night for two to six people; *www.rentinprague.com*). I rented an antiques-filled apartment, with oil paintings on the walls and a shared bathroom and laundry facilities in a quiet neighborhood filled with embassies (from $75 a night; 800-860-0571, *www.castlesteps.com*). In terms of neighborhoods to stay in, I also recommend Letna in Prague 7, Old Town Prague, or Vinohrady in Prague 2. The latter is a well-off residential spot where you'll find ex-pats who came to Prague and never left. You never know, the same could happen to you. Skip the area of Prague 1, filled with pubs, bars, and hostels, where the nonstop noise will keep you up at night.

DO IT YOURSELF

If you'd like to arrange your own customized artistic girlfriends' journey (apart from Artbreak), you can take pottery and ceramics classes on your own through Muddum Art Space. Muddum offers an adult pottery class the last Saturday of the month. Some classes focus on specific subjects, like teapot- or vase-making, ($20 a class; *www.muddum.cz/eng*).

Once a summer, the Prague Academy of Fine Arts hosts a ten-day intensive workshop with drawing, painting, and sculpture instruction. These all-day classes allow you to fully focus on your work. You'll have a turn at several disciplines during your time (about $343 for classes; *www.avu.cz/en*). If you opt for this workshop, renting an apartment will be cheaper than staying in a hotel.

EVENTS TO FLY IN FOR

If music's your thing, time this trip to the Prague Spring International Music Festival, a classical music extravaganza held in May. The literary artists among you should consider a visit in June for the Prague

Writers Festival—you'll catch both book buzz and the streets of Prague filling with summer students and international travelers. And crisp fall air, the opera, and symphony kick into high gear in September.

WHAT'S INCLUDED

Artbreak's program includes six nights' hotel accommodation, art classes, tours, and evening activities (starting at $2,600; *www.artbreak.org*).

ONE CLICK AND YOU'RE OFF

For more on Prague, visit *www.pragueexperience.com*.

Canada

Making a trip out of an international film festival is the ideal vacation for ladies who love the silver screen. Not a school, perhaps, a film festival is still a place to learn: You can gain an understanding of the art from actors and directors, watch various genres of new movies, and explore the host city's neighborhoods, shops, and museums. Maybe you're a sucker for the craft of filmmaking, maybe you just like the red-carpet fashion glitz. The Cannes International Film Festival is paramount, but it's nearly impossible to get tickets or navigate the crowds. The Toronto Film Festival, held each September, is far less overwhelming, easier to get to, and just as exciting. The city of Toronto, on the northwestern shore of Lake Ontario (Niagara Falls is less than a two-hour drive away), combines all the things I love about Canada—safe, welcoming neighborhoods with friendly locals who are far too modest about their dynamite cosmopolitan city. But it's also surprisingly diverse: You'll find Greek, Italian, and Indian hot spots, and hear more than a hundred languages and dialogues spoken by residents strolling along the tree-lined streets. Toronto is a big city composed of diverse little neighborhoods that are easy to explore on foot.

Don't miss Little Italy, a chic and trendy, ethnically diverse district filled with outdoor cafés, restaurants, bars, and small boutiques along College Street. The streets are jammed in the summer and on good-weather weekends, so sip an espresso and people watch at one of the outdoor patios.

The narrow streets around Kensington Market are filled with bicyclists, local shoppers, and foodies searching for inexpensive cheeses, fresh fruits, vegetables, sweets and eclectic gourmet products. Sample regional cheeses at a food stall, relax in an upscale café, or dine at one of the many trendy restaurants.

Toronto is a short jaunt by plane or even car from many parts of the United States, and once you're there, you'll find an easy-to-navigate subway, bus, and streetcar system. The ten-day film festival has events throughout downtown—with a lot of the excitement centered on Bloor and Bay Streets. Bloor Street is known as Toronto's Fifth Avenue because of the number of high-class shops, and Bay Street is lined by upscale shops, restaurants, and hotels. You'll see movies by first-time and seasoned Canadian filmmakers and, if you buy your tickets early enough, you may catch high-profile premieres of both international and North American films (in 2007, the People's Choice Award went to the thriller *Eastern Promises* with Viggo Mortensen).

GETTING TICKETS

Tickets go on sale in early July—check the festival's website early in the month of July to jump on the tickets to the films you want to see. If you buy ticket packages or passes in advance (both of which give you entry to multiple films), you'll have first choice of movies when the film schedule is released, in August. You can order tickets online (*www.tiffg.ca*), by phone (877-968-3456), or in person at the box office at Manulife Centre downtown. If you're a Visa card member, ticket passes and packages are available to you a week before they go on sale to the general public. One of the best ways to see the festival with friends is the 10-Film Package (about $166). For films people will be talking about, invest in the Gala package (about $350), with eight premieres (and the stars that accompany them). Same-day tickets are sometimes available if you're a fly-by-the-seat-of-your-pants type of gal.

SHOP TILL YOU DROP

Hit the historic Bloor-Yorkville district for boutiques. You'll find familiar names like Prada and Gucci as well as Canadian favorites like Harry Rosen. The posh restaurants are perfect for ladies' lunches and celebrity sightings. Bargain shoppers will want to hit Chinatown for discounts on porcelain, teas, and more. Find deals on the latest from local designers in the Fashion District along Spadina Avenue. Women with a penchant for trendy little shops will feel at home in Kensington Market, a multicultural neighborhood with cute independently owned boutiques and unique cafés.

LAUGH OUT LOUD

Chicago's renowned Second City theater company has a branch in downtown Toronto. Head over to the theater for a night of live comedy—Canadian-style. Sketch comedy is Second City's hallmark (*www.secondcity.com*).

FINE DINING

The swanky Bymark, with its extensive wine cellar and an airy, gallery-like setting, creates a special and fun evening out. (You can reserve a private room here for a special celebratory evening with girlfriends.) Indulge in their signature Bymark Burger—an eight-ounce patty with porcini mushrooms, Brie, and truffle shavings, plus a side of onion rings and truffle aioli to share with friends (main dishes from $38; *www.bymark.ca*).

BEST PICNIC

Head to the family-owned Cheese Boutique, which was featured on The Food Network, for plenty of free samples to help you select from

HOW TO FIND A LANGUAGE SCHOOL

౪

I wanted to improve my Spanish, but I didn't know how to find a good, affordable Spanish study program. Limiting my search to Guatemala, I did an Internet search for "Spanish Language School/Guatemala" and reviewed all the websites I found. I wrote to the schools, asking for a list of references. Then I emailed past students. I asked about the schools and the host families. They were very honest with me. After all, if you've had a fabulous travel experience, you love to talk about it, and if you had a bad experience, you want to warn others. I learned which schools to avoid. My advice is to email for references.

—Kelly Westhoff, 31, Former Teacher, Writer,
Plymouth, Minnesota

their huge array of exotic artisanal cheeses and other goodies. Add to your basket treats like Turkish figs and chocolates, and then take your finds to nearby High Park for a gourmet picnic among friends (*www.cheeseboutique.com*).

WHERE TO STAY
Several hotels can be found in proximity to the festival's venues that offer discounts for festival-goers. Sutton Place, on Bay Street, has a film-festival package that includes three nights' accommodation, two tickets to the Closing Night Gala, and six tickets for films of your choice (starting at $1,234; 866-378-8866, *www.toronto.suttonplace.com*). The Hotel Intercontinental Toronto is located in the heart of the exclusive Yorkville neighborhood, right across the street from the Royal Ontario Museum and close to art galleries. Canada's Fashion Mile, located on Bloor Street, begins just steps from the hotel's front doors (starting around $200; 800-267-0010, *www.toronto.intercontinental.com*).

ONE CLICK AND YOU'RE OFF
For festival information, visit www.tiffg.ca. General information on Toronto can be found at *www.torontotourism.com*.

∂ Denmark ∿

The International People's College is a Scandinavian concept that dates back to the 1800s, when Danish philosopher and social reformer N. F. S. Grundtvig decided that learning should be a practical, life-long process and should be open to all and free for all Danes. The diversity of the school's curriculum and students has changed since the late 19th century. These days, the International People's College in Elsinore (also known as Helsingør)—about an hour on a north-bound coastal train from Copenhagen—attracts all types: Japanese, Chinese, Palestinian, Israeli, African, and Russian students. And the teachers are just as diverse, hailing from Lebanon to Mexico. They present captivating lectures and leading intellectual discussions that can spill into hours spent at a local coffee shop. Courses range in subject from human rights to European history to world politics—and are offered in three-week sessions as well as intensive longer courses (from a semester to a year). The college is located on more than five acres of rolling hills, meadows, and extensive lawns punctuated by a forest and a lake. Elsinore is best known as the setting for Shakespeare's *Hamlet*. (And because of this, it's attracted great actors including Laurence Olivier, Vivien Leigh, John Gielgud, and Kenneth Branagh.) The town is a Danish port city with cobblestone streets, quaint churches, monasteries, theaters, and scads of coffee shops. You'll be amazed at the number of bicyclists you'll see on city streets and country lanes. Denmark is reputed to have more bicycles than people, and cycling doesn't get any better than on the flat, well-maintained roads. Elsinore is on the coast at the eastern end of a 35-mile stretch of beach, but of course this isn't the Caribbean, and the water can get pretty darned cold. If you don't have the polar-bear-club mentality, I don't blame you. Instead stick to sightseeing, shopping, or sipping coffee at an outdoor table with the girls. And with 17-plus hours of daylight during most of June and July, the night always feels young.

CULTURAL CURRICULUM

If you enroll in the autumn or spring term (from 8 to 22 weeks long), you can chose from a myriad of stimulating subjects: analysis of economic trends affecting globalization; world religions; development in former communist countries; an introduction to capitalism in China; the impact of the World Trade Organization (WTO); and, of course, Danish language and culture. If you're short on time, consider the three-week summer course Danish Language, Culture, and Society. Students from all over the world, who don't speak Danish, converge for the two-week classes to learn the basics of the language, as well as Danish art, design, film, and literature and to mingle and exchange ideas with fellow students.

STUDENT LIFE

The international school culture is immersive and group-oriented—probably even more than your school days, because fellow students are from all continents, countries, and cultures of the world. You might find specific classes devoted to leadership skills or group theater projects or debates as part of your courses. During "Human Rights Week" offered during the longer courses of study, you'll learn from movies, documentaries, open forums, and lectures by international professors from European countries. Most of the participants in the programs are in their 20s; however, students range in age from 18 to 80 years old. Two Elderhostel trips to the northern European countries include five days of classes at the college (see below for details).

WHAT'S INCLUDED

All courses, dorm-room accommodations, all meals, sightseeing tours, bike rentals (starting at $1,670 for three weeks, $2,700 for eight weeks, $3,050 for ten weeks. Longer stays are $4,200 for 14 weeks, $4,330 for 18 weeks, and $5,620 for 22 weeks; *www.ipc.dk*).

Elderhostel offers two trips each spring to the northern nations of Norway, Denmark, Sweden and Finland. The "Nordic Nuances" itinerary includes five nights at the International People's College, where you'll study Swedish society, visit local families in their homes and learn about Norway's folk music from musicians in live performances (from $4,474; 800-454-5768, *www.elderhostel.org*).

LOCAL FOOD

If you're heading to the beach for a picnic, stock up on local favorites at a local grocery: artisanal cheese, a traditional *smørrebrød* (open-face sandwich), and, of course, the Danish staple, herring! It's a little touristy, but it's hard to beat Restaurant Ophelia for traditional Danish cuisine. The charming interior showcases photos from international productions of *Hamlet* and other Shakespeare memorabilia (*www.hotelhamlet.dk*).

BEST SIGHTS

The longer courses at International People's College include a five-day tour of many of the highlights of Denmark and Sweden. But if you've signed on for a shorter course, you'll want to explore the area on your own with your friends. An Elsinore must-see is Kronborg Castle, or "Hamlet's Castle," considered one of the most important Renaissance castles in northern Europe with marble fireplaces, ceiling paintings, tapestries, and cannon, pigeon and trumpeter's towers. Look for the graves of Hamlet and Ophelia—a nod to Shakespeare—and then find the statue of the mythic Holger the Dane, in the castle dungeon (*www.kronborgcastle.com*).

On European trips my feet often ache at the end of the day after walking miles on paved sidewalks or cobblestones. In my hotel room, I put a tennis ball under my bare feet and roll it around, massaging the pads, instep, and heel. It's almost as good as having a foot massage!

—Marybeth

EVENTS TO FLY IN FOR

I can't think of a better place in the world to watch a production of *Hamlet*. Lucky for you, in September, Kronborg Castle hosts a Shakespeare festival, where you can watch *Hamlet* performed in the Grand Ballroom, along with ballet, acrobatics and more (*www.hamletsommer.dk*).

GET OUT OF TOWN

Elsinore, once a crucial port town, sits on the sound that separates Denmark and Sweden—take a 20-minute ferry ride, and you're in another country. Before you hop aboard, take a moment at the waterfront to absorb the amazing view of the Swedish coast. Copenhagen, Denmark's capital is less than an hour by train—visit the royal family's home at Fredensborg Castle; if you're there in July when the Queen is away, you can tour the inside.

ONCE CLICK AND YOU'RE OFF

For information on the International People's College in Denmark, visit *www.ipc.dk*. The Denmark tourism site is *www.visitdenmark.com*.

CHAPTER EIGHT

Floating Fantasies

❧ CORY AND LAUREN'S STORY ❧

For her 50th birthday party, Cory wanted to bring together all of the important women in her life for a once-in-a-lifetime trip. She had her heart set on a biking and barge trip in Holland because she loved the idea of cycling through fields of tulips in full bloom, navigating adorable villages, and returning to a hotel barge each night for private, intimate dinners with her closest friends. She asked around, did some research, and discovered an affordable hotel-barge capable of comfortably accommodating 24 guests, equipped with a cook, cycling guide, and bicycles. She sent out an email invitation to her nearest and dearest girlfriends—ladies from her book club, her fellow PTA volunteers, work colleagues, college roommates, and childhood playmates. The deal was this: The first 23 friends to respond would get to join her on a barge in Holland.

When they received the invitation, Cory's pals sprang into action, rearranging their work schedules, doctor appointments, and children's team practices. Their motivation to be on that barge was impressive, to say the least. And in late April, at the peak of the tulip season, 23 of Cory's friends made their way from Australia, England, and all corners of the United States to board a barge in Amsterdam for her biking-and-barge birthday celebration.

While they all knew Cory, many of them didn't know each other. So she made the introductions during an epic 12-course Indonesian Rice Table dinner in Amsterdam. And right then and there, the group made a pact: No one would talk about children or significant others for the whole week. Cory wanted everyone to simply be friends, on the same level—not assuming their roles as mothers, wives, or someone defined by another person.

The birthday party set sail from Amsterdam and cruised on canals in a clockwise loop south into the interior of the country, then west and up the coast to return to Amsterdam—covering what seemed like every inch of this small country. And once they got moving on the water, the girls fell into a rhythm. Every morning after a hearty breakfast, each packed her own picnic from the boat's supply of healthy breads, meats, cheeses, and fruit. They stashed their lunches in their bike saddlebags, and they cycled off behind their lanky, quiet, gray-haired guide, John Paul. They peddled through landscapes that looked like the Old Dutch masterpieces, along canals, past working windmills, down cobblestone streets lined with thatch-roofed cottages, and through fields upon fields of flowers. The ladies would hop off their bikes at the same time, breathe deeply, and absorb the beauty of millions of red or yellow tulips. "The color of the flowers was so intense you almost had to squint," remembers Cory's friend Laurel.

The weather posed some challenges—most days it was damp, clammy, and cold. But the ladies came up with a few creative solutions for dealing with the weather. A team dynamic developed among them. "We wore lots of layers, drank lots of wine, and ate pounds of chocolate," Laurel explains of their camaraderie. And she's not kidding: The parade of 24 women pedaling caused a traffic jam in front of more than one chocolate shop.

Late in the afternoon, after long days of biking 20 to 40 miles, they would gather on the barge, which was parked in a new location each day—often in the center of a small town. They would congregate before dinner in the lounge, sprawl out on the comfy couches, sip wine, and share stories from the day. Some women bundled up

Packing for a barge trip is easy. It is not a cruise where you will have a cocktail party to meet the Captain or need to dress for dinner, so you can leave all the fancy clothes at home. Think comfort, informal, and layers. Shorts, slacks, T-shirts, a fleece shell, maybe a skirt and athletic shoes are all you need. You may not have a lot of storage space in your room, so carry only what will fit into a small suitcase.

in warm clothes to watch the sun set over a village from the open-air deck. After a hearty dinner of Dutch cuisine, four women were given the floor to tell their personal stories. The rule was that it had to be a story no one else in the group already knew. Some stories were funny, others tragic, but all were deeply sincere and offered a glimpse into each woman's inner self. A few women had lost a child or a spouse; others had been through divorce, cancer, or other major life disappointments. "Not one of us had experienced the life we'd expected to live," says Laurel. By sharing their stories, they shared their strength. And being far removed from their responsibilities, by being together and in such an idyllic setting, they found that opening up to new experiences, new perspectives, and new friends came easily to each of them. Between the nightly storytelling and the hours pedaling together in the mist day after day, an intense solidarity developed. To an outsider, it would appear these women had known each other for decades.

They also made each other laugh—hysterically. In fact, as Laurel remembers it: "We laughed till we cried at least once a day." One evening they danced with each other for hours in a barn, swaying and giggling to turn-of-the-20th-century organ music. They got a reminder about the hilarious things that happen in the company of other women. And traveling has a way of really exaggerating that: You're in a place where no one recognizes you or will ever see you again!

On the last night, all 24 women crammed into a tiny bar in Amsterdam and raised a toast of gratitude to Cory. She told them the trip had exceeded everything she had hoped it would be. What more could a woman ask for than close girlfriends who would bike soaking wet with a smile on their faces?

⪻ France ⪼

When you board a boat together, you and your girlfriends create a captive audience of, well, yourselves. And aboard a barge in France you'll feel you've been transported back to an era when life was simpler, journeys were slower—and boats were the main modes of transport. You'll glimpse scenery you'd never see from the road, the gentle movement of the boat will rock you to sleep at night, and perhaps best of all, you'll be catered to by a French chef! Hotel barges on the waterways of France sleep between 4 and 20 guests, and are usually outfitted with small living rooms, libraries, dining rooms, and private or shared cabins. The cruising options are practically endless in this country, where there are more than 5,000 waterways, including

I've cruised three times on different sections of the Niverne Canal in Southern France. We cruised one week one way and probably went no more than 60 miles. It was very relaxing and the people along the way were friendly. Speaking broken French to the lock keepers was a great experience. It is so easy to get a barge without a crew or cook and do it on your own. You get on the boat the night before you take off, and they show you how to maneuver it in the harbor. It's fun to decide for yourself where and when you want to go or get off. Every town has its own bakery so you'll have fresh croissants and bread daily. We loved doing our own cooking and going out to eat in small restaurants along the way. Remember, the locks close from one to two each afternoon, so plan to be in a town, or have your lunch aboard. One evening, docked in Auxerre, as we were sitting on the deck sipping wine, the bells at two cathedrals on the hillsides above us chimed in harmony. I said to my girlfriend, "We couldn't have bought this experience at a Five Star Hotel."

—Cathy Robertson, 60, Golfer, Sailor,
San Anselmo, California

a network of canals created to connect the country's major rivers and to serve as a passageway for cargo barges navigating from the Atlantic to the Mediterranean Sea. Here, you and the ladies might traverse the fertile wine regions of Bordeaux or Burgundy, sail along the opulent southern coast, or trace the German border. Along the way, you can take guided tours of cavernous wine cellars, colorful markets, and tiny mom-and-pop craft shops. Or spend your days stretching your legs on a bike ride (equipment is provided on board), gabbing over lunch in an outdoor café, or simply lazing about in the sun. The water sets a leisurely pace, allowing you to catch up on old times or get to know each other—or a little bit of both—without feeling rushed. You can either gather your best friends and charter an entire boat (they range in size from 80 to 200 feet), or join a group of other like-minded travelers for a relaxing river journey. France's barge season runs from mid-March through early November, with temperatures ranging from the mid-60s to high 70s. And what I like about the waterways in the south of France is that they have the advantage of longer fall and spring seasons.

THE ULTIMATE ROUTE FOR LADIES

For a wine-lovers' reunion, the Burgundy Canal, coursing through east-central France, couldn't be more perfect. And you'll have a choice of several companies that lead tours of this route. You and the girls will take in the Burgundy region from north to south (the canal links two major rivers, the Yonne and Saône) stopping at medieval villages en route to Dijon, Burgundy's capital. Gothic castles with colorful tiled roofs soar into the sky, gentle rolling hills emerge cloaked in forests of maple and pine, and fields reveal splashes of poppies, lilacs, or sunflowers (depending on the season). In Dijon, you'll sample some of the world's finest reds at the Clos de Vougeot vineyard, where a stone wall surrounds the vines that were first planted by 12th-century monks. And I would be wildly remiss if I didn't insist that you take a detour in Dijon to the famed Les Halles market, the largest covered market in the region. Here you and the girls can hone your haggling skills over the local produce, seafood, meat, and clothing.

BEST REASON TO STAY ANOTHER WEEK

If there are true foodies among you, it's worth heading farther east to the fairy-tale Alsace and Lorraine regions, along the German border. The rolling Vosges Mountains, dotted with small timber houses among heavily wooded forests, provide a majestic backdrop for a cruise along the Canal de la Marne au Rhin. In the Alsatian town of Colmar, you and the gals can spend an afternoon strolling the cobblestone lanes and then reserve a table for dinner at one of Alsace's many Michelin-starred restaurants (it has the most of any region in France). Once you reach Lorraine, you and the girls will swoon over the French treat that inspired Proust—the madeleine cookie—and try the bacon-and-Swiss-cheese quiche named for the town.

BEST TOUR OPERATORS
For a ladies-only trip, sign on with U.S. outfitter Adventure Women, which charters the *Litote* on the Burgundy Canal for seven days (starting at $2,895; 800-804-8686, *www.adventurewomen.com*). Barge tour coordinators Special Places Travel offers seven-day cruises of Alsace on the *Lorraine* (starting at $2,090 per person, or groups of 22 can charter the barge starting at $41,800; 877-642-2743, *www.bargesinfrance.com*).

DESIGN YOUR OWN TRIP
You can indulge your independent streaks by getting together and designing your very own itinerary in the south of France on the 300-year-old Canal du Midi. The *Fandango* and *Tango*, small sister luxury barges that each accommodate six people, can be chartered separately or together for six days (starting at $4,500, up to $47,000 to charter both barges for 12 people; 866-550-3447, *www.canalsof france.com*). Sycamore trees shade the way as you cruise past fields of sunflowers and vineyards. You'll encounter stone bridges and aqueducts at what seems like every turn. The region is rather hilly, and in order to navigate the elevation gains, you'll pass through locks that lift you from one level to the next. Stop at your leisure at open-air markets, private vineyards, and the olive-oil mill l'Oulibo, which produces one of the finest cold-pressed extra-virgin oils in the world. A mother-and-son team—both trained French chefs— own and operate the boats. They use fresh ingredients to prepare all of your meals on board, and they can also arrange culinary barge tours with hands-on cooking seminars. Savor the Provençal and Mediterranean-inspired food and wines of this region: The canal is a conduit between the Atlantic Ocean and the Mediterranean Sea.

CAPTAIN YOUR OWN BOAT
You've got to love the laissez-faire French attitude. Combine that with the chutzpah we seem to muster when with our girlfriends en masse and at the helm of our own barge. Several barge companies will let

you sail a barge without a crew even if you don't have any boating experience (professional barge captains refer to these as "Tupperware Boats," due to their light, easily navigable construction). But not to worry, they provide hands-on training, teach navigational techniques, and give you detailed routes highlighting places of interest and lists of restaurants. The canals have several lock passings, gated sections that control water levels. It can take up to 30 minutes for a lock to empty out or fill up before you can move the barge to its desired level. Don't give up the idea if this sounds too complicated: You'll get instructions on how to move the barge up- or downstream. I recommend taking this opportunity to chat with the lockkeepers—they have great stories and an intimate knowledge of the region. You won't have any trouble finding mooring spots along the waterways—marinas may charge a small fee, but most other docking areas are free. The France-based Locaboat Holidays rents out barges, which accommodate 2 to 12 people (starting at $1,315 per week; *www.locaboat.com*).

ONE CLICK AND YOU'RE OFF

The French Government Tourist Office can be found online at *http://us.franceguide.com*.

❧ China ❧

The longest river in China and the third longest in the world, the Yangtze flows 4,000 miles from the snowy glaciers of Tibet to the East China Sea, acting as the unofficial divider between north and south China. Cruising the Yangtze in the company of friends is an ideal way to see this massive country, which is home to a dizzying dichotomy of high-energy cities and an old-world countryside. Since rural China is still fine-tuning its tourism industry, a Yangtze cruise is certainly less shocking to your senses than traveling solo or on land. In the company of your friends, you'll be more at liberty to open yourself up to the unfamiliar. A river trip delivers you to pre-industrial China, minus the Prada stores, traffic jams, or glass highrises of its urban centers. But if you're in the market for jade, silk, and freshwater pearls, not to worry, there will be plenty of opportunities to shop on the Yangtze. You'll also have a lot to keep you busy while you're sailing because most ships have an on-board gym, sauna, shops, and a beauty salon. You can take a group calligraphy lesson, hone your mahjong skills, or sign up for a workshop on Chinese herbal medicine. Traditional Chinese performers take the stage most eve-nings, but on karaoke nights, you and the ladies may find yourselves grabbing the mic and providing the entertainment yourselves! Your best bet weather-wise is early autumn and spring, when the climate is dry and temperatures rise to the mid-70s. Try to avoid summertime travel as July and August can get extremely hot.

BEST CRUISING ROUTE

I recommend taking a three- or four-day trip on the Yangtze down-stream from the city of Chongqing to Yichang, or vice versa. If you're up for a longer cruise, you can go from Chongqing all the way into

PICKING THE RIGHT BARGE

∽

Here's what you should ask about the barge before you book:

Does each cabin have a toilet and a shower in the room?

If the weather is hot, are the cabins air-conditioned?

Is there a separate lounge, or does the dining room serve as the get-together space when not in use? Are there comfy couches to chat in? Are books and music available?

Are you offered a choice of entrees at meals? Is wine or beer included in the price?

Are bicycles available on board? How many?

If you're feeling energetic, can you get off the barge at a lock, then walk, jog, or bike along the water and get back on the barge at the next lock?

—Marybeth

Shanghai, on the East China Sea coast. Yangtze cruise ships sail at a slow pace—only about 20 miles an hour—making stops in multiple villages and farms to give you and the ladies an up close look at the temples, palaces, ruins, and other cultural treasures of rural China. You'll be thrilled that your friends are with you to share in the Yangtze's most spectacular stretch: the Three Gorges area. Otherwise you'd be hard-pressed to convey the beauty of it to them back at home. You'll sail between imposing rugged cliffs blanketed by layers of mist and light at the convergence of the towering gorges. The ship will pass right through the jungle-covered walls of the deepest gorge, Qutang, which rises to an astonishing 4,000 feet. But to explore the so-called Lesser Gorges, you'll board a small motorized boat. As you zip past these canyon walls, be sure to look at them closely: The ancient coffins of the Ba people (475-220 B.C.) hang from the walls. This region has made headlines in recent years with the construction of the Three Gorges Dam, a large-scale hydroelectric engineering project that is expected to become operational in 2009. Besides submerging ancient temples and tombs, the rising waters are expected to displace about 1.4 million people. If cruising the Three Gorges of the Yangtze is a dream trip of yours, put it at the top of your list: It won't be in its natural state for too much longer.

BEST SHORE EXCURSIONS

If you were fans of Indiana Jones, you'll love the adventure of exploring the Snow Jade Cave, an underground limestone labyrinth laced with winding streams and brilliant, jewel-like stalagmites and stalactites formed over thousands of years. The cave is in Fengdu, a town on the north bank of the Yangtze 110 miles downstream from Chongqing. Farther downstream is another otherworldly dazzler: Shibaozhai, the Precious Stone Fortress. You can help each other climb up the spiral staircase into the fortress, which is a 12-story, wooden red pagoda that was built in the 17th century entirely without nails against a craggy, 700-foot hill. The stairs are steep, so take them slowly and pause to admire the paintings and sculptures on each level. All that huffing and puffing will be worth it once you take in the spectacular view of the great river and rolling countryside below—and get your best group photograph of the trip.

BEST TOUR OPERATORS

A ten-year veteran on the river, Victoria Cruises specializes in Yangtze-only trips, which means a cheaper vacation that doesn't include land tours of Shanghai and Beijing (four-day cruises start at $675, eight-day round-trip cruises start at $1,200; 800-348-8084, *www.victoriacruises .com*). Soft adventure tour company Intrepid Travel has a 14-day "Best of China" tour, which includes a three-day Yangtze River cruise, along with land tours in Shanghai, Nanjing, Xi'an, and Beijing (starting at $1,890; 866-847-8192, *www.intrepidtravel.com*). Viking River Cruises, a luxury outfitter, offers a 12-day "Imperial Jewels of China" land and water tour, which includes 5 nights on the Yangtze River (starting at $2,699; 877-668-4546, *www.vikingrivercruises.com*).

If you're tempted to save money by booking your own river cruise directly through the wharf in Chongqing or Yichang or through a hotel reservation desk, don't do it. These boats are slightly cheaper, about $130 to $400 for a three- or four-day trip, but safety standards are lower, and the tour guides likely won't speak English. Without a doubt, I recommend signing on with a U.S.-based company.

BEST SIDE TRIPS

If you've chosen a Yangtze-only trip, you can extend your China adventure by flying to cosmopolitan Shanghai for some museum-hopping and tours of sites such as the Jade Buddha Temple (with a six-foot, white-jade Buddha) and the 88-floor modern skyscraper masterpiece, Jin Mao Tower. In Beijing, peek in on the so-called Forbidden City—a complex of gardens, pavilions, and a palace that was off-limits to the world for 500 years. Girlfriends love exploring these hubs of opulence, modernity, art, fashion, and architecture. To be witness to the blistering pace of development in these cities gives you a firsthand perspective of China to share with those at home. If you'd like to see both Shanghai and Beijing, take a scenic train ride between the two cities (find timetables and fares at *www .tourismchina-ca.com/trains.htm*). You've come all the way to China, so why not?

ONE CLICK AND YOU'RE OFF

Visit the China National Tourist Office's website at *www.cnto.org*.

❧ Holland ❧

There's more to Holland than windmills, tulips, and clogs. But a trip here wouldn't be complete without sampling each of these Dutch icons and taking a few days to kick up your heels in Amsterdam. For my money, I think the best way to see it all is from the deck of a boat. Until a hundred years ago, nearly half of this northern European country was submerged in water, and today it still has the densest network of waterways in all of Europe, with about 50 percent of the country below sea level. Over the years, ambitious projects involving barriers and dikes have fought back floods from the North Sea and channeled the water into an extensive system of navigable canals, lakes, and rivers. Because the Dutch waterways were designed for commercial barges, they're plenty wide enough to accommodate a hotel barge. All of this qualifies Holland (aka the Netherlands) as one of the best places in the world to hop on a boat for a week. Add to that picture-perfect villages, cool weather, cheese, and tall, handsome men and I guarantee there won't be a girlfriend of yours who won't want to join you. When you all are planning your tour, be sure to coordinate the itinerary with the time when the tulips are in full bloom, from early April to early May.

BEFORE YOU BOARD

If you've never been to Holland's capital city, Amsterdam, by all means meet the girls there for a one- or two-day stay prior to setting sail. My favorite way to tour the city is the same way the locals get around—by bicycle. There are nearly a million bikes within the city limits, and rental shops are as ubiquitous as tulips (about $26 for a half-day; *www.bikes.nl*). Form an all-girls bike-touring gang for quick and easy travel between quintessential landmarks such as the Anne Frank House, the Van Gogh Museum, and the Rembrandt House. Let your hair down and visit less conventional cultural phenomena like the red light district and the coffeehouses.

BEST CRUISING ROUTE

You can indulge every single one of your Dutch fantasies by cruising on Holland's most popular route, the "tulip cruise," which connects a series of rivers and canals through the central region of the country. These trips originate in Rotterdam harbor (40 miles southwest of Amsterdam) and head northeast on the River Ijssel to the town of Gouda. No doubt you've munched on this town's signature product: a yellow cheese with a distinctive red rind. Now's your chance to also taste the other local delicacy, *stroopwafel*. A wafer-and-syrup pastry sandwich served atop a steaming cup of coffee, stroopwafel slowly transforms into a warm, soft treat. Savor it while you and the gals kick back at an outdoor café along the water. Back on board the boat, you'll enjoy an ever changing, wraparound view of green fields, narrow waterways, ponds with ducks and other waterfowl, and neat little homes with lace curtains, vegetable gardens, and toddlers playing in the yard. You'll sail northwest to the cosmopolitan city of Haarlem and the village of Zaanse Schans, where you'll find enough windmills and clogs to last a lifetime. Hop off the boat to get a closer look at the traditional wooden houses lining the Zaan River, watch shoemakers show off their clog-making skills, and get to the source of the yeasty scents of fresh-baked bread and stroopwafel wafting through the air. Next up is the city of Amsterdam, with its canal houseboats and soaring bridges, and after that, the famed Keukenhof gardens. When you pull into the town of Schiedam, your final destination on the tulip cruise, I doubt any of you will want the tour to end.

STOP TO SMELL THE FLOWERS
You'll love the massive flowerbeds of Keukenhof so much that you might fantasize about pitching a tent in the 70-acre floral wonderland (unfortunately, that's not allowed). Located in the town of Lisse, Keukenhof is far and away the highlight of every canal journey. From late March to mid-May, more than seven million flowers spring to life, including a thousand types of tulips and bounties of crocuses, hyacinths, and daffodils. If this visit inspires the gardener in you, you can bring home a part of Keukenhof by buying bulbs and having them shipped home to you in time for autumn planting (*www .keukenhof.nl/nm/english.html*).

BEST TRIP EXTENSION
If you're organizing a girlfriend reunion, you might prefer a longer, more leisurely cruise to give you time to catch up. You can do a portion of the central loop, and then extend your trip from Haarlem to the southern route. You'll get your fill of tulips and windmills, but you'll also have the added bonus of a border crossing into the French-influenced medieval towns of Belgium, including Antwerp, Ghent, and Bruges. You'll indulge in gourmet Belgian cuisine and lounge on the sundeck, making up for lost time with your friends and becoming the rare tourists to leave Holland with suntans. A trip to Belgium is not complete without tasting the country's award-winning beers. There are scores of cute outdoor cafés pouring hundreds of Belgian beers. My favorite is a brew called Leffe Blonde, a summery beer originally brewed in a monastery.

BEST TOUR OPERATORS

You'll have good luck with Dutch-owned Barge Connection, a luxury barge provider that leads a "tulip cruise" through central Holland on the *Absoluut 2* (from $3,450 per week; 888-550-8580, *www.bargecon nection.com*) and the southern route, between Haarlem and Bruges, on the *Marjorie II* (from $3,800 per week; *www.marjorie2.com*).

BIKE AND BARGE TRIPS

A bike-and-barge tour has that alluring mix of relaxation and exercise—it allows you the flexibility to explore the countryside on your own and provides you with a floating hotel as a comfy home base. A few boats sail the lesser-traveled region of northern Holland, delivering you to fishing villages and small towns that date back to the 12th century. Each day, you and the gals can choose a route and set off at your own leisure for a self-guided ride (averaging between 15 and 40 miles a day). If you can, pedal through the town of Alkmaar on a Friday—the locals don traditional costumes to re-create an authentic Dutch cheese market in the summertime. You might choose a cheese you've never heard of before, pair it with some crusty bread and a few bottles of Amstel, and have a quintessential Dutch picnic lunch by the water. Another highlight of the region is the largest Dutch island, Texel (pronounced Tessel), which has an extensive network of bike paths. As the trip winds down, you'll stop in several northern seaside resorts, like Schoorl and Bergen, where you can meander through miniscule Danish hamlets like Oterleek (population 192). U.S.-based Bike Tours Direct works with the Dutch company Channel Cruises to arrange seven-night bike-and-barge tours

---

PACKING TIP

≪৯

Ladies, stuff your empty shoes with feminine hygiene supplies. Although they are available in Jaipur, Prague, Paris, Killarny, aboard cruise ships, and countless other places, who wants to spend valuable vacation time tracking down an open drug store, or be obliged to pay exorbitant prices?

in northern Holland (from $910 per week; 877-462-2423, *www
.biketoursdirect.com*).

CAPTAIN YOUR OWN BOAT

Feeling audacious? Impress your husbands and friends back home by
captaining a small self-drive barge from the northern ports of Sneek
and Strand Horst. The U.K.-based Crown Blue Line offers weekly
boat rentals with accommodations for four to ten people. You don't
even need previous boating experience: The company gives you
hands-on lessons and detailed maps with recommended stops along
the way (from $1,085 per week; *www.crownblueline.com*).

ONE CLICK AND YOU'RE OFF

Go to the Netherlands Board of Tourism and Conventions' website,
www.visitholland.com.

Egypt

One of the most profound history lessons of your lives is what's waiting
for you on a Nile cruise. Egyptian civilization wouldn't exist without
the river—every major Egyptian city and nearly all significant cultural
sites were built on the Nile's banks. It used to be that you could only
visit the elaborate temples, imposing pyramids, and lavish tombs by
sailing the river, and I still think the traditional route is the best way to
learn, take in the ancient sites, and shop in the busy markets. And on
a group river tour, girlfriends can feel more at ease about being in this
mysterious (albeit very welcoming) nation. Most river cruises operate
in southern Egypt between the cities of Luxor and Aswan, covering
about 125 miles of the river's 4,000-mile length. (Flights from Cairo to
both cities run frequently.) Navigating the ancient waterway, your boat
will pass through rocky, desert land along fertile riverbanks lined with
lush greenery and swaying palm trees. As you cruise farther and farther
from the major cities, hundreds of years of civilization peel back: Cars,
honking horns, billboards, and electricity disappear. You'll glide by
simple hamlets with mud huts and see farmers slowly working fields of
wheat, cotton, and rice behind wooden plows pulled by oxen. Women
and children walk on paths carrying water or wood on their backs.

I urge you to read up on Egypt before you visit. Knowing the
captivating tales of pharaohs, festivals, feasts, and famines as well
as its present-day struggles with modernity will give you a greater

appreciation for the sights and experiences of your journey—and a chance for deeper bonding among friends. Form a mini-book club to pore over such contemporary hits as *Down the Nile*, in which author Rosemary Mahoney rows solo down the river, exploring its history as she goes. Or see modern Egypt through the eyes of its most famous author and Nobel literature laureate, Naguib Mahfouz. While you're planning your trip, keep in mind that there are only two seasons in Egypt: one is hot and the other is hotter. Between May and October, temperatures can reach into the 90s, particularly in the more southerly areas like Luxor. Weather is milder from November to April, but beware that March and April are prone to violently dusty and sandy desert storms, or khamsin. Regardless of when you go, dress conservatively, wearing long pants or skirts and keeping your shoulders covered (short sleeves are okay, tank tops are not).

BEST CRUISING ROUTE

The most popular route, from Luxor to Aswan, takes four or five days. As you cruise out of Luxor, keep your eyes peeled for temples on both sides of the riverbank. The Temple of Luxor, which dates

A NIGHT AT THE OPERA HOUSE

Have a free evening in Cairo? You can head for the Opera House, which has classical music, dance, or some such program almost every night. Even if the big hall is sold out, a chamber music concert is usually going on in the small hall. Schedules are posted and detailed in the English-language *Egyptian Gazette* daily newspaper. When you hire a cab, remember to negotiate taxi fees before you step inside the taxi. I usually sit up front and chat with the drivers. They'll typically ask for a tip as you step out, but the agreed upon price is enough. Try to have the exact change handy, or your driver will take his own tip.

—Marybeth

back to 1400 B.C., is on the east bank; on the western shore, you can explore the tombs of pharaohs and their wives—including King Tutankhamun's—in the Valley of the Kings and Valley of the Queens. When you disembark to explore the temples and tombs, be sure to snap some photos of yourselves. (What could make for a better Christmas-card picture than you posing in front of a row of sphinxes?) In Idfu, you'll be shocked at how well preserved the Ptolemaic sandstone Temple of Horus is, and you'll marvel over Kom-Ombo, with its unique "double temple." On board the cruise ship, there's nightly entertainment, including Nubian dance performances, slinky belly dancers, and cheesy-but-fun discotheques where you and your girlfriends can let loose. For a quieter evening, skip the entertainment and head out to the deck for an informal astronomy session—the stars sparkle more brightly in the unpolluted sky here.

STRIKE OUT ON YOUR OWN

If your group feels like a solo mini-excursion, you can arrange to spend an afternoon on a felucca—setting sail on one of these traditional, wind-powered vessels will make you feel like Egyptian queens. You'll bask in the sunshine by yourselves, buy jewelry, cotton scarves, and woven wool blankets from floating merchants, and explore small islands.

MUST-SEE MARKETS

The sky's the limit in the souks (markets) of Luxor and Aswan; you can buy anything from handmade slippers to gold bracelets to spices and incense. You may be surprised to see butchers standing out in the streets displaying sliced-open carcasses, but you should

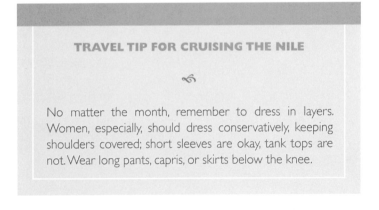

TRAVEL TIP FOR CRUISING THE NILE

No matter the month, remember to dress in layers. Women, especially, should dress conservatively, keeping shoulders covered; short sleeves are okay, tank tops are not. Wear long pants, capris, or skirts below the knee.

be even more wary of the brilliantly colored fruits and vegetables spilling over market stands—uncooked, unpeeled food is a no-no for foreigners. You're much better off snacking on lamb *shawarma* or roasted chicken from the sidewalk stands. And of course, haggling is not only expected, but a practiced art form and an age-old way for two cultures to communicate. Have fun with it!

BEST TOUR OPERATORS

Lindblad Expeditions, experts in educational travel and adventure cruising for nearly 50 years, runs excellent 10-day and 15-day Egypt tours, including four to five days on the Nile aboard the *Triton* (starting at $4,480 and $6,680, respectively; 800-397-3348, *www .expeditions.com*). Egypt-based Sonesta Cruise Collection leads Nile River–only trips from Luxor to Aswan for three, four, six, or seven nights (starting at $414; 800-766-3782, *www.sonesta.com/nilecruises*). A nonprofit travel company for adventurous folks over 55 years of age, Elderhostel offers a ten-day tour of Egypt, including a four-night Nile cruise (starting at $3,491; 800-454-5768, *www.elderhostel.org*).

ONE CLICK AND YOU'RE OFF

Get more information from the Egyptian Tourism Authority at *www .egypt.travel.com*.

Eastern Europe

Floating on the Danube River, you can explore many Eastern European countries without the hassle of connecting from one famed city to the next, searching for good hotels—or even carrying your luggage, for that matter. The Danube is the second longest river in Europe, flowing from Germany's Black Forest through eight countries and into the Black Sea. A cruise lets you tour this emerging travel destination without having to lift a single bag. All you need to do is show up and be ready to step off the boat when it docks in Vienna, Budapest, or Belgrade (the season is March through December). Groups of women love the itinerary because it packs in so many historic cities, varied terrain and activities, shopping in mom-and-pop shops, as well as captures the irresistible charm of an untapped Eastern Europe. Most Danube cruises start in Passau, Germany, and end roughly 400 miles later in Budapest, Hungary, an itinerary that includes the seven bridges of Budapest, the world-famous Vienna State Opera House, and the enormous Bratislava Castle. But the Danube also rushes past picturesque Eastern European villages and towns that have yet to be combed over by tourists. In Germany's Rüdescheim village, for example, you'll be the rare visitors to stop in at one of the vineyards that blanket the hills around town, take some time in the wine museum, and then hit a local tavern to sample the region's famous Rieslings. Back on board your ship, there are daily activities for you while you're cruising. As you make your way through the countryside of Germany or Austria, for instance, the crew of your boat might lead an apple-strudel-making demonstration (with hot samples, of course) or host a glassblowing demonstration by a local artist. You may also have the chance to close your eyes and absorb the sounds of Mozart in a chamber orchestra concert, or bop around to upbeat regional folk music.

TAKE YOUR HOLIDAY CELEBRATION OVERSEAS
If Christmas in Vienna sounds like bliss to you, you'd be hard-pressed to find a better way to spend the winter holidays than on a Danube cruise. One thing that sets the Danube apart from other rivers is the length of the travel season: March through December. The winter extension, while icy cold, gives you access to the most spirited Christmas celebrations in the world. In Vienna, Salzburg, and Nuremberg, for example, you can wander the famous Christmas markets, where the scent of roasting sausage mingles with fresh gingerbread. You and the girls can keep warm by sipping on *glühwein*, hot sweetened wine, buying wooden carvings and handmade toys, and cheering on the local children performing in pageants and concerts.

BEST TOUR OPERATORS
Founded in conjunction with AARP in 1958, Grand Circle Travel leads a 12-day "Old World Prague and Blue Danube" tour (from $2,095; 800-959-0405, *www.gct.com*). The deluxe cruise company Amadeus Waterways offers a 23-day "Grand Danube" package, which includes a 14-day float all the way from Germany into Romania with stays in Prague and Istanbul on either end (from $3,498; 800-626-0126, *www.amadeuswaterways.com*).

BIKE AND BOAT TOURS
The Danube Bike Path is one of the most celebrated cycling routes in all of Europe, running adjacent to the river all the way from Passau into Vienna, a total of 230 miles. As you coast next to the river, cycling along the mostly flat ground (except for the bridges),

the countryside flies by, peppered with picturesque cottages, working farms, and rolling vineyards. Peter Deilmann Cruises, a small-ship pioneer, hosts weeklong biking cruises along the Danube (from $3,897; 800-348-8287, *www.deilmann-cruises.com*).

CRUISE INTO THE BLACK SEA

Put on your explorers' caps for this trip extension: A couple of outfitters run Danube cruises all the way to the river's terminus, the Black Sea. Few Westerners travel this far, but those who do are rewarded by spectacular scenery and a glimpse into a postcommunist culture still steeped in history. European-vacation specialist Globus Journeys offers a 12-day trip starting with a tour of Budapest, followed by seven nights on the lower Danube, venturing into Croatia, Serbia, and Romania, and ending at the Black Sea (from $3,730; 866-755-8581, *www.globusjourneys.ca*).

ONE CLICK AND YOU'RE OFF

Check out information on the Danube from the Austrian National Tourism Office, *www.austria.info*; the German National Tourist Board, *www.cometogermany.com*; and the Romania National Tourist Office, *www.romaniatourism.com*.

CHAPTER NINE

Glorious Gardens

∾ KATHY'S STORY ∾

Kathy, a businesswoman from Connecticut, is known in her community as the Flower Lady. Her idea of a perfect weekend is working hard in her garden and making trips to the local nursery.

This horticulture hobby began in her youth when she and her family lived on a large estate with her grandmother in rural New York. Kathy and her sisters played in the apple orchards, rose gardens, and vegetable beds on the property. Kathy's grandmother shared her love of flowers and took great pride in teaching the girls how to arrange them artfully. "When mom wanted fresh asparagus for dinner, they would ask us to go dig it up," Kathy explains. "And gardening was a treasure hunt for us kids. We never knew what we'd discover. One day I found a whiskey crock dating from the Revolutionary War."

One memorable summer during her childhood, Kathy and her family visited the Butchart Gardens in British Columbia, Canada. "It was the first garden that I adored almost as much as my grandmother's garden," she remembers of this oasis outside the city of Victoria on Vancouver Island.

Years later through her business, Kathy met a German widow named Anne who led garden tours in England and Ireland. Their shared interests led to an immediate friendship, and they began corresponding overseas. They exchanged letters on politics, economics, their favorite books and music.

After writing back and forth for several months, they planned a garden tour of southern England. "We went in June to catch the roses in bloom from Sissinghurst, in Kent, through the Cotswolds," Kathy says. To their surprise, each garden was very different. She learned that English gardens have very old rose varieties and that many of them are bicolored, just like peonies. During the trip, Kathy fell in love with David Austin's roses (bred by the English horticulturalist). She liked the old-fashioned scent so much that she filled her garden back home with them.

During their trip to England, Anne and Kathy discovered that gardeners use dead trees as support for large climbing roses and clematis. So Kathy adopted the practice and used a dead dogwood tree to support her Constance Spry rose in her front yard. "Another Constance Spry now covers the front arbor and is climbing up live trees," she says. "Every June we wait with baited breath for the dynamic show."

Kathy and Anne's botanical travels have continued for the past two decades. They meet once a year to tour some of the most beautiful gardens in Europe, spanning from Isola Bella and Isola Madre in Lago Maggiore to Baden-Baden, and from the Channel Islands to the wine regions of France and Germany.

Their remarkable friendship cuts across international borders and cultures. "Our different points of view make for stimulating conversations," Kathy says. They talk about gardening, international politics, business, history, landscape architecture, books, and authors. But it's their love of gardens and gardening that brings them together and strengthens their bond.

On the final night of these vacations, Kathy and Anne begin to plan the next year's trip. "We have a list, probably several pages long, of places we want to visit," says Kathy. "I don't know if we'll live long enough to cover them all, but we're going to try."

Arabella, a lifelong horticulturalist and floral designer from New Hampshire, travels the globe to be enveloped in the world's most celebrated gardens, to inspect them carefully, to be moved by them. Over the past 15 years, she has traveled both with her girlfriends and with her husband to dozens of countries across six continents in order to immerse herself in one-of-a-kind gardens. Arabella feels that gardens are evidence of someone's imagination and passion, and that entering a garden allows you to engage in the gardener's fantasy. She loves looking for the correlation between the cultivated and the wild in these gardens and views gardening as an art form. "The creativity in each garden is the vision of its creator and his muse," Arabella says. "Success is only limited by time, money, and the gardener's ability to collaborate with Mother Nature."

At home, during the winter, she pores over botanical, history, and landscape books to study the plants, flowers, and geography of the gardens she visits. Inspired by her growing knowledge, Arabella began volunteering for garden clubs and horticultural societies, and became so involved that a few years ago she served as the chairman of the American Horticultural Society. One of her favorite volunteer jobs is to host tours for the American Horticultural Society's foreign excursions. On these trips, she leads women on visits to private homes and gardens, natural landscapes, public parks, castles, and World Heritage sites. Professional lecturers come along to educate the travelers on the history and culture of the country they're visiting, and an horticulturalist lectures about gardens and plants.

For her, it's a wonderful experience to share garden tours with other women and to make new friends around the world who share the same fixation and sense of wonder about gardening. Arabella admires and praises the Canadian gardening approach: "The colors and textures in the Butchart Gardens give you the same sensual hit as smelling freshly baked bread," she says. "The Canadians plant flowers in the top of their baskets, as we do, but they also position flowers to poke through the bottom of their hanging baskets, so when you look up you see a hanging garden. The flowers float in the air like an aerial garden." It's this kind of passion, appreciation, and knowledge of gardening that Arabella shares with her fellow travelers, whether they be her husband, pals, or tour clients.

Now Arabella is the incoming president of the World Association of Flower Arrangers, and she's busy reading up on exotic plants and botanical gardens in Singapore. The remarkable friendships she's made along the way motivate her to travel as much as she can, near and far. She's planning a trip to Asia to visit her daughter, who lives there—and of course, to see the gardens. "Our world is filled with negativity, pain, and conflict," she reflects. "But gardens celebrate beauty and nature's bounty."

Kent

In southeast England's county of Kent, about a 30-minute trip from London, the rolling countryside is dotted with hearty forests, orchards, and the occasional hop-drying house (a curious but charming brick structure). You'll find a picture-perfect haven for the garden lovers and Anglophiles among you. Kent is after all the Garden of England and as prim and proper as you'd expect. The 180 gardens and the incredible castles and estates that are open to the public make for a weekend (or week) full of photo ops, a dose of English history, idyllic walks, picnics, and ideas for your gardens back home. And the variety of the gardens holds something for everyone in your group, whether you're a traditionalist, a topiary buff, or an avant-gardener. This land is also shared by some of England's premier sights, such as the White Cliffs of Dover, overlooking the English Channel from on high, as well as the rolling hills of the High Weald, a protected wilderness filled with some of Earth's more peculiar land features. It's easy to cover a lot of ground in a short time here thanks to a convenient railway system, affordable taxis, and bike rentals. And you'll find it a very walkable region—on foot you'll pass bluebell-strewn woods, fields of lavender, antiques shops, and boutiques en route to the grounds of castles and apothecary gardens. At the end of the day, over a meal of shepherd's pie or fish-and-chips with a pint of beer in a snug pub, you can brainstorm about the changes you'd like to make to your gardens back home. Bellies full, you'll retire to your cute-as-a-button bed-and-breakfast for the night. If you're a sucker for English roses, you'll catch the best blooms and most divine scents in June. Many of Kent's gardens open their gates from April through September, so plan accordingly.

BEST CASTLE GARDENS
Sissinghurst Castle Garden earns the top spot in Kent's order of gardens, with a 16th-century Elizabethan castle, the remains of a moat from the early Middle Ages, and world-renowned landscaping.

Writer and poet Vita Sackville-West bought the property in 1930 and spent the next three decades designing and planting ten exquisite gardens, each of which has its own theme. Roses were Vita's favorite flowers; so if you're rose aficionados, too, visit in June when they're in full bloom. Another notable is the White Garden, decked out with white primroses, lavender, and pale foliage. Sissinghurst spreads over 400 acres, so you'll need a boost after walking much of it: Take high tea in the afternoon at its café ($16; *www.nationaltrust .org.uk*). At Scotney Castle Gardens—which was designed around a 14th-century castle with a moat—the blooming azaleas, rhododendrons, and wisteria helped it earn its reputation as the country's most romantic garden. But it's also an archaeological site, built with sandstone from a quarry on the grounds. And extra treat is a fossil of a giant dinosaur footprint (*www.nationaltrust.org.uk*).

MOST EDUCATIONAL GARDEN

Many of us feel a tad intimidated by the English garden—its perfection and scale can seem unattainable. To better learn all about the evolution of this art form, visit Yalding Organic Gardens. Here 14 separate gardens trace the history of English gardening from medieval times to the present. At the Apothecary Garden, which features plants used for medicinal purposes and cooking from as early as the 13th century, there could be some ideas for your own herb garden. You and the girls can also learn more about water-conserving plant species at the Low Water Garden and how to attract friendly critters to your yard at the Wildland Garden (*www.gardenorganic.org.uk/gardens/yalding.php*).

TRAVEL TIP

∽

Avoid camera calamities. If, by accident, you leave the shutter open, or the flash on overnight, your battery will be dead in the morning and you may not be able to buy the size and brand of battery you need in a foreign country. Bring your digital camera recharger, a converter, and extra memory cards with you. Also pack extra batteries.

LITERARY STOPS

Jane Austen began *Pride and Prejudice* shortly after staying at Goodnestone Park, which at the time was her brother's home and is now open to the public. The Walled Garden here displays rows of jasmine and roses and hanging purple blossoms of wisteria. The view of the church tower through the central archway of the garden is one of my most cherished memories of Kent ($9.50; *www.good nestoneparkgardens.co.uk*). The bookshelves of the serious gardeners among you may already contain a volume or two by renowned British gardener and writer Christopher Lloyd. If not, I recommend picking up his recent work, *Cuttings*, for gardening inspiration. His educational tome, *The Well-Tempered Garden,* will help you better appreciate Lloyd's own gardens, which are for show at the Great Dixter House and Gardens in nearby Sussex. You'll be wowed by the arts-and-crafts-style gardens, which include topiaries, intricate mixed borders, and a native plants meadow (*www.greatdixter.co.uk*).

LUNCH BREAK

Fill up on a traditional plowman's lunch or munch on fresh-baked bread and homemade chutney at Pashley Manor Gardens, on the border of Sussex and Kent. The restaurant here uses local ingredients, including greens from its own vegetable garden for salads and pates, and trout plucked from nearby rivers. Walk off your hearty, healthy lunch while inhaling the wondrous scents of sweet peas and lilies, which bloom here in July ($13.50; *www.pashleymanorgardens.com*).

SPECIAL BREW

Vineyards are gardens of sorts, aren't they? You can ponder the question over a glass or two of the region's increasingly popular sparkling wines. Book a tour at Chapel Down Winery to taste award-winning whites, reds, and sparkling wines (guided tours are $13.50; *www.new wavewines.com*). Follow it up with lunch at the winery's bistro. If beer is more your thing, plan a visit to Shepherd Neame, Britain's oldest brewery, for a two-hour tour and samples of their ales and lagers ($15.70; *www.shepherdneame.co.uk*).

SHOPPING SIDETRIP

The charming town of Rochester, located in northwestern Kent, has a shop-filled Victorian High Street that's perfect for strolling and window-shopping (*www.cometorochester.co.uk/shopping*). Here you could lose an entire afternoon in England's largest second-

Try to time your trip to Britain to indoor or outdoor flower shows such as the Hampton Court Flower Show, London (July); the Rose Festival in St. Albans, Herfordshire, England (July); the Chelsea Flower Show, London (May); and the British Garden Festival, Glasgow, Scotland (May–Sept.).

hand bookstore, Baggins Book Bazaar (*www.bagginsbooks.co.uk*). Then on the eastern side of Kent, the medieval city of Canterbury, a UNESCO World Heritage site, boasts two castles, six museums, and St. Martin's Church, the oldest parish church in England still in constant use, and, of course the setting for the legendary medieval work *The Canterbury Tales*. Take time to peruse the bohemian boutiques, art galleries, and scads of specialty shops with antiques, classical music, and rare books (*www.canterbury.co.uk*).

WHERE TO STAY

The owners of Church Gates Bed and Breakfast, in the southern Kent town of Cranbrook, will send you off for the day after pancakes topped with blueberries or Scottish smoked salmon with scrambled eggs and toast (from $115 for doubles; *www.churchgates.com*). They'll also arrange garden tours (see below). For eyefuls of gardens just out your bedroom window, try the Gardeners Rest in Kingsdown—just north of the White Cliffs of Dover. With just two bedrooms, each with a balcony for prime views both of the garden and of the English Channel, you and the girls can have the place to yourselves (from $145 for doubles; *www.gardeners-rest.co.uk*).

BEST GUIDED TOURS

To learn more about the big personalities behind England's great gardens, sign up for the "Gardens, Homes & Haunts of English Artists, Writers & Horticulturists" tour with Coopersmith's One-of-a-Kind Tours. Over the course of the 11-day trip, you'll visit several gardens and homes in Kent, including Chartwell, Winston Churchill's family home, which has a beautiful rose garden ($4,795; 415-669-1914, *www.coopersmiths.com*). Church Gates Bed and Breakfast also hosts small groups on customized garden day tours. Girlfriends wishing to experience the authentic English garden are treated to a morning garden tour, followed by a late lunch, an afternoon tour, and then a glass of bubbly and dinner with the knowledgeable guides ($300 per person per day; *www.churchgates.com*).

For information on Kent, visit *www.visitkent.co.uk*.

⤳ Victoria ⤳

If you want to experience the romance of an English garden, but don't have the time or budget for a transatlantic flight, the city of Victoria, in British Columbia, is the next best thing. On the southern end of Vancouver Island (less than two hours by ferry from the city of Vancouver), Victoria boasts perks similar to those of its Commonwealth cousin towns over the pond: red double-decker buses, afternoon tea servings, and well-tended gardens. But it's singular in the beautiful views of Washington State's snowcapped Olympic Mountains. For maximum flexibility, you'll want to rent a car in Vancouver and bring it over on the ferry. That way you can freely access Victoria's nearby spas and wineries and the world of British Columbia's First Nations people. You can also take a 30-minute flight to Victoria from either Vancouver or Seattle, settle into a hotel, and explore the area by bus and foot. Take time to visit the Royal British Columbia Museum, which show-cases human and natural history from fossilized palm trees and woolly mammoths to satellite imagery (*www.royalbcmuseum.bc.ca*). And meander through Victoria's colorful Chinatown, the second oldest in North America—only San Francisco's is older—and Thunderbird Park, with an amazing display of 15 impressive totem poles. There isn't a bad time of year to be outdoors on Vancouver Island—the weather is surprisingly mild, and spring can start as early as February. Its botanical crown jewel, the Butchart Gardens, is where you will want to begin this horticultural expedition. Flowers fill the Blue Poppy Conservatory here from winter to spring, and starting at Christmastime, there's car-oling, concerts, and ice-skating; summer means spectacular blossoms, picnicking, outdoor music, and weekly fireworks.

THE GARDEN OF ALL GARDENS
Butchart is a rarely found four-season garden. You'll want to spend days here—you may even prefer to escape altogether into the gardens. (At least that's how I felt when I came here as a girl.) A quick 14-mile drive from Victoria, the Butchart Garden's 55 acres were the gift of Robert Pim Butchart, a 19th-century cement industry titan who built his factory and home in a limestone-rich spot on the grounds. As the limestone quarry began to empty out, Butchart's

wife, Jennie, hit upon the idea of transforming it into a garden. The Sunken Garden you see today was built in the quarry. And over the years, the estate transformed into an international garden destination with exceptional stylized landscaping—Japanese, Italian, and rose gardens among them. During high season (June–Sept.), you can avoid the crowds by arriving in the late afternoon or early evening—and take afternoon tea or dinner on the grounds (888-824-7313, *www.butchartgardens.com*).

BEST URBAN GARDENS

The Butchart Gardens gets all the buzz, but the city parks are worthy of your attention too. Government House Gardens is a free park in downtown Victoria enjoyed by locals and tourists. The 36-acre grounds at the Government House are blanketed with rose and lily gardens, a waterfall, Mediterranean-style terrace gardens, and a lovely showcase of British Columbia's native plants. If you have the time, their tours are very worthwhile (*www.ltgov.bc.ca/gardens*). Designed by a Scottish architect in the late 1800s, Beacon Hill Park, also in Victoria proper, welcomes you with winding paths and stone bridges for group walks, morning jogs, and carriage rides at dusk—while showcasing its native plant species, manicured gardens, and many avian residents, including swans (*www.beaconhillpark.com*). In spring, pay a visit to the Finnerty Gardens at the University of Victoria to witness for yourselves over 500 rhododendron species and hybrids in all of their blooming glory (*www.uvic.ca/garden*).

TEA TIME

During a long day of garden touring, there should always be time made for sitting down, taking a breath, and sipping tea. The regal Fairmont Empress Hotel, which looms over Victoria's Inner Harbor, serves an opulent afternoon tea service, offering its own secret blends along with all of the traditional accoutrements, including cucumber and salmon tea sandwiches and warm raisin scones with clotted cream. Be sure to get a reservation in advance (from about

Typically garden tours sponsored by horticultural societies or botanical gardens are intended for the more serious gardener. If that's you, be sure to inquire about the lectures included in the program. If it's not, sign on for a tour geared toward hobbyists.

$51; *www.fairmont.com/empress*). The Butchart Gardens also offers afternoon tea at its Dining Room Restaurant, complete with savory sandwiches and indulgent sweets ($26.25).

BUTTERFLY GARDENS

Along with brightly hued flowers come equally colorful birds, bees, and butterflies that pollinate them. At the Butterfly Gardens, located five minutes from the Butchart Gardens on Saanich Peninsula, 14 miles north of Victoria, look for the legendary blue morpho butterfly among the 50 species fluttering about. Flamingos and Amazonian parrots call the gardens home, too. Orchid lovers will drool over the collection here—but the real question is, will the carnivorous plant exhibit drool over you (877-722-0272, *www.butterflygardens.com*)?

BEST SHOPPING

The 8,600-square-foot seed shop at the Butchart Gardens is a wonder to behold. I can't think of a better—or bigger—place to stock up on seeds, gardening tools, books, and gifts (the floral calendars are a personal favorite of mine). Back in the city, peruse the shop windows in the stately Victorian buildings along Government Street, where you'll be tempted by artisan chocolates, native art (including handmade masks), linens, and jewelry.

THE FOOD

You won't go hungry at the Butchart Gardens, especially in the summer, when coffee carts, a gelateria, and a gazebo café serve hungry horticulturists throughout the park. Those are in addition to three tasty restaurants. For dinner, I like the Dining Room Restaurant (open April 1–Nov. 30 for lunch, June 15–Sept. 15 and Nov. 30–Jan. 6 for dinner), which serves local fare such as juicy free-range chicken, freshly caught trout, and delicious British Columbia wines, of which the Pinot Gris tends to be my pick.

BEST SIDE TRIP

You might not equate Vancouver Island with wine, but the same fertile soil and mild climate that produce such beautiful flowers also work wonders on the island's grape vines. This region is very similar to Napa Valley in that regard. Plan a day trip to the Saanich Peninsula, a short drive from Victoria, to visit the vineyard and buy a few bottles of Pinot Gris and Pinot Noir at Church & State Wines (*www.churchandstatewines.com*). At the small, family-owned Chalet Estate Winery, you and the girls can arrange a private winemaker's dinner accompanied by a sampling of the vineyard's limited-edition wines to celebrate a birthday or just as a treat (*www.chaletestate vineyard.ca*). And for something truly different, head to Marley Farm Winery, which specializes in unusual fruit wines (raspberry, loganberry, and kiwi) along with traditional varietals (*www.marleyfarm .ca*). There's always the option of hiring Crush Wine Tours to take you on tours of local vineyards and farms (from $84 per person for an afternoon tour; 877-888-5748, *www.crushwinetours.com*).

WHERE TO STAY

The Magnolia Hotel & Spa, in Victoria's Inner Harbor, provides fluffy down bedding, in-room gas fireplaces, and guided tours of Victoria's public and private gardens as well as Aveda spa treatments (the "Victorian Garden" package, including one night's stay, breakfast, and four-hour tour for two, starts at $348; 877-624-6654, *www.magnoliahotel.com*). At the Brentwood Bay Lodge Resort and Spa in the city, rooms look onto ocean views. After a day exploring Victoria's gardens, unwind with a wrap or massage (a two-night spa getaway package, including breakfast and $100 spa gift certificate starts at $464; 888-544-2079, *www.brentwoodbaylodge.com*). Moderately priced Royal Scot Suite Hotel, is well located near the harbor, the ferry to Port Angeles, Washington, the government buildings, and the Royal British Columbia Museum. Choose from suites to studio apartments (from $164; *www.royalscot.com*).

ONE CLICK AND YOU'RE OFF

For information on travel to Victoria, visit *www.victoriatourism.com*.

⊱ Japan ⊰

There's something therapeutic about a Japanese garden. The silence and order one finds in a classic Japanese raked-pebble garden will astound you. So will the perfect ponds, manicured gardens, and blossoming cherry trees found in Kyoto, in the central region of Japan's largest island. Kyoto, now associated worldwide with environmentalism, actually became Japan's capital in 794 and remained the emperor's home for more than a thousand years. Because Allied bombings spared Kyoto during World War II, the city and its gardens serve as a window into its ancient history. The city, while quite modern, has the feel of a small town and a sense of its past; around every corner of Kyoto's easy-to-navigate grid you will find a treasure: hidden temple pagodas with their upturned roofs, shrines, museums, and of course, tidy raked-pebble gardens.

By exploring Kyoto on foot or bicycle, you will be treated to a glimpse of private gardens tucked behind traditional screens and down narrow alleyways. You and the girls will feel like you're being ushered into a secret world. Dedicating a trip to the gardens of Kyoto, girlfriends traveling together find it a cathartic experience—from the wholesome and distinctive cuisine that will undoubtedly result in some experimenting to the aesthetic and intellectual balance between nature and man-made beauty. Summer can be quite hot and humid, so if you can, arrive in spring, when the blossoms are absolutely breathtaking. November is another peak month for a visit, when maple leaves ignite with bright-red leaves. Kyoto is one of Japan's most romantic cities; a place where you can easily imagine the opulent lives of geishas in regal kimonos, powerful nobles, shoguns, emperors, and samurai.

ROYAL GARDENS

Formerly the domain of the Japanese shoguns (the highest class during the 17th-century Tokugawa period), Nijo Castle is protected by no fewer than three stone walls and two moats. And cloistered between the moats one finds a garden. Delve further, and come across footbridges linking three islands within a tranquil pond shaded by cherry and pear trees. And in the inner sanctum of the castle, you'll find a surprise—another garden with two teahouses. Sprawled before the Imperial Palace, the Japanese national garden, Kyoto Gyoen, presents guests with chrysanthemums and cherry trees, a French garden, a Japanese garden, and a tropical greenhouse (*www.kyoto gyoen.go.jp*). The Imperial Palace, where the royal family lived from 1331 until 1868 when they moved to Tokyo, has two free English-speaking tours daily on weekdays; to sign up you'll need to register online (http://*sankan.kunaicho.go.jp/english*). Although the tours do not go inside the palace, you'll learn about the palace architecture and 500 years of court life.

ZEN GARDENS

You don't need to be a practicing Buddhist to appreciate the stark, calming beauty of a Zen garden. These enclosed rock gardens made with tiny pebbles and accented with larger stones are a study in restraint and perfection. And there's no better place to view a perfect example of Japan's famous Zen gardens than at the Ryoanji Temple. Here, 15 rocks sit like islands among raked white gravel. You could very well lose an hour or two simply sitting and absorbing the garden's lines and textures as well as the serenity enveloping you—and ponder how it's possible that you can only see 14 of the rocks from any one vantage point (*www.ryoanji.jp*). Kyoto's other exemplary rock garden can be found at the Daisen-in Temple. The garden here conveys a mountainous landscape and a dry river that "flows" through the garden through the arrangement of the rocks.

TEA TIME

Tea is as much as an institution in Japan as in England—although perhaps more healthful. What this means for women travelers is an excuse to seek out a daily spot of tea, plop yourselves down, and use the time to catch up on stories. We've all heard about the benefits of green tea, and maybe you've worked it into your routine. But nothing you've had before will stack up to a powdered green tea called *matcha*, typically served as a creamy, frothy concoction. The Westin Miyako's Shikunshi teahouse offers an exceptional traditional tea ceremony in which powdered green tea is prepared

SHOPPING SMARTS

෨

Before you leave, make a list of the family members and friends for whom you wish to purchase a gift. Ask for the clothing sizes of children or teens and record that information. Also note what *colors* and *styles* family members do not like. You may be tempted to buy a gorgeous green pashmina shawl for your mother, who thinks that green is "not her color" and would never wear it.

by a skilled practitioner and served to a small group of guests in a tranquil setting (from $10; *www.westinmiyako-kyoto.com*). The Women's Association of Kyoto also hosts tea ceremonies—along with courses in flower arranging, cooking, kimonos, and Japanese language ($127 for tea ceremony, which includes a Japanese-tea history lesson; *www.wakjapan.com*).

BEST GARDEN CAFE

While in Japan, eat as the Japanese do. Much like the gardens, Japanese food is meticulously prepared, clean, and light. At the Ryoanji Temple's Seven Herb Tofu Restaurant, *yudofu* is the restaurant's signature—and only—dish. This simple yet tasty creation consists of tofu cooked in hot broth and seasoned with herbs, along with sides of pickles, vegetables, and sticky rice (*www.ryoanji.jp*). Nanzen-ji Temple, in Kyoto's eastern foothills, is also known for its yudofu—and its beautiful dry-climate garden (*www.nanzenji.com/english*).

In the heart of old Kyoto (on the west side of Fuyacho, north of Sanjo), try Misoka-An Kawamichiya, a 300-year-old soba and *udon* noodle shop renowned for hot or cold buckwheat noodles, as well as noodles with fish cakes, quail eggs, yuba, tempura and chicken, onions, or Japanese mushrooms. Or enjoy the house specialty; a one-pot noodle dish prepared at your table called *hokoro*, which includes vegetables, chicken, mushrooms, and vegetables. An English menu is available (noodle dishes are $5 to $14; *www.kyotoguide.com*).

MUST-SEE MUSEUMS

The fashionistas among you will find the Costume Museum worth the visit to Japan along: It displays clothing worn during various periods of Japanese history, with a special focus on costumes and noble life during the Heian period, from 794 to 1185 (*www.iz2.or.jp/index.htm*). Summer kimonos and Buddhist icons were recently on display at the Kyoto National Museum, home to one of the most extensive collections of premodern (pre-1800) Japanese and Asian art in the world; during your visit you will be treated to a extensive collection of endemic ceramics, paintings, calligraphy, and lacquerware (*www.kyohaku.go.jp*).

TAKE A STROLL

For some morning exercise, lace up those sneakers and strike out on the Walk of Philosophy, a pathway lined with cherry trees stretching nearly a mile along a canal. Located in eastern Kyoto, it runs from Nanzen-ji to Ginkaku-ji (Silver pavilion). The path was named in homage to the philosopher Nishida Kitaro, founder of the Kyoto School of Philosophy, who meditated as he walked this route in the early 1900s. In springtime, you too may do your own version of mediation with friends surrounded by cherry blossoms—and in summer, fireflies.

BEST CULINARY EXPERIENCE

Referred to as the kitchen of Kyoto, the Nishiki Food Market still, after 400 years, satiates the appetites of the city's residents. This covered market is replete with more than a hundred vendors selling mounds of fresh produce and seafood as well as freshly prepared local dishes. Friends should make a pact in the morning to each try something a little wild: It's a great way to seal your memories of Kyoto (via your taste buds) and to likely have a few laughs. Sample fresh octopus balls or Japanese pickles, which might include soft *umeboshi* (plums), and *matsutake* (pine mushroom), crispy tart radishes, pickled slices of *saba* (mackerel), cucumbers, young shoots, or red peppers. Rarely is a meal served without Japanese pickles. They are part of breakfast, packed into bento boxes for lunch, and accompany dinners and feasts. You'll also see them served in bars and restaurants as appetizers. Sometimes the traditional Japanese tea ceremony includes pickles, too, so have some fun and sample all kinds at the Nishiki Food Market.

It's also a fantastic place to stock your kitchen with serious culinary gear, such as Japanese steel knives (not to be packed in your carry-on, of course). You may want to plan your visit to Nishiki around the famous confectionery shop Tsuruya Yoshinobu, where you can watch artisans create impeccable flower-like cakes, which you may sample with your tea.

HOT SPRINGS HAVEN

The Japanese, you may notice, are serious people and they take their hot springs ritual very seriously—it's an age-old therapy. To partake in the tradition, you and the girls can take a 45-minute train ride to the town of Kurama, in the mountains to the north of Kyoto. You'll all find relief (maybe even healing) in steaming indoor and outdoor tubs at Kurama Onsen. The website for Japanese Guesthouses has a list of hot springs across the country and detailed transportation information (*www.japaneseguesthouses.com/db/kyoto/kurama.htm*).

BEST SHOPPING

There are a few items I wouldn't want to leave Kyoto without, namely: textiles (kimonos included), ceramics, lacquerware, and folding fans.

SMALL THINGS I ALWAYS PACK FOR AN INTERNATIONAL TRIP:

* A rubber door stopper for added security in hotel rooms.

* A large safety pin or a clothespin to fully close the hotel drapes.

* A washcloth because most hotels do not provide them.

* A bottle opener and corkscrew. Although I can find these in almost all countries, it's nice to have one ready for picnics or in my hotel room for a drink before dinner.

* Individually wrapped chocolates, unless I'm going somewhere really warm. Chocolate or candy is a nice gift to offer to a desk clerk or someone who has been especially kind or helpful. If I am going to be hosted by a family, I always take a gift box of fancy chocolates.

* Photos of my family, pets, garden, holiday celebrations and home. In my experience the people I meet are as curious about my life as I am about theirs.

—Marybeth

To find the best selection of these in one area, visit the specialty shops along the street of Shijo-Dori. The multistory Kyoto Handicraft Center is a great resource as well. If you've got the stamina and the skill, you should plan your trip around Japan's biggest flea market at the Toji Temple, held on the 21st of each month. If you're looking for a less expensive but stunning kimono, you may find one here.

WHERE TO STAY

It's a splurge, but the 30-room Hiiragiya, a luxury *ryokan* (traditional inn) in Kyoto's center is worth every yen. The wooden private bath in your room you may try to bring home with you (starts at $271, including breakfast and a multicourse Japanese dinner; *www.hiiragiya.co.jp /en*). For something easier on the credit card, try Yoshi-Ima, where you'll curl up on a futon placed upon a tatami mat. You can also enjoy the hot baths and a candlelit tea ceremony with your dear friends. Another fine attribute is its location in the Gion neighborhood (the geisha quarter), located near some fabulous art and antiques shopping on Shinmozen street (from $162 per person double occupancy, including dinner and breakfast; *www.yoshi-ima.co.jp*).

BEST GUIDED TOURS

The Japanese gardening magazine *Sukiya Living* sponsors two-week garden tours of Kyoto and its surrounding regions led by bilingual garden experts in the spring and fall. Getting a group together for this trip won't be hard when everyone finds out about taking part in Japanese traditions such as calligraphy, flower arranging, and Noh mask carving ($3,950 including accommodations, breakfast, garden admissions, and daily meal at a garden restaurant; *www.rothteien .com/tour/info.htm*).

EVENTS TO FLY IN FOR

The best focal point to a girls' garden getaway is the peaking of Kyoto's cherry blossoms in late March and early April. Although there is no official "festival," you can join the locals in celebrating the season by heading to Maruyama Park, the centerpiece of which is a lighted *shidarezakura* (weeping cherry tree). Maruyama Park is a public, free park, and the most popular location in Kyoto for informal picnics and parties under the blooming trees.

ONE CLICK AND YOU'RE OFF

For more information on Kyoto, visit *www.kyoto.travel*.

Portugal

Madeira has graced the pages of many wine lists worldwide, but a little-known secret about this Portuguese island is that it's also a garden paradise. Known as "the floating flowerpot," Madeira is the largest island in the Madeira archipelago, smack between mainland Portugal and the coast of northern Africa. And the flora here is a reflection of their cultures—a mix of European and tropical. Girlfriends looking for an island getaway with an exotic bent will adore this Atlantic gem. Madeira's capital city, Funchal, is on the island's southern coast, wedged between the sea and the mountains. White buildings with red-tile roofs are spread along cobblestone streets stretching from the water up toward the foothills, which eventually rise to nearly 4,000 feet. The city's name is thought to come from the abundance of fennel growing here. You'll sniff the plant's sweet licorice scent in the air. For a group of ladies, the way to go is to rent a comfortable home base in Funchal (90 minutes by plane from Lisbon), or stay in one of the beautiful villa-like hotels in the surrounding foothills. Either way, you and the girls will pile into taxis or buses to explore the fertile grounds all around the island, flush with vibrantly colored orchids and bougainvillaea, trees bursting with bananas and dates, and roses and topiaries. And be sure to end your days with a glass of that Madeira wine.

Madeira's subtropical climate makes it a year-round destination with temperatures varying only a few degrees throughout the year. Spring is the best time to see the island in bloom. Summers are very hot and cruise ships and hordes of European visitors descend upon the islands.

GREAT GARDENS

Here's a sight you won't find too many other places in the world: a garden that resembles an intricate quilt. It's one of the many displays at the 12-acre Botanical Garden, about two miles from central Funchal. The garden burgeons with 2,500 plants—both Madeira natives and rare species from around the world. Take a stroll with the gals along palm-lined paths, past camellias and fuchsias, stopping in at the bromeliad greenhouse, pausing to admire the ponds and streams filled with water-loving plants, and oohing over the sculpted topiaries. Your admission ticket to the garden also gets you into the Museum of Natural History and Loiro Park (*www.sra.pt*). Take a 15-minute cable-car ride into the hills to visit Monte Palace

Tropical Gardens, which are like the United Nations of flowers, with Scottish heather, cycads from South Africa, orchids and azaleas from the Himalaya. When you're there, you'll be walking the 17-acre grounds in good company—black and white swans glide across the central lake and peacocks display their iridescent colors as they strut the garden's paths (*www.montepalace.com*).

FOR ORCHID LOVERS

Madeira's Orchid Garden (next door to the Botanical Garden) is home to 50,000-plus orchids. It's an intoxicating, year-round destination dedicated to the species thanks to behind-the-scenes propagation and laboratory work that keep the flowers continually in bloom. You'll get a December-to-May dose of intense color from slipper orchids, cymbidiums, and lycastes at this award-winning garden. Throughout the year, you can witness the peak of the hybrids and South American bromeliads, Australian martinets, and African aloes. You and the girls can try your hand at keeping an orchid alive: Buy a bottled baby orchid at the garden (*www.madeiraorchid.com*).

BEST STROLLING

A good pair of shoes and a love of walking will go a long way on Madeira. The island's many small canals (which are called *levadas* and date back to the 16th century) are lined with walking paths. Collectively, the paths create a network of miles and miles of walkways through the island's countryside. Madeira Explorers offers several guided levada walks to suit casual cruisers and high-energy hikers alike (*www.madeira-explorers.com*).

BEST VIEWS

The Palheiro Estate is situated at about 1,640 feet above sea level in the hills to the east of Funchal. The sweeping views from here of Funchal below are almost as breathtaking as the renowned camellias in the estate's gardens (*www.palheiroestate.com*).

BEST DINING

Much like the island's flora, the cuisine here is bright, bold, and delicate all at once. In Funchal, the casual Ristorante Villa Cipriani at the luxury hotel Reid's Palace presents fine Italian dishes served in old-world elegance with views of the Atlantic (*www.reidspalace*
.com). At the Adega da Quinta (Adega means "wine lodge") at the Quinta do Estreito hotel—a short ride to the west of Funchal in the

village of Estreito de Câmara de Lobos—you can treat yourselves to delicious country fare like homemade sweet-potato bread and savory pot-roasted chicken (*www.quintadoestreitomadeira.com*).

FOR WINE LOVERS

Were you wondering when I'd get back to talking about Madeira's wine? The local wine is usually made with the *tinta negra mole* grape and blended with other varietals and served primarily as an aperitif or dessert wine. On a 90-minute Funchal Winewalk, you get to explore the city's streets and wines (get the details about this walk and more at the blog *www.madeirawineguide.com*).

SHOP TILL YOU DROP

At the Mercado dos Lavradores, in Funchal, you can browse stands selling fresh produce and crafts—it's especially crowded on Fridays. The pedestrian, cobblestone streets in the market are packed with shops selling embroidery, trinkets, and fresh Madeiran flowers (orchids, birds of paradise, and flamingo flowers). Most shops will offer to pack the flowers for you in protective boxes to preserve them on your flight home if you'd like to bring a piece of Madeira back with you. You'll see a lot of wicker for sale around Funchal, but resist the temptation to buy anything until you visit the village of Camacha, near the Palheiro Estate in the hills to the east of Funchal. Camacha is a wicker town, and it has the biggest selection of items. If you're in the market for a basket, hat, chair, or toys, this is the place to spend your money.

WHERE TO STAY

Perched in the hills above Funchal, Choupana Hill Resort and Spa is the garden isle's most relaxing retreat. In addition to lovely rooms and landscaped grounds, the resort offers outstanding spa services, among them hot-stone massages, Rasul (a Moroccan mud massage followed by exfoliation), facials, and yoga classes (garden-view doubles start at $400; *www.choupanahills.com*). The Estalagem Quinta da Casa Branca's award-winning modern building is surrounded by 30 acres of lush gardens. The renowned Casa da Quinta restaurant serves innovative seafood dishes, like sautéed scallops on a vanilla and green asparagus risotto. Take advantage of a health club with weights and cardio equipment, a Jacuzzi, sauna, and Turkish bath (doubles are from $270; *www .quintacasabranca.pt*). At Casa Velha do Palheiro, golf lovers will

Many private garden owners will not host big groups, so be sure to find out how many participants are in your group. You don't want to be denied access.

be delighted by this Relais & Chateaux hotel's close proximity to the Palheiro Golf Course. About six miles east of Funchal, the 37-room hotel has its own hibiscus and bougainvillaea-filled private gardens for strolling. The "Madeira Garden Splendour" package includes entries to several of Madeira's gardens, an afternoon tea and a dinner at the hotel restaurants, and private shuttle service into Funchal (from $655 for a three-night stay in a double room; *www.casa-velha.com*).

BEST TOURS
U.K.-based Bright Water Holidays has been offering garden tours for 15 years to Madeira, Japan, Brazil, South Africa, Holland, Lake Como, Namibia, Costa Rica, Sweden, and the United Kingdom. They offer an eight-day Madeira tour, with bed-and-breakfast at three- or four-star hotels, airfare from the U.K., and admission to all gardens from $1,181 (*www.brightwaterholidays.com/ostours.htm*). Daylong and abbreviated tours of gardens are available from Madeira Wind Birds (from $41 for a three-hour biodiversity tour to $61 for a five-hour flora-and-fauna tour; *www.madeirawindbirds.com*). And those gals who want a little more help planning, but prefer to stick to their own schedule once they arrive, will be happy to know that it's easy to book a simple tour once you arrive or book a customized fly/drive tour from U.S.-based Magellan Tours (*www.magellantours.com*).

EVENTS TO FLY IN FOR
The island's breathtaking New Year's festivities require a commitment—you'll need to get there a few days before Christmas and leave after January 6, the Day of Kings (celebrating the day when the "three wise men," known at the magi kings in Portugal, arrived in Bethlehem). But with fireworks (according to the *Guinness Book of World Records*, it's the world's largest display) and nonstop parties, you won't want to leave even then. Another event to plan this trip around is the annual Madeira Flower Festival, two weeks after Easter, when houses and shops are covered in floral displays, and a parade winds through the streets with costumed dancers and opulent floats decorated with flowers.

Visit Madeira Tourism at *www.madeiraislands.travel.*

❧ Italy ❧

Italy is known for fantastic food, warm and lively people, art history, fashion, and *il dolce far niente*—the pleasure of doing nothing. In the Lake Como region you can add to that list intricately designed Renaissance gardens, the sparkling waters of a 26-mile-long lake, and pomegranate, fig, and olive trees shading the shoreline. In northern Italy, near Milan and the Swiss border, stately lakeside villas and decadent resort towns are all strung around Lake Como's shores. It's a romantic place, where the snowcapped Alps frame the jewel-blue lakes ringed by forests and lavish Mediterranean gardens—an emotional place to dream, to brood, to be unapologetically sentimental. You won't be alone: The Lake District has been praised and cherished for centuries—by poets (Lord Byron), novelists (Flaubert to Shelley), and composers (Verdi and Rossini).

Start easing into Italian time with a four-hour train ride from Zurich, Switzerland—the Milan airport is closest but the flights are more expensive. Plus, I think you'll agree that the Alps scenery is worth the extra time on the train. Book a few rooms with the girls in one of the lake's small, friendly resort towns—two of my favorites are Bellagio and Varenna—then spend your days taking ferries to other towns to explore their terraced gardens and tree-lined shores. Days begin with strong espresso and end around a café table with glasses of wine and a feast composed of pastas, meats, and cheese accented with fresh ingredients from the area. Local favorites you can look forward to include polenta with *missoltini* (dried lake fish), porcini mushrooms, and sweet *miascia* (mixed fruit tart). For beautiful azaleas and rhododendrons as well as blissfully cool days, springtime is best, but rest assured that many of the gardens display their fabulous colors in summer and fall as well.

GREAT GARDENS

The 40-acre park encircling Villa Carlotta is home to 500 plant species. And there's a good story here to take home to your daughter about a mother's love: This estate, completed in 1690, was a wedding gift from Princess Marianne of Prussia to her daughter, Princess Carlotta, in 1843. Some gift! From Bellagio or Varenna guests approach the gorgeous villa on the lake's western shore by ferry. Springtime visitors are treated to 150 varieties of rhododendrons and azaleas in bloom; and year-round feast your eyes on the camellias, venerable cedars and sequoias, ferns, and rock and bamboo gardens. If you've got an extra hour to spare, stop in at the museum on the grounds, which specializes in 19th-century art ($11; *www.villacarlotta.it/sito/indexx2.php*). Over in the town of Bellagio, the white Villa Melzi, built in the early 1800s, was originally the lakeside home of an Italian vice president. The villa has French-influenced neoclassic detailing, and outside, there's a lively botanical garden. You can wander its paths, visit the Japanese pond dappled with water lilies, and relish the estate's springtime blossoming of azaleas and rhododendrons.

STRETCH YOUR LEGS

In the town of Como, the Piazza Cavour neighborhood gives those on foot plenty to experience: charming cafés, grand belle-époque hotels, and historical treasures such as Il Duomo di Como, the 18th-century cathedral. Lakefront promenades give the city an elegant 19th-century ambience. For an extended walk and unfettered views of the lake, ride Como's funicular up to Brunate. From there, walk to the Volta lighthouse and continue to the Sanctuary of Santa Rita for a stunning panorama of the lake and the Alps. The lake town of Varenna presents you with cobblestone streets and steep stairways, which allow you to walk back to another era. Get the girls to make a day of exploring this village on foot: Pack a picnic in town then hike up to the Castello de Vezio, a medieval fortress surrounded by olive groves. When you arrive, catch your breath and savor your reward: Yes, the lake views are absolutely breathtaking. Settle for your Italian picnic feast, and when you're done, take a peek around the ruins of the castle, the tower, the drawbridge, and the underground vaults created during World War I. The absolute best views of the lake are from the highest point, from the castle tower, of course (*www.castellodivezio.it*).

FROM GARDEN TO TABLE

If you're staying in one of Lake Como's luxurious hotels, you'll find plenty of fine cuisine just steps from your room. But when you're out and about in the towns along the lake, there are a few restaurants that you and the ladies should make it a priority to plan a night around. In Varenna, try Vecchia Varenna, an adorable waterfront restaurant known for its fabulous (and relatively affordable) local cuisine. Sip a glass of *prosecco* on the terrace and try a local specialty like the risotto with perch (*www.vecchiavarenna.it*). In Como, share dishes at Ristorante Colombetta of wonderful fish and pasta, including a lobster tagliolini (*www.colombetta.it*). Il Gato Nero, in Cernobbio, is reportedly one of George Clooney's favorites—incredible cuisine served with a side of sunset view.

SHOP TILL YOU DROP
If you love silk, you'll love Como. Boutiques here are swimming in the stuff: Bring back gorgeous scarves, ties, and bedding. (To help calibrate your budget, an exquisite duvet or bed cover starts at around $400.) La Tessitura Concept Store, near the center of Como, works silk like no one I've ever seen, designing espadrilles, hats, bowls—you name it, they've thought of it—in silk (*www.lates situra.com*). And if you're really looking to overdo it, there's always the fashion axis of the world—Milan is only an hour's drive away.

HOTEL IN BLOOM
A Russian empress and a Napoleonic general used to call Cernobbio's Villa d'Este home—and Queen Caroline of England owned the property in the early 1800s. Ladies today, no doubt, will appreciate their taste. The rooms of the villa are lavishly decorated with silk drapes, period furniture, and oil paintings, and many have private balconies. The grounds are a sprawling 25-acre park with a Renaissance garden brimming with jasmine and oleander bushes, olive and magnolia trees, topiary hedges, and sculptures (from $690 for a double; *www .villadeste.com*).

RENT A PRIVATE VILLA
If you'll be traveling in a group, there's no better option than renting a villa. You'll help cook your own Italian feasts and then dine in your own private garden. The six-bedroom Casa Rosore Passalacqua is contained by fountain-filled gardens, among them an olive garden, an orchard, vegetable and cutting gardens, a rose garden, and a classic Tuscan garden (price on request; *www.thevillapassalacqua.com*). Rental company Cottages to Castles rents out several properties with views of Lake Como (from $3,400 for a three-bedroom villa for a week; *www.cottagestocastles.com*), and Parker Company specializes in Italian villas and apartments and has several options in Bellagio ($1,500-$5,000 per week; *www.theparkercompany.com*). Owners Direct offers villa and apartment rentals on Lake Como (from $616 for a two-bedroom villa for a week; *www.ownersdirect.co.uk/Italy.htm*).

BEST TOURS

On U.S-based Wilderness Travel's seven-day "Hiking in Italy's Lake Districts" trip, you'll spend several days in the Lake Como area, exploring gardens, nearby trails, and local food. During moderate hikes, you'll enjoy great picnic lunches, and you'll also see a private folk museum and have time to shop and stroll around Como and Bellagio (starting at $4,095 for groups of six to nine; 800-368-2794, *www.wildernesstravel.com*).

ONE CLICK AND YOU'RE OFF

For information on the town of Como, visit *www.comune.como.it*; for Bellagio, *www.bellagiolakecomo.com*; for Varenna, *www.varen naitaly.com*.

CHAPTER TEN

Lending a Hand

TO VOLUNTEER OR NOT TO VOLUNTEER

Being an observer is a cinch when traveling: You board the plane, you ride the bus, and you watch the scenery go by. But the most soul-satisfying travel experiences come when you make a difference in the lives of the people within that landscape. You might teach English to children in Brazil, lead art projects with Nepalese orphans, help African women learn to use computers. Volunteering is, for lack of a better term, true total immersion. It's more like living in a country than being a tourist. You interact with people on a more intimate level, you see the country through the eyes of its inhabitants, and you understand their traditions, customs, language, day-to-day joys, and struggles. If you really want to get beneath the surface of a culture, live with the local people in a village. In Mexico, for example, if you're a polite guest, you'll be invited to join a family birthday party where the teenagers will teach you the samba, and you'll sample the homemade mole Grandma spent five days preparing. In Cambodia the matriarch of the family may ask you to join her shopping at a local market and you'll meet her lady friends, or you may go to school with her son and speak to his class about the United States. You'll find that doors swing wide open for volunteers.

And you won't have any trouble finding a volunteer opportunity. Dozens of U.S.-based nonprofit organizations send volunteers abroad for as little as a week and as long as a year. It's a safe and meaningful way for women to visit far-off countries on their own—you'll meet other volunteers and form bonds with the locals. Or if you round up a group, it can be a great opportunity to bond with your girlfriends. But here's the surprising part: Volunteering isn't always free. Most of these nonprofits charge a fee, with the proceeds funding the operating costs of the organization and often benefiting the communities you're working with. The upshot is that the fee and any related travel are usually tax-deductible, and your living expenses are often covered. Some programs even cover language classes, weekend outings, and daily cultural activities. Most volunteer organizations send you orientation packs to help familiarize you with the country you're visiting, and they'll also pick you up at the airport and bring you to the neighborhood or town where you're volunteering. The experience, I assure you, will be priceless.

⤳ JACKIE AND MARCIA'S STORY ⤳

When Jackie and Marcia met more than 20 years ago in San Leandro, California, they never imagined they would voluntarily use up vacation days, leave their significant others at home, travel all the way to Central America, and volunteer in a school next to a city dump. The two had taken vacations together with their partners—shopping, museum hopping, lying on the beach. But they were interested in a more meaningful experience and seeing the mostly hidden-from-tourists side of a nation. They began searching for a program that would allow them each to get involved in a community and make a difference in the everyday lives of the underprivileged. With full-time jobs and few vacation days, they needed a short-term volunteer program.

A quick search on the Internet landed them on the AARP website where they found the heading "Making a Difference." One click offered lists of short volunteer projects in Costa Rica, Russia, South America, and Guatemala. "I felt like a kid in a candy shop," says Marcia of the possibilities. They both had visited Mexico before and taken some

Spanish classes, so they felt comfortable with Latin culture and were intrigued by Guatemala, a place they had never been. So they booked a one-week program in Guatemala City with a volunteer organization that provided accommodations, meals, transportation to and from the volunteer site, and afternoon excursions. The organization assigned work projects for every volunteer based upon their skills and interests.

A week before their departure, Jackie and Marcia were notified of their volunteer duties: They were to set up a library in a remedial school for underprivileged children. They were thrilled with the assignment, but when they arrived, they weren't quite prepared for the extreme poverty. The school was in the poorest neighborhood in Guatemala City, across the street from a dump. The residents lived in cardboard shacks, selling and recycling garbage from the landfill. It was utterly overwhelming, shocking, and immediately began to fit their view of the world into a new perspective. But having each other to go through this transformation with made it all more manageable.

Jackie and Marcia went on to enthusiastically tackle their project. Every day from 8 a.m. to noon they painted the library walls, covered the bookshelves with colorful paper, and sorted, stacked, and cataloged hundreds of donated books. They were creating a safe, quiet reading area for the children of the dump workers eagerly awaiting the library's opening day. No one at the school spoke English, so Marcia and Jackie improvised. "We gestured and used what little Spanish we had to communicate," Marcia says. "A smile and handshake are part of a universal language," Jackie adds. While they worked, they got to know the children. Young girls came in to give them hugs and offer their help; boys hid behind the bookshelves and giggled as they popped out to surprise the ladies.

The "home base" where Jackie and Marcia lived for the week was a quaint middle-class house in a residential neighborhood with seven modest bedrooms filled with bunk beds for 22 volunteers from across the United States, ranging from 20-year-old students to grandmas. A motherly, bilingual Guatemalan woman welcomed them at the house and provided insights into cultural events and pointers on safety. Meals were traditional Guatemalan fare, authentic and very indulgent with its rich flavors: stews, pastas, beans, green salads, and handmade tortillas.

Jackie and Marcia began to feel the difference between being a tourist and being a volunteer. It was a subtle distinction that allowed them to get involved in the everyday lives of the townspeople.

continued on page 242

HELPING OUT IN THE HIMALAYA

✿

One of my reasons to travel is to help women in developing countries," Vivien, a 47-year-old substance-abuse counselor from Adelaide, Australia, explains. So when she planned a trip to India she searched on the Internet for volunteer organizations where she could donate time and energy and discovered the Women's Alliance of Ladakh. From Delhi she flew northwest to a harsh land located deep in the Himalaya on the Tibetan Plateau. She just showed up at their office in Leh and asked: "What can I do?" They put her to work helping to organize workshops and festivals that showcased traditional Ladakhi Buddhist culture, cuisine, dance, music, weaving, and handicrafts. Vivien volunteered for five hours a day, five days a week for four weeks.

"It's hard to say what I enjoyed most. I loved promoting and staffing the two-day festivals where the local women proudly wore their traditional dresses, tapestry shawls, and tall hats. They sold their weavings and homemade food; apricot jam, whole wheat noodles, vegetable *mok moks*—Ladakhi dumplings,"Vivien says, "and they invited everyone to join in the slow dancing. The workshops were equally fun." Village women came in from the countryside and taught their traditional ways to tourists: spinning, weaving, dyeing, making mud bricks, and preparation of indigenous foods such as organic vegetable noodle soups.

Vivien discovered that volunteering is a two-way experience. "I was not just giving—I was getting so much back," she says. "I got to hang out with the local women, partake in their jokes and teasing, learn about their ancient ways of living, and share in the joyfulness of their everyday lives." These women have hard lives but they find joy in the camaraderie of each other. They have a lot of fun as they weave, cook, farm, make apricot jam or dumplings.

"They are very connected to their community and they welcomed me into their lives. I felt connected, not like a tourist on the outside observing," Vivien adds.

Two local staff members ran the Women's Alliance along with volunteers from France, Poland, Slovakia, Austria, Brazil, and Israel. "I made a wonderful network of girlfriends from all over the world," says Vivien. Her daily work varied from writing media releases to showing tourists movies about Ladakhi culture to chopping vegetables in the restaurant kitchen. The Alliance's projects reach more than 6,000 women members from almost a hundred different villages.

Adjusting to the high altitude, dry climate, and basic living conditions was part of the adventure for Vivien. She stayed in a simple Ladakhi guesthouse with a lovely family. Every morning the 93-year-old grandma greeted her and then nodded off to sleep while sunning in her chair on the roof porch. "Although the home had no hot water, the *ama-leh* (mother of the house) cheerfully heated a bucket of water for me and I learned how to make every drop count for my 'bucket bath,' " recounts Vivien. The guesthouse was at the top of the valley, outside of town, and Vivien enjoyed her walk into town on pathways with donkeys, dogs, and farmers carrying produce to market and through people's vegetable patches, along irrigation canals, and through stone passageways under homes. People waved, called hello, and seemed genuinely pleased to see her.

"I felt like I was living in another world, in another time," Vivien says. "I left India a changed woman. I learned that the simple things in life are deeply meaningful; weaving, cooking, singing, dancing. I connected with local women and even though we were from very different cultures, we have so many similarities in our lives. The most important things are our families and friends." While Vivien was in India, her 25-year-old daughter wrote to her saying; "I'm so proud of you, Mum, for traveling to places like India and giving back to the world." Smiling, Vivien adds, "I'm proud to be that kind of Mum for my daughter."

This transparency gave Marcia and Jackie the opportunity to see through the eyes of these Guatemalans and experience typical days for them: To see the same sights, taste the same flavors, hear the same sounds, and live in a residential neighborhood. A touristy hotel's version of Guatemala City would have been disappointingly myopic compared to this immersion.

At lunchtime the organization's van picked up Marcia and Jackie to take them home for a hearty meal and a siesta—often they sun-bathed or read under the trees in the courtyard, serenaded by the vocal pet parrots. This free time helped balance the work-vacation ratio and allowed them to reflect on the intensity of their surroundings and encounters. After siesta, they joined other volunteers for afternoon outings to folk-art museums, pottery workshops, tortilla-making classes, and shopping trips in the colonial town of Antigua. Marcia and Jackie appreciated being tourists for a bit but always looked forward to the next morning at the school. Their favorite excursion was a visit to the homes of the school's students. "We saw entire families—babies, toddlers, teens, and grandparents—truly enjoying each other," says Jackie. "Their laughter, hugging, and teasing showed how much togetherness and love they share. We realized that poverty means you don't have money, but it doesn't necessarily mean you're unhappy."

Clearly, this was unlike any vacation either of them had taken. They took a journey well beyond a destination: They got to live through the lives of a native people. And even though it only lasted a week, they felt they made a significant contribution to the school and the children. On their last day, when the library was finally complete, a seven-year-old boy named Juan and his two friends sat on the cement floor of the new library, fascinated with the illustrations and words in a Little Golden Book. Jackie observed how looking through the book was magical for the kids. "I really had the opportunity to touch people," Jackie says. "My life is richer from this experience. It opened a door and I'd like to go back and volunteer again."

Jamaica

Reggae, rum, and beach resorts come to mind with the mention of Jamaica. But at the heart of the Caribbean island, beyond the hubbub of spring-break hot spots Montego Bay and Negril, you can discover one of Jamaica's last authentic cultural and natural outposts. It's an area of rounded mountains and bowl-shaped valleys, an underground cave system, and the headwaters of the island's three biggest rivers (the source of most of its water). This region of western Jamaica, called Cockpit Country (so named because the holes in the limestone topography resemble cockfighting pits), consist of about 110,000 acres of former sugar, coffee, and cotton plantations with Great Houses—British-style estates built in the 1800s by slave owners—and three main towns. Trust me: It's the kind of place you and your friends will want to help protect from overdevelopment. The local Maroon people here, whose ancestors escaped slavery back in the 1600s, need help growing a viable ecotourism economy of their own. You can lend a hand to the Maroons, who have begun clearing their rivers, marking trails, and helping raise awareness about environmentalism and sustainable-tourism practices. Perhaps the best component of volunteering here is the homestay program. You'll live in simple houses (not to worry: they have electricity and running water), play dominoes with your host family, and try to pick up the sweet-sounding Jamaican-Creole patois. The foodies among you won't be disappointed in the cuisine: Every meal will be a feast of local specialties like breadfruit, yams, spicy "jerk" chicken, dumplings, rice and peas, salt fish, and curried goat. They are served everywhere and you'll likely get the chance to participate in the cooking of them. The benefit of visiting Jamaica is that it's a relatively small island. In your free time, you can cover a lot of ground in a day or a weekend and explore varied terrain and towns. You can look forward to touring the island with your girlfriends or new friends in a rental car and maybe hitting the beach, going for a horseback ride, or touring a traditional Jamaican Great House.

WHERE TO SIGN UP
U.S.-based nonprofit Globe Aware, which specializes in international volunteer trips that raise cultural awareness among Americans, runs a "Jamaica Undiscovered" trip every month of the year ($1,180 per week; 877-588-4562, *www.globeaware.org*). You can expect your group to range in size from 2 to 15 other volunteers also there to teach environmental education classes at local Maroon schools. The trip fee covers accommodations, meals, medical insurance, emergency medical evacuation, program coordination, and transportation within Jamaica—but not airfare to the island. A volunteer coordinator will meet you at the airport in Montego Bay, which is just a couple of hours in the air from Miami.

TAKE A BREAK

Globe Aware plans for you to have one weekday free and the entire weekend off from volunteering, so corral some girls and trot over to Good Hope Stables, based at an 18th-century plantation perched in the mountains above Cockpit Country, for a horseback-riding tour of the area. It's a birding hot spot up there, be sure someone in the group packs binoculars. You can chase endangered black-and yellow-billed parrots, along with endemic butterflies and 78 other bird species around the thick jungle dotted with wild orchids and bromeliads. After your ride, make a beeline for the Good Hope plantation house. This is one of Jamaica's glorious Great Houses with 14-foot-tall windows, polished rare wood floors, and gardens of papaya, breadfruit, banana, and orange trees ($35 per person for a 90-minute ride; *www.goodhopejamaica.com*).

A BIT OF GLITZ

The British actor and playwright Noël Coward was so enchanted by Jamaica in the 1940s that he bought property on a bluff with a stunning view of the Port of Santa Maria, east of the town of Ocho Rios on the northern coast. When you take a tour of his estate during a weekend outing, you can share in his romance with the place—and glimpse his photo-guestbook, featuring the likes of Marlene Dietrich, Laurence Olivier, Elizabeth Taylor, and Winston Churchill. (Be sure to document your own visit to the estate.) Coward had so many guests that he eventually purchased a second property as a retreat from his retreat. Both estates are open to the public. The first, Blue Harbor, is a bed-and-breakfast (from $100 per person per night, including meals; *www.blueharb.com*). And the second, Firefly, is now a museum preserved as it was when Coward died in 1973 (his paintings, his library, and his grave are here). After a hard week of work, this is an ideal spot to indulge in Jamaica's decadent side with an overnight stay.

JUST LIKE IN THE MOVIES

Jacques Cousteau dove to the bottom and Brook Shields swam it in the buff. Yes, that's right, I'm talking about the Blue Lagoon. On the northeastern shores of Jamaica—a 140-mile drive from Cockpit Country—is the town of Port Antonio and this legendary, spring-fed, 180-foot-deep pool of glorious clear water. You and the girls should hop into the car, turn up the contagious reggae tunes from a local radio station, and discover the Blue Lagoon for yourselves. It's no secret anymore and it can be a challenge to access, but the lagoon is certainly something you want to experience while in Jamaica. (It's a good idea to ask your host family for any insider tips about the place before you go.) Just past the Blue Lagoon, take your pick of Port Antonio's relaxing, sugar-white beaches below the lush Blue Mountains as well as markets, seafood cafés, and a promenade along the harbor.

SOAR TO NEW HEIGHTS

I can guarantee that peering down at the Caribbean Sea from the cockpit of a helicopter will make your personal top-ten list of greatest moments. Tours lift off from the town of Ocho Rios, on the north shore, and soar above the undulating mountains and sandy coastline of the island. The best part about taking a helicopter tour with your girlfriends is that it's actually affordable when you go with a group—plus there will be witnesses to vouch for this outrageous experience (about $95 per person for 30 minutes for a group of four; *www.carib bean-travel.com/helitours*).

EVENTS TO FLY IN FOR

Join the Maroons for traditional singing, dancing, and drum-playing at the Accompong Maroon Festival. Each year on January 6, the descendants of Cockpit Country's 17th-century runaway slaves gather to celebrate their victory over the British. Or plan your visit around the Ocho Rios Jazz Festival, which draws international musicians each June. The raucous sessions by Rastafarian blues musicians are out of this world and will get you and the girls to your feet. Not to be missed is the scenic "Jazz and Coffee in the Mountains" session set in a national park near Kingston and accompanied by Blue Mountain coffee—a major Jamaican export (*www.ochoriosjazz.com*).

I've melted curling irons, blown out hair dryers and almost ruined my cell phone because I didn't have the correct plugs and adapters. To find out what plugs and adapters you may need for your particular destination, a worldwide guide is available at this website: *www.interpower.com/ic/guide.htm*. To purchase phone and plug adapters, surge protecters, and voltage converters check out Magellan's, an online travel store: *www.magellans.com/store*.

—Marybeth

Visit Jamaica Tourism's website at *www.visitjamaica.com*. And for more detailed information on Cockpit Country, go to *www.cock pitcountry.com*.

⤳ Kenya ⤳

If you've always had your sights set on the Peace Corps but could never find the time, volunteering in Kenya might be your second chance. Located in East Africa, Kenya is known both as the cradle of humanity (the earliest evidence of humankind's existence was discovered here), and it is one of the most spectacular wildlife destinations in the world. But it's also a country where more than 50 percent of the population lives below the poverty line. The challenges for Kenyans are many: HIV/AIDS, gender inequality, lack of education, and poor maternal health. Volunteers are welcome to spend from one week to several months on programs in Mombasa (Kenya's second largest city, with nearly one million inhabitants) dedicated to sustainable development, education, and women's empowerment. Swahili is the predominant language in Mombasa, which has the largest port in East Africa. Volunteering with your girlfriends may be a more comfortable option for delving into Kenya. And if you're a solo traveler, it will give structure to your days and an instant community. Either way you'll find it easy to recruit companions to discover the wonders of Africa in your free time. Portuguese explorer Vasco da Gama landed here in the 15th century, and you can visit the forts built by the Portuguese in the 1600s. And since you're in Africa, girls, you must round out this epic journey to Kenya with a trip to the 3,000-mile-long Great Rift Valley, a geological wonder, and a safari in the region of the Serengeti, home to the Masai people and some of the planet's most exotic animals, among them zebras, lions, leopards, rhinos, and elephants.

WHERE TO SIGN UP
Based in San Francisco, the Foundation for Sustainable Development (FSD) offers volunteer opportunities year-round with its Kenya Women's Empowerment project ($1,150 for one week; 415-283-4873, *www.fsdinternational.org*). In your travels, I suspect that you've never returned home with the satisfaction of having taught women skills to launch businesses and earn a living. FSD

strives to do just this. As one of their volunteers, you'll come in and teach job skills, help women understand budgeting, and share your business-development acumen. There's a lot of other work to go around here as well. You can help teach basic health education, participate in hospice work for the elderly, and offer trauma counseling. The best way to grasp Kenyan culture is to live with a family and share in local traditions—a key component of the FSD program. Accommodations, meals, language lessons, emergency evacuation, all volunteer coordination fees, and airport pickup are included; airfare (flights via Nairobi, and then on to Mombasa) is not.

MUST-SEE IN MOMBASA

Mombasa is an island city. Surrounded by two creeks and the Indian Ocean, it's accessible by boat or bridge. For a quick beach break, you'll adore an area to the north of the city called North Beach. It's fringed with powdery white sand and protected waters teeming with tropical fish, and is home to the magnificent Serena Beach Hotel and Spa, a reproduction of an old Swahili village fringed with palm trees (from $200 for a double; *www.serenahotels.com*).

BEST SAFARI

For many of us, Africa is a once-in-a-lifetime trip. If you've come this far, I absolutely insist that you extend your journey at least another couple of days to go on safari—especially if you're traveling with girl-friends. The word safari is, in fact, Swahili for "journey." And that it is: You'll come home with stories of lions, hippos, and zebras that you and the girls will be recounting for years to come. As you may know, one of East Africa's most fascinating cultures is the Masai tribe, members of which live in the Serengeti, in Kenya and Tanzania. The Masai are a seminomadic ethnic group; they wear distinctive woven red fabrics and brightly colored beaded necklaces. In the Serengeti, a nearly 15-million-acre savanna spread across Kenya and Tanzania, you'll have a chance both to interact with Masai communities and view some of the most extraordinary wildlife left on the planet. This is where you'll find the famous Ngorongoro Crater—an enormous caldera that serves as a pen, of sorts, for rhinos, elephants, zebras, giraffes, hyenas, and lions. And it's also where the annual wildebeest and zebra migration takes place. There are numerous safari companies to choose from; it can be overwhelming to decide. The one that I recommend, and with whom I have traveled with twice, is U.S.-based Thomson Safaris. With 27 years of experience, they specialize in guiding smaller groups, sustainable luxury, and tours steeped in the cultures of the areas they visit (from $4,490 for 11 days; 800-235-0289, *www.ThomsonSafaris.com*).

BEST BEACH DAY

To fully transport yourselves back to another era—and a completely different culture—visit the tropical island of Lamu, 150 miles north of Mombasa in the Indian Ocean. After arriving by plane or ferry, you'll immediately sense that ancient traditions live on: Donkeys are the primary mode of transport in this former port, which was an important exporter of ivory, amber, spices, and timber as far back as the 1500s. You won't be able to resist the laid-back vibe here while you stroll the narrow streets of the Old Town, gazing at Swahili architecture and the intricately carved doors adorning most buildings. It's a predominantly Muslim island, so you should dress modestly in town. In the more touristy parts of the island, such as the popular powdery beaches, shorts and swimsuits are just fine.

BEST DINING EXPERIENCE

If you have a taste for meat, and you're flying through Nairobi, you must make a special trip to Carnivore, a world-renowned barbecue restaurant that many consider to be a destination in itself. From the minute you walk in, you're greeted with the sizzling smells of beef, chicken, and pork cooking by the flame of an enormous charcoal pit at the entrance to the restaurant. It's spectacular. If you're feeling adventurous, try the gamier meats like ostrich and crocodile.

For $30, you'll get all you can eat—and then some (*www.tamarind .co.ke/carnivore*).

EVENT TO FLY IN FOR

People have likened the great wildebeest migration to a religious experience. I don't know if I'd go that far, but I will tell you not to miss out if you can fit in into your schedule. In July and August, millions of wildebeest (picture antelope) travel in a giant parade with thousands of zebras tagging along from the Serengeti north in search of food, and then head south again in October. It's a fascinating biological spectacle, with lions, cheetahs, and hyenas following close behind. The best place to watch the migration is in neighboring Tanzania's Serengeti National Park—another must-see if you can fit it into your itinerary—which has some of the most awe-inspiring quantity and variety of wildlife on the continent (*www.serengeti.org*).

ONE CLICK AND YOU'RE OFF

Learn more on Kenya's Ministry of Tourism and Wildlife information portal at *www.tourism.go.ke*.

❧ Cambodia ❧

You can make a very noticeable difference volunteering in Cambodia. Women find it satisfying and empowering work. This Southeast Asian country, which borders Thailand, Laos, and Vietnam, was embroiled in a devastating civil war until 1991. Khmer is Cambodia's official language, but English is fast becoming the dominant second language, and learning it is critical for the children of Cambodia. Your hearts will go out to the survivors of the oppressive Khmer reign of terror, but you'll be amazed at the resiliency and grace with which they're emerging from such a dark period in their history. And you and you friends are plenty qualified to help Cambodian kids with their basic English skills, an important step toward progress for this nation. One of the best places to volunteer is in the schools of the budding tourist town of Siem Reap, in northwestern Cambodia. The lush jungle topography of Siem Reap will embrace you, and the towering ancient Hindu temples of nearby Angkor will astonish even the most well traveled among you. Siem Reap is the fastest growing city in Cambodia, with both old and new architecture—all of it accessible by foot or rented bicycle. There are French colonial and Chinese buildings and modern hotels alike, and restaurants of every kind springing up at a blistering pace. But traditional culture is still very much alive. Evidence of this is the traditional Khmer dance, in which women wearing golden-hued headdresses and costumes use graceful hand movements to tell stories (similar to hula). You'll go back in time perusing the stalls at Siem Reap's Old Market, overflowing with vegetables like bamboo shoots, banana blossoms, and yard-long beans, as well as through touring the nearby rice paddies and silk farms. The tropical environs here add to its exotic mystique, but it makes for tricky weather—it's dry but very hot (hovering around 100°F) from December through April, and wet but cooler (around 80°F) from May through October.

WHERE TO SIGN UP

Globe Aware's "Cambodia Rediscovered" trips run every month of the year, with dedicated volunteers working a solid six to eight hours each day ($1,200 per week; 877-588-4562, *www.globeaware.org*). In the village school, you'll teach English, computer skills (how to send emails, how to use word-processing programs, etc.), and basic first aid to the local population of children with extremely limited access to education. You'll stay in modest hotel rooms and gather at night with old and new friends for Cambodian specialties (much like Thai food) such as grilled freshwater fish wrapped in lettuce and salads with coriander, lemongrass, and mint. The trip fee covers accommodations, meals, medical insurance, emergency medical evacuation, program coordination, side trips, and transportation within Cambodia, but not airfare to Siem Reap, although you will be picked up at the airport. Several Asian airlines fly there via Bangkok or Phnom Penh (Cambodia's capital city).

SACRED SITES

There's no way to fully prepare you for the beauty and vastness of Angkor. Simply put, it's massive. Angkor comprises a collection of more than a hundred Hindu temples built between the 9th and 12th centuries across 40 acres of jungle north of Siem Reap. At the time the temples were constructed, the Khmer kingdom stretched from Vietnam to China to the Bay of Bengal. Today, you might see Buddhist monks with shaved heads and brilliant orange robes streaming into the temples to worship. (Today, Buddhism is the official religion of Cambodia and most temples house some Buddhist statues.) I recommend you spend no fewer than three days exploring the Angkor temples. You're best off seeing Angkor with a guide—the hotel can arrange for an English-speaking guide for about $25 per day. Specifically ask to see Angkor Wat, the world's largest temple, taking turns to pose for the camera in front of the gigantic, three-tiered pyramid topped by five flowering lotuses. A great way to see—and photograph—the temple complex and nearby Tonle Sap Lake is by hot-air balloon either at sunset or sunrise. Trips leave a half-mile west of Angkor Wat ($15 per person for an hour; *www.phnompenhtour.com*).

CULINARY DELIGHT
Siem Reap is buzzing with backpacker-friendly restaurants, but you and the gals will appreciate the upscale elegance of Khmer Kitchen. It serves up regional Cambodian fare with a special twist. You'll savor flavors new to your taste buds, such as mussaman curry, baked pumpkin, and chicken soup with mint, lemongrass, and lime (dinners are $2–$3; located on an alley north of the Old Market).

BEST DEAL IN TOWN
Most hotels rent bikes for a dollar a day—a self-guided bike tour is probably the best bargain in town. But on the days you're interested in a different sort of adventure, have a seat (in pairs) in one of the town's ubiquitous motorcycle rickshaws (called *tuk tuks*) to take you around the sights for about $10 per day.

BEST HISTORY LESSON
It'll be a sobering experience to visit the Cambodian Landmine Museum, located a mile from Siem Reap, but it's one of the best ways to learn about the devastation of the 1970s Khmer Rouge regime. Consider an afternoon outing to the museum (which consists of a string of shacks filled with decommissioned mines and shell casings) to be a must-see educational experience for you and your girlfriends. The story of the museum's founder is fascinating in itself: He's a former Khmer fighter who became a landmine decommissioner and began storing the mines in a shack on his property. His collection grew, and the museum was formed (*www.cambodialandminemuseum.org*).

EVENTS TO FLY IN FOR
The Khmer New Year festival, a three-day nationwide celebration in mid-April, marks the end of the harvest season and infuses the nation with a celebratory vibe. Take the opportunity to immerse

continued on page 254

MOST FREQUENTLY ASKED QUESTIONS
ABOUT VOLUNTEERING

෯

What type of accommodations and food can volunteers generally expect?

It depends on the type of program and cost. Less expensive and often longer-term programs have accommodations such as: dormitory-style or shared accommodation with shared bathrooms, staying in local homes, different levels of camping, as well as cafeteria- or family-style food preparation.

In Europe some volunteer programs, like Rempart or the British Trust for Conservation Volunteers, house volunteers in special interest accommodations such as castles, monasteries, or period houses.

Some programs offer a surprising level of privacy and physical comfort—with air-conditioning, private rooms, and gourmet chefs.

Ask if the program's cost is based on a shared room. Often this is the case.

Are there short-term programs with traditional sightseeing?

"Voluntours" are hybrid experiences that combine traditional sightseeing, entertainment in the evenings, free time, and/or the chance to learn about the culture and activities of your host country with the opportunity to volunteer. These can be anywhere from one afternoon to one to three weeks. Some are trips where you don't actually volunteer in a hands-on way, but the trip has a service component, such as delivering books, school supplies, or medicine, and more opportunities to engage with the local people.

Some companies charge high fees for a volunteer experience. Why pay?

In return for higher fees comes the comfort and safety you pay for: extensive pre-trip reading materials, someone to escort you from the airport, security when using public transportation in high risk areas, on-site training, hotel accommodation, prepared meals, a volunteer coordinator on-site at all times. Some organizations use part of your program fee to pay for supplies donated to the community being served.

Generally, if a program charges a high fee, you want to ask what percentage of your money goes toward the local community, in-country staff, and project.

Are there less expensive volunteer options?

"Workcamps" exist around the world and allow people to live and volunteer together for a few weeks on grassroots projects often organized by local sponsors. Such volunteer projects are often most beneficial for the community, since income remains local and the cost of training volunteers is very low. Two organizations with searchable online directories are Volunteers for Peace (www.vfp.org) and World-Wide Opportunities on Organic Farms (www.wwoof.org).

What happens if I get there and find out the experience is really not for me or that I am not ready to handle it?

To minimize the chances of this happening, be sure you understand the environment and the type of work. Will there be physical labor involved, with there be electricity, what are the primary risks in the area, are you emotionally prepared for the challenges, how rugged are the conditions? Ask about the refund policy before you book. Choose an experience within your comfort zone the first time around.

—Sherry Schwarz, 29, Editor & Publisher, *Transitions Abroad Magazine* and Director of The Abroad View Foundation, Bennington, Vermont yourselves in the Cambodian festivities found on nearly every street corner through games, singing, and dancing. (But be careful, April is the hottest month of the year, with temperatures tipping more than 100°F.) If you love full moons, fireworks, and muscular men, the Bon Om Tuk water celebration is for you. In early November, timed to the end of the wet season and the full moon, you and your travel buddies can gather on the banks of Chaktomuk River, in front of the Royal Palace in the capital of Phnom Penh, to watch hundreds of boats converge for three days of dragon-boat racing and fireworks. The boats themselves are works of art: long and narrow with a brightly colored dragon's head and tail painted on the bow and stern.

ONE CLICK AND YOU'RE OFF
Visit Cambodia's official tourism site at *www.tourismcambodia.com.*

✂ Guatemala ✂

With a large indigenous population still utilizing farming, cooking, and weaving techniques they've used for centuries, the Central American country of Guatemala provides a fascinating cultural experience. But poverty is rampant, and the Maya-descended indigenous people (40 percent of the entire population) are very much still rebounding from centuries of oppression and a brutal, decades-long civil war that only ended in the mid-1990s. There's no better humanitarian excursion to be had in Guatemala than in the city of Quetzaltenango, nestled in the mountains 130 miles northwest of Guatemala City. If you're having trouble pronouncing Quetzaltenango, you're not alone. Most people refer to the city by its nickname, Xela. It's is the second largest city in the country and a lively college town (hosting seven universities) with cobblestone streets and colonial belle-époque architecture mixed in with plenty of modern buildings and amenities (including Internet cafés, which come in handy if you like to stay connected with your family back home). In the mornings your volunteer work may involve visiting with elderly indigenous women in a nursing home or playing games and helping kids with their homework at an orphanage for boys. Then you'll have your afternoons free to explore the city. It's inevitable that your stay here will be dominated by the delectable food, a variation of Mexican cuisine. But it's easy to burn off the calories with hiking trips to surrounding volcanoes, hot springs, and mountain towns. I also recommend striking out for the famous crafts market at Chichicastenango, and taking a weekend trip to the towns strung along Lake Atitlán. The most common form of local transportation is something called a "chicken bus," which is a converted American school bus that provides a cheap, safe mode of transport. Be prepared to wedge yourselves between men and women in traditional dress—and yes, the occasional chicken.

WHERE TO SIGN UP
New York–based Cross-Cultural Solutions' Quetzaltenango program requires you to fill out a pre-trip form describing your interests and skills. It then taps its vast network of grassroots partners in the area (including orphanages, nursing homes, and schools) and matches your skills to the local community's needs, and places you with whichever program best suits your abilities. Programs are a minimum of one week (from $1,695; 800-380-4777, *www.crossculturalsolutions.org*). You'll live in a house with other volunteers—you might even want to fill the whole house with your friends for a group volunteer vacation. The fee includes room, board, cultural activities, emergency medical evacuation, and transportation from Guatemala City to Xela. International airfare is not included.

BRUSH UP ON YOUR SPANISH
How many of us couldn't use a little refresher on our high school Spanish? You'll have a fantastic opportunity to practice your conversation skills and bone up on your grammar during a trip to Quetzaltenango, which is home to at least two dozen incredibly well-priced language schools. Signing on for even just a couple of days of instruction before you start your volunteer work can make all the difference in your communication with locals. Casa Xelaju is one of the top schools in town (from $165 per week; *www.casaxelaju.com*).

SHOP TILL YOU DROP
If you only go to one crafts market in your life, Chichicastenango should be at the top of your list. Maya vendors from all over Guatemala make a biweekly pilgrimage to Chichi on Thursdays and Sundays to sell the best textiles, blouses, pottery, and masks in the country. (It's a five-hour bus ride from Xela so you'll want to make a weekend of it.) Since precolonial times, the market has been a key hub for Maya commerce. Hundreds of stalls line the cobblestone streets snaking in and around the plaza. Seasoned buyers can identify

vendors' hometowns based on what they're wearing—each village has its own distinct style of dress. You can pick up a few bright additions to your wardrobe to spice it up. The brilliantly colored fabrics are also ideal for making pillows, tablecloths, and quilts. And you won't go hungry at this market: Produce stands are plentiful, and meat sizzles on wood-burning grills alongside pots of chile-flavored soups. For one of the most pagan church experiences you'll ever have, stop in at the 400-year-old chapel, where candles burn on the floor, incense clouds the air, and the occasional dead chicken is offered to the gods.

BEST WEEKEND GETAWAY
The dazzling waters of volcano-ringed Lake Atitlán, a two-hour bus ride from Xela, are a must-see. The town of Panajachel is touristy, so I'd recommend passing through it just long enough to peruse the shops selling handicrafts, but then continuing on via ferry to Villa Sumaya, a yoga retreat on the banks of the lake. Guests ride across the lake on a traditional *panga* boat to get there, and then zen out in thatch-roofed rooms with private verandas overlooking the water (from $50 per night; *www.villasumaya.com*). It's an unparalled setting for your yoga practice. When you pass back through Panajachel, stop for coffee before you board the bus back to Xela. Most of Guatemala's finest coffee beans are exported, which means your morning brew is often the bitter second-tier stuff. Not so at Panajachel's Crossroads Café. This place serves some of the best coffee anywhere in the world—and that's probably because they get the finest beans not only from Guatemala, but also from Ethiopia and Indonesia. Share a slice of the homemade cheesecake, baked by the friendly American expat owners—it's to die for (*www.crossroadscafepana.com*).

EVENTS TO FLY IN FOR
Guatemalans takes Lent seriously and they don't skimp on the festivities. The week before Easter, known as Semana Santa, or Holy Week, is the biggest event of the year. Thousands of Guatemalans don purple-and-white tunics and join in processions through the streets. You're in for a real treat in Quetzaltenango, where the city's celebration of the high holiday offers a special blend of Catholic and Maya influences.

ONE CLICK AND YOU'RE OFF
You'll find the ultimate source for information on Quetzaltenango at *www.xelapages.com*.

❧ Romania ❧

Communism is not as much a relic of Romania's past as I wish it were. Poverty is still rampant in this Eastern European nation north of Bulgaria and south of the Ukraine. And the children are as affected as anyone. Luckily, they have Romanian Orthodox priest Father Nicolae Tanase working on their behalf. In 1991, after the fall of communism, Tanase took in a single orphaned child; three years later, he and his wife started a nonprofit committed to caring for homeless children, kids with disabilities abandoned at hospitals, and unwanted babies. Today, Tanase and his staff house 280 orphans in Romania's Carpathian Mountains, several hours from the capital city of Bucharest. It won't be too difficult to recruit your girlfriends for this trip. You'll all find rural Romania irresistible. It's a fairy-tale land of castles, horse-drawn carts, apple orchards, and the remnants of Roman buildings and Greek ports. The Romanian countryside hasn't quite caught up to the 21st century yet; you still might see women in traditional dress (white flounced blouses, headscarves, thick black skirts, and slippers) spinning wool onto a spindle or folk artists carving elaborate wooden spoons and embroidering wool bags. If you come in the fall or winter, pack light and then purchase handmade wool blankets or sweaters to wear during your visit—the climate is similar to that of the northeastern United States, so it can get very cold. One of your jobs at the orphanage is to help prepare meals for the kids, so you can consider your trip an informal cooking class as well. Romanian food is an amalgamation of cuisines: roasted eggplant and peppers (Bulgarian), moussaka (Greek), hot pretzels and schnitzel (Austrian), and hot pastries (Hungarian). As much as you'll indulge the children at the orphanage, there are countless ways Romanian will pamper and fascinate you.

WHERE TO SIGN UP

Help Father Tanase's mission and enroll with American nonprofit United Planet, which sends volunteers to more than 150 countries ($1,295 for the first week, $200 for each additional week; 800-292-2316, www.unitedplanet.org). As a volunteer, you'll live in a wing of the orphanage, helping the kids with their homework, playing games with them, and soaking in a culture rich in folklore, music, and dance. The Romania programs are offered year-round and include lodging, food, transfers from the Bucharest airport, and volunteer administration fees. International airfare is not included.

MUST-SEE CASTLE

Images of Dracula will leap to mind when you arrive at Bran Castle. It has been featured in many film adaptations of the Bram Stoker tale. Almost directly in the center of Romania, 125 miles northwest of Bucharest, Bran Castle is one of the most important examples of Romanian medieval architecture and has become a museum. If the mystery and intrigue of the place start to set your imagination running wild, stick close to your travel companions as you gaze at the turrets and spires—it's a little creepy. Don't get too close to the courtyard fountain, which hides a web of spooky underground passages (*www.brancastlemuseum.ro*). While you're in Bran, further your journey deeper into medieval times with an overnight at Pensiunea Andra, a rustic guesthouse with wooden beams, arched doorways, and a stone fireplace (from $47 for a double; *www.andratour.ro*).

BEST CITY ESCAPE

I'm not the first to say that Bucharest reminds me of a mini version of Paris (it's nickname was Little Paris in the early 1900s). Part of the reason for the similarities is that French and French-trained architects descended upon the city and contributed neoclassic buildings, parks, and mansions—and even gave Bucharest its own version of the Arc de Triomphe. The Royal Palace is definitely worth a visit—it houses the Romanian National Art Museum. I don't recommend taking the full tour of the Palace of Parliament—at 3.5 million square feet, it's the world's second largest building after the Pentagon—but I do suggest a visit to the small Parliament Hall to take photos of yourselves under the three-ton crystal chandelier. If you thought your power bill was high, this fixture has 7,000 lightbulbs. Then for an inexpensive and memorable (and caloric) meal of Romanian soul food, visit Bucharest's Crama Culmea Veche, whose menu includes stews, grilled meats, and peppery sausages (dinners ranges from $3 to $7; Strada Culmea Veche 2).

WINE-TASTING WEEKEND

If you and the ladies feel like blowing off a little steam before you head back to the United States, what better way than a wine tour? Romania has one of the oldest winemaking traditions in all of Europe thanks to its rich soil. The Tarnave region in Transylvania combines a rare combination of cool climate, high altitude, and humidity to create fruity white wines, such as the Pinot Gris and Italian Rieslings of the Medias and Zagar wineries. Or bask in the sunshine while you sip supersweet whites and reds at Cernavoda vineyard in the sunny Murfatlar wine region, near the Black Sea. Learn more about the different wine regions and customize your own vineyard-to-vineyard itinerary through Go Romania Tours (*www.goromaniatours.com*).

EVENTS TO FLY IN FOR

Old habits die hard in Romania, which makes for festivals that are fascinating windows into the past. Shepherds traditionally met their future wives at the Fundata Fair, held each June in Fundata, the highest village in all of Romania. These days, the shepherds still bring their sheep for a day out in the Carpathian foothills, where they sell crafts and take part in traditional singing and dancing. And who knows, maybe you'll find love. Another festive celebration is Medieval Days, a two-week-long arts, crafts, and music festival in August in Sighisoara, a 12th-century medieval village recognized as a UNESCO World Heritage site.

ONE CLICK AND YOU'RE OFF

Go to the Romania Tourist Office website at *www.romaniatourism.com*.

Travel Companies for Women

AAA SOJOURNS
877-222-6036
www.csaa.com

ADVENTURE ASSOCIATES
888-532-8352
www.adventureassociates.net

ADVENTURE WOMEN
800-804-8686
www.adventurewomen.com

ADVENTURES IN GOOD COMPANY
877-439-4042
www.adventuresingoodcompany.com

ADVENTUROUS WENCH
866-419-3624
www.adventurouswench.com

ARCTIC LADIES
877-783-1954
www.arcticladies.com

BUSHWISE WOMEN
61-266-840178 (Australia)
www.bushwise.co.nz

CALL OF THE WILD
888-378-1978
www.callwild.com

CANADIAN WOMAN TRAVELER
888-830-5324
www.cwtraveller.ca

CANYON CALLING TOURS
928-282-0916
www.canyoncalling.com

GIRLFRIENDS GO TOURS
435-513-0659
www.girlfriendsgo.com

GOING PLACES TOURS!
707-935-0595

GUTSY WOMEN TRAVEL
866-464-8879
www.gutsywomentravel.com

MARIAH WILDERNESS EXPEDITIONS
800-462-7424
www.mariahwe.com

SOUTH SEA MERMAID TOURS
4-973-0675 (New Zealand)
www.southseamermaids.co.nz

THIS GIRL'S GONE TRAVELLIN'
877-846-2831
www.womentravelling.com

TRAVEL WITH WOMEN
617-254-1729 or 508-904-5843
www.travelwithwomen.com

WALKING WOMEN
44-1926-313321 (U.K.)
www.walkingwomen.com

WOMAN'S WORLD TRAVEL
800-651-5008
www.womansworldtravel.com

WOMANTOURS
800-247-1444
www.womantours.com

**WOMEN TRAVELING
TOGETHER**
410-956-5250
www.women-traveling.com

WOMEN'S TRAVEL CLUB
800-480-4448
www.womenstravelclub.com

WOMEN'S TRAVEL NETWORK
888-419-0118
www.womenstravelnetwork.ca

Garden Tours

**AMERICAN HORTICULTURAL
SOCIETY**
800-777-7931
www.ahs.org/events/travel_study.htm

**AUSTRALIAN PACIFIC
TOURING**
800-290-8687
www.aptouring.com.au

**COOPERSMITH'S GARDEN
TOURS**
415-669-1914
www.coopersmiths.com

**HORTICULTURE MAGAZINE
GARDEN TRAVEL PROGRAMS**
617-742-5600
www.hortmag.com/garden_tours.asp

JEFF SAINSBURY TOURS
800-748-9685
www.jeffsainsburytours.com

Volunteer Opportunities for 1 to 2 Weeks

**CENTER FOR GLOBAL
EDUCATION**
800-299-8889
www.augsburg.edu/global

CROSS-CULTURAL SOLUTIONS
800-380-4777
www.crossculturalsolutions.org

EARTHWATCH
800-776-0188
www.earthwatch.org

GLOBAL EXCHANGE
415-255-7296
www.globalexchange.org

GLOBAL SERVICE CORPS
415-788-3666 ext.128
http://GlobalServiceCorps.org

GLOBAL VOLUNTEERS
800-487-1074
www.globalvolunteers.org

GLOBE AWARE
877-588-4562
www.globeaware.org

HABITAT FOR HUMANITY
229-924-6935
www.habitat.org

TEACHING & PROJECTS ABROAD
888-839-3535
www.teaching-abroad.co.uk

INTERNATIONAL VOLUNTEER PROGRAMS ASSOCIATION
914-380-8322
www.volunteerinternational.org

WORLD TEACH
800-483-2240
www.worldteach.org

Volunteer Websites

WWW.VOLUNTEER ABROAD.COM
Volunteerabroad.com offers comprehensive searches for volunteering abroad.

WWW.IDEALIST.ORG
Action without Borders is a clearinghouse for tens of thousands of nonprofit organizations worldwide.

WWW.VOLUNTEERINTER NATIONAL.ORG
International Volunteer Programs Association (IVPA) features a searchable database of volunteer-abroad programs.

WWW.SCI-IVS.ORG
Service Civil International has listings for low-cost, short-term volunteer options in more than 50 countries.

WWW.TRANSITIONS ABROAD.COM
Transitions Abroad covers all aspects of international volunteering.

WWW.VFP.ORG
Volunteers for Peace provides over 3,000 low-cost, short-term voluntary service placements in more than 100 countries.

WWW.WEVOLUNTEER.NET
The Building Bridges Coalition website for international volunteering.

Volunteer Resources

Alternatives to the Peace Corps: A Guide of Global Volunteer Opportunities by Paul Backhurst. 2005 (11th ed.).

How to Live Your Dream of Volunteering Overseas by Joseph Collins, Stefano DeZerega, and Zahara Heckscher. 2002.

Volunteer Vacations: Short-Term Adventures That Will Benefit You and Others by Bill McMillon, Doug Cutchins, and Anne Geissinger. 2006 (9th ed.).

Helpful Travel Websites

WWW.GUTSYTRAVELER.COM
Women travel tips, (solo travel, family travel, teen travel, serious defense tips, packing, and more), resources for women's trips, stories about girlfriend weekends, reunions, and more.

WWW.AAA.COM
Click on "travel" to find maps and travel information.

WWW.TRIPADVISOR.COM
The most comprehensive collection of unbiased, reader-generated hotel reviews, plus reviews of restaurants, destinations, and tour companies with links to guidebook reviews.

WWW.BUDGETTRAVEL.COM
Last minute sales, and special promotions—all tested and approved by editors.

WWW.CRUISECRITIC.COM
Ship reviews, readers' ship ratings and reviews, news, bargains, tips, and message boards.

WWW.THEBATHROOM DIARIES.COM
Rates more than 9,000 public rest rooms worldwide in the areas of safety, hours of operation, aesthetics, handicap accessibility, including talking toilets for the visually impaired, and cost (if there is a charge).

WWW.SEATGURU.COM
Airplane cabin diagrams showing space and legroom, entertainment options, ergonomics, and armrests.

WWW.WHICHBUDGET.COM
Dozens of low-cost airlines from Asia to Europe and the list is organized by route.

WWW.RAILEUROPE.COM
Comprehensive selection of train tickets, from single fares to complicated multicountry passes. Real-time booking allows you to reserve a seat on specific sectors, rather than buy an open ticket and reserve a seat at a later date.

WWW.WEBFLYER.COM
Detailed information about airline, car rental, and hotel loyalty programs including ratings and reviews, and up-to-date promotions.

WWW.TRAVEL.STATE.GOV
Official U.S. government site for travel warnings and country-by-country consular information. Educates travelers on topics from political news to medical facilities and road conditions.

Founded in 1888, the National Geographic Society is one of the largest non-profit scientific and educational organizations in the world. It reaches more than 285 million people worldwide each month through its official journal, NATIONAL GEOGRAPHIC, and its four other magazines; the National Geographic Channel; television documentaries; radio programs; films; books; videos and DVDs; maps; and interactive media. National Geographic has funded more than 8,000 scientific research projects and supports an education program combating geographic illiteracy.

For more information, please call
1-800-NGS LINE (647-5463)
or write to the following address:

National Geographic Society
1145 17th Street N.W.
Washington, D.C. 20036-4688 U.S.A.

Visit us online at www.nationalgeographic.com/books.

For information about special discounts for bulk purchases, please contact National Geographic Books Special Sales: ngspecsales@ngs.org.

For rights or permissions inquiries, please contact National Geographic Books Subsidiary Rights: ngbookrights@ngs.org.

Library of Congress Cataloging-in-Publication Data

Bond, Marybeth.
  Best girlfriends getaways worldwide / by Marybeth
Bond.
    p. cm.
  Includes index.
  ISBN 978-1-4262-0226-1 (pbk.)
  1. Women—Travel—Guidebooks, I. Title.
G153.4.B66 2008
940.4082—dc22

    2007045185

Cover and Interior Design: Peggy Archambault
Production Assistant: Al Morrow

Illustrations: Sheila Aldridge/Swell-Art

Printed in U.S.A.